18 IN AMERICA

*A Young Golfer's Epic Journey to Find
the Essence of the Game*

DYLAN DETHIER

SCRIBNER

New York   London   Toronto   Sydney   New Delhi

SCRIBNER
A Division of Simon & Schuster, Inc.
1230 Avenue of the Americas
New York, NY 10020

First Scribner hardcover edition May 2013

SCRIBNER and design are registered trademarks of The Gale Group, Inc.,
used under license by Simon & Schuster, Inc., the publisher of this work.

For information about special discounts for bulk purchases,
please contact Simon & Schuster Special Sales at 1-866-506-1949
or business@simonandschuster.com.

The Simon & Schuster Speakers Bureau can bring authors to your live event.
For more information or to book an event, contact the Simon & Schuster Speakers
Bureau at 1-866-248-3049 or visit our website at www.simonspeakers.com.

Manufactured in the United States of America

1 3 5 7 9 10 8 6 4 2

Library of Congress Cataloging-in-Publication Data is available.

ISBN 978-1-4516-9363-8
ISBN 978-1-4516-9365-2 (ebook)

To all those who play

Contents

18 IN AMERICA

Prologue

If you're an eighteen-year-old kid in desperate need of money, living out of the back of your parents' filthy Subaru wagon three thousand miles from home, and if you find yourself sharing a Las Vegas driving range with a guy who looks (and smells) like a homeless Johnny Depp, and that guy offers to play a round of golf against you for a substantial amount of money, just say no—before things go terribly wrong.

As I stared at Vegas Johnny on the driving range at the Painted Desert Golf Club, I was unimpressed. Physically, he wasn't much to look at—five nine, maybe, and so thin that his clothes hung off of him like he was some undersized, back-of-the-store mannequin. It was hard to see his face, which he kept hidden behind a mountain-man beard, a low-slung fedora, and a pair of sunglasses that screamed *I'm hungover.*

His golf game looked even less imposing. One shot would careen off to the right, the next would boomerang hard left, then another one to the right, then off to the left again. He continued this mixture of shanks and yanks in nearly rhythmic fashion, not one of his efforts getting more than ten feet off the ground before it crash-landed among thousands of other range-ball misfires.

Another guy was leaving the practice tee and walking toward the first hole, and I saw Johnny motion him aside and gesture toward himself and to the course; I guessed this was an offer for a match. I could see the other guy taken aback, could easily read his "No, thanks" body language, and saw Vegas Johnny turn away and slam his club into the turf, upset at being turned down. Who *was* this guy? Poker pro with cash to blow? Somebody who'd seen the *The Big Lebowski* too many times? It didn't matter, really—I figured this was a chance to make some much-needed money.

I cleared my throat.

"I'm going out next," I said. "You looking for a game?"

He hit another grounder before responding. "Sounds good, brother."

Back in Massachusetts, I'd play buddies on my high school team for clubhouse drinks, sometimes Snickers bars. As I shook Vegas Johnny's hand on the first tee, though, he was proposing some higher stakes: fifty a hole, hundred a side, two hundred for the eighteen. *Whoa.* I'd never done anything like this. Then again, I was in Sin City—and since I wasn't old enough to hit the casino floors back on the Strip, here was my chance to strike it rich. Plus, the odds were in my favor. Or so I thought.

Through three holes, I was two up—and I was confident that two down was just the start of a long day for my bedraggled opponent. Our next hole was a tricky par-3. I hit first, into the front right bunker. *Damn.* I walked back to my bag to watch Mr. Vegas, the generous part of me hoping he'd at least keep it in play, the greedy part hoping for water left. Just as he stood over the ball, he glanced back at me, checking to see if I was watching. Was that a smirk on his face?

And then Vegas Johnny made a perfect golf swing.

The neck-scratching hitch he'd been making the first three holes had vanished. Instead, he whipped the club hard and aggressive through impact, holding a low follow-through to keep the ball down; in complete control. The shot began at the right bunker and drew in at the flag, taking one hard bounce forward before spinning to a halt, leaving about eight feet for birdie. He held his finish as the ball was in the air, admiring its flight, leaning just to the left, urging the ball to pull toward the hole.

The Dude had suddenly turned into Sergio Garcia, and I suddenly realized that over the next fifteen holes, I could lose *a lot* of money. Vegas Johnny was a hustler. And now I had only two options: I could play out the round.

Or I could run.

How does a nice East Coast teenager find himself on a course in Vegas betting hundreds he can't afford to lose against a golf shark? I asked myself that question a lot as that afternoon wore on.

After all, this was nothing like the game I had grown up playing. The course where I fell in love with golf—a shoes-optional par-30 near my grandparents' house on the Maine coast—was a world away from the Painted Desert. From age five, my older brother, Evan, and I traipsed carefree down the ocean-lined fairways during our August vacations there, playing three or four or five rounds a day. We would wander the rocky beaches alongside the ninety-three-yard peninsular fifth hole, where the ocean had washed up more Pinnacles than we would ever know what to do with.

As our stash of golf balls grew, so too did our fascination with the game. Seven-irons began to tear up a section of the backyard at our home outside Williamstown, Massachusetts. As we got older, the Pinnacles flew deeper and deeper into the back woods, and junior sets replaced the persimmons we had found in Maisie and Gramps's attic.

Golf didn't exactly run in our blood, however. Mom and Dad didn't play. Gramps had a nice history with the game, including a legendary round at the Old Course in which he scored either 72 in a typhoon or 82 in clear blue skies depending on the day, but he'd bagged his clubs for good by the time we'd started playing in earnest.

I was the son of a geologist and a pioneer in the field of renewable energy—not exactly a recipe for country club fanaticism. Golf lessons weren't going to be a priority in this family. So I focused my energy on honing my lash of a swing that I'd learned playing Little League baseball—more Mark McGwire or Sammy Sosa than Mark O'Meara or Sam Snead.

Before long, a twenty-one-year-old named Eldrick Woods was fist-pumping his way around Augusta National, and then around Pebble Beach, and all of a sudden golf looked as if it might be sort of *cool*. A poster of Tiger joined the Red Sox on the wall of my room.

Over the years, my game didn't mature as much as it adapted. I would come out of baseball season fighting a vicious hook, so I learned to slice. I didn't have a sand wedge, so I learned to open my pitching wedge way up to blast out of bunkers. My hits were big and my misses were bigger. Each round felt like driving a car with no steering.

But golf is famously a game not of how but of how many, and for some reason I was getting good. I could make par from two fairways over or hit a skip slice across the surface of a lake, and I had such soft touch with a wedge that I could get up and down from the beverage cart. Plus I had a knack for rolling in those six-to-ten-footers that are the difference in any good round of golf.

"My buddy was right about you," one junior golf opponent told me after I took the lead with a particularly outrageous par-4 that took me from the woods to the bunker to thirty feet to the bottom of the cup. "You're not really that good, but damn, you make par from anywhere." Competition helped focus me and elevate my game. Still, things sometimes went awry. At one tournament I hit six provisionals in a row into the left swamp and ran out of golf balls. At the state championship my junior year, I ricocheted my way around the woods for the better part of twenty minutes, stubbornly refusing to punch out to safety a half dozen times. I ended up draining a twenty-footer for 11.

It was a radical style of play that not only made me really good at apologizing (*Sorry about hitting your cart, sir, I had no idea the golf course even extended this far to the right*) but also gave me some comfort-by-separation from the country club range rats of the junior golf world. The distinction no doubt pleased my parents as much as it did me, and I could always fall back on the fact that

Prologue

I wasn't a golfer—I was an athlete. A skier and a baseball player and a pickup football star. Golf was just something I did.

I deflected everything I hated about the game onto the rich kids I would run into at tournaments. I hated the way they wore thick white sunglasses when it wasn't sunny and the way they matched their turquoise hats to their turquoise pants. I hated the way they laid up and pitched out and had no creativity, no imagination. I hated the way they talked about the putting greens in their backyards but still managed to suck at putting. I hated the way they talked about golf courses they had been to and where their fathers were members and how *this* was nothing. So I learned to love how I *wasn't* them.

And then, after high school, I hatched an unlikely plan: spend a year playing golf.

The idea: play a round in each of the lower forty-eight states. Why? I'd just spent nearly fifteen years in a Williamstown classroom, and I needed to get out. I'd play the three-buck courses of the country, maybe some three-hundred-dollar ones too, and meet all kinds of Americans. SMALL-TOWN MASSACHUSETTS KID SEEKS ADVENTURE. Somehow I'd get my parents to agree. College could wait for a year.

In the months that followed, as I traveled the country in Subi, my rattling, dusty old Subaru, playing rounds with a range of individuals with increasingly fancy pedigrees, I began to be seduced by a different kind of golf, the kind that was beyond even the rich kids I knew. I encountered the golf played by America's elite on velvet fairways hidden behind high walls. I'd meet CEOs and the PGA Tour commissioner, walk inside the ropes with Phil Mickelson. And I'd make some mistakes, too. (See *Johnny, Vegas*.)

When the year began, I had no idea how far I would stray from the ideals of the barefoot five-year-old who started hitting golf balls as an excuse to hang out with his big brother. By year's end, though, I would discover many different Americas and, eventually, find the way back to the heart of my game.

CHAPTER 1

The First Drive

We were three silhouettes walking up the eighteenth fairway, the late summer sun already sinking behind the mountains.

"So you're really gonna do this, huh?"

This was Taylor, one of my closest friends for nearly a decade. He was on my right, purple golf bag slung carelessly over one shoulder, and he was looking at me even though he and I both knew the answer to his question. He was a few inches shorter than I, a smiley boy with mussy blond hair and wide blue eyes that always told you exactly how he was feeling.

"Yeah," I murmured. "I guess I am."

We stopped at Taylor's ball.

"You nervous?" This time it was my brother, Evan. Two years older and three inches taller, Evan was a razor-thin giant with broad shoulders and a mop of dark brown hair that fell haphazardly to one side of his face or the other, depending which way he swiped it with his hand.

"Nervous?" I responded. "Nah. Just excited to get out on the road."

I wondered how many summer nights we'd spent this way—driving the ten minutes from home to Taconic Golf Club to tee off at five P.M., Evan and Taylor and I, playing till we couldn't see the ball. That was the time of day when the wind had died and left us in a quiet stillness, when the air was cool but comfortable, when the light was getting lower and the shadows longer, all of us in the sunset, feeling as if nights like these would last forever even as the gathering darkness warned that they wouldn't.

We putted out and I shook each of their hands, because that's what you did after a round of golf. And then I gave them each a long, choked-up hug—because that's what you did when you were seventeen years old and didn't know the next time you were going to see your best friends.

What I had told Evan was true, but it wasn't the whole truth. I *was* excited. But I was still coming to grips with the fact that leaving meant leaving stuff behind—everything I had ever loved: the people, the places, my home.

We went our separate ways—Evan off to his college dorm, the beginning of his junior year; Taylor to his house, one of the last nights before the start of his senior year of high school; and me, home, one final time.

Dinner was unusually quiet that night. Dad had gotten steak and Mom made pesto pasta, with corn on the cob from Chenail's Farm. My favorite meal.

From the outside, it was a perfect picture: the All-American family gathered around the table for a late summer dinner. But as we were sitting down I realized I still didn't know exactly how my parents felt about what I was about to do. And at this point, I was afraid to find out.

It was a simple idea, really: Me and Subi, our 2002 forest-green Subaru Outback station wagon, would drive around the country, and I would play at least one round of golf in every state—Hawaii and Alaska excepted. I'd be gone for the length of the school year, the beginning of September to the beginning of June. Then we'd come home, Subi and I, and I'd start college the next fall.

Home was Williamstown, Massachusetts, a town of fewer than eight thousand people and also the home of Williams College, a small liberal arts school where I had been accepted the previous December and was on track to spend the next four years of my life. Williams is among the most selective schools in the country, and I had done well to get in. But enrolling there meant I wasn't exactly leaving the nest. I would become a freshman at the college where my brother was a junior and my father taught geology, all of eight minutes from the house I had grown up in.

I'd been mulling the idea of a year of *something else* since the moment I applied to Williams. My childhood had been happy and fulfilling, but since I'd started thinking about life after high school, I'd dealt with the persistent feeling that I had never really *done* anything. Staying in town for college wasn't really going to shake things up—I needed something that would.

My mom was in favor of the trip, I figured. I could almost always tell when she disapproved of something Evan or I was doing, and this didn't seem like one of those times. Plus we were usually on the same page—if I was really, truly excited about something, I could count on Mom to get on board.

Her job was built on hopefulness, after all. She worked for a company called the Center for EcoTechnology, which helped individuals and small towns acquire things like solar panels and wind turbines. Nothing screams blind optimism like battling pollution and global warming.

That's why I'd told her first, before I had all the details worked out.

Before I told Dad, though, I'd really need a plan. I knew he would appreciate part of it: the independence, the road trip, the rugged adventure. He was a mountain man, after all—a geology professor who spent his summers working in the Rockies, a father who used to take us hiking every Sunday. Exploring was my dad's thing.

Growing up, I came to realize that not everyone had a father like mine—starting with his appearance. From my earliest memories, Dad has had a full head of wavy, bright white hair and a thick, dignified mustache that gives him the look of George Washington or Mark Twain or Albert Einstein, going from least to most windy outside.

He was a warm, caring man who smiled a lot and was always proud of us. But he could be inscrutable, too. He rarely gave a clear, strong opinion unless he was asked directly, and even then he tended to speak in riddles, allusions, or roundabout responses that only he truly understood. I think he wanted other people to arrive at answers themselves, like any good professor, and hoped merely to lead us in the right direction.

He'd grown up in the Philadelphia suburbs and had gone to the all-male Haverford School. Since then he'd utterly rejected any sort of boys' club. As an adult, he'd been to more Grateful Dead concerts than golf courses. He was far more comfortable in a ratty T-shirt and a pair of old, tight, fuzzy ski pants than he ever would be in a polo and khakis. He exclusively wore sneakers, except for once, when he had to go to a wake—and then he borrowed my dress shoes. Here was a man wholly unimpressed with the appearance of things and fully enthralled with what lay below the surface.

Golf, ironically, was the only thing my parents and I ever fought about—never bad grades, juvenile misadventures, or other turbulent teenage behavior. When I wanted to join the high school team in ninth grade, it nearly tore apart the family. To my parents, golf was too white, too rich, too preppy, too exclusive. Couldn't I wait fifty years, they asked, until I had run out of other activities?

Mom and Dad were always eager to let Evan and me know what they thought, but they'd also always allowed us to make our own decisions, to figure out firsthand that they had been correct the whole time. So I was allowed to join the golf team. Maybe they thought I would miss soccer or develop a love for cross-country running or, best yet, realize that pursuing golf meant pursuing a life that was morally and physically against our family values. I didn't quit. But there was no question that they had won. I learned to think that there were two types of golf—the cheap, unrefined public course versus the private, stuffy country club—and that the former was the only type I would ever want to play.

Still, I *loved* golf. I wanted to keep playing, in college and beyond. And I didn't want to feel guilty for that. So really, secretly, I hoped that the sport, so famous for stratifying social classes, would show me something to justify my involvement in it. For the time being, the only way I was able to enter its world with a clean conscience was by establishing my role as an outsider—not a golfer, just a kid who happens to play golf—and sticking to it. That's what this trip was going to be all about.

I knew I would need a concrete plan before going to Dad so I could defend against any skepticism, show that this wasn't just a whim but a plan with depth and purpose.

Except I never really made a plan.

To be fair, I did devise some basic rules. I would play at least eighteen holes in every state in the lower forty-eight. I would pay for the whole thing myself, using my savings and whatever I could scrounge up along the way. My first leg would take me across the northern states in the fall, and then I'd move back across the South in the winter and use the spring to fill in the gaps. My goal was to experience all the golf America had to offer, from the worst city municipal to the locked-gate country club and everywhere in between. I wanted to seek out golf where I didn't belong and golf where nothing at all belonged. I had to survive the whole thing—and I had to do so without coming home, except for Christmas.

Foolproof, right?

Except I didn't know *how* I would do these things. I didn't know how I was going to pay for the trip. I had exactly $4,720 saved up and didn't have to use a calculator long to determine how quickly that could disappear.

Where would I sleep? I had a station wagon, so I could probably fit in the back when I needed to. I packed a two-man tent and I solicited contacts from family friends and made a list, state by state, of potential hosts. I soon found that the constant problem was not with the number of offers but with geographic concentration. Everyone had a friend in Chicago and a cousin in L.A.

Everyone "had me covered" in New York. Everyone had a golf-ing grandpa in Tampa.

I was touched by how eagerly people volunteered to look up old friends or call their least favorite relatives, but I was discour-aged by just how clustered these folks were. Hell, *my* grandfather lives in Tampa half the year. Dude loves golf.

I began to make a list of the lower forty-eight in the order in which I would tick them off, attempting to hone in on the approximate date I would arrive in each—but I soon realized that I couldn't really figure that out, either.

I wasn't a planner at all. If I decided to do something, I gener-ally just did it—and figured out *how* as I went along. So as excit-ing as it was to try to figure out the specifics of what and where and when, I didn't really want to have to answer to any schedule. I wanted this to operate on my terms; I'd confront issues as they arose.

As departure day—September 1—drew near, though, I real-ized I was leaving home with zero tee times, exactly one golf course lined up, and no idea where I would spend my first night on the road—knowing only that it had to be free.

Dad arrived home with a fresh roll of duct tape one late August afternoon. "There's not much you'll run into," he told me, dead-pan, "that a few strips of this can't fix." That was as close as he'd come to actually giving me his blessing for the trip, but it made me happy. *You'll be all right,* the gesture seemed to say. I took the tape. I was really doing this.

Urged on by Mom's insistence that I "just never knew" what I was going to need, I erred on the side of bringing too much. I took all the collared shirts I had—mostly yard-sale buys and hand-me-downs from my cousin Mark—and stuffed them into a low plastic crate alongside dozens of T-shirts, a smattering of shorts and pants, and my entire collections of socks and boxers. I stuffed winter clothes into a bag, jackets and gloves and hats, that went beneath the folded-up backseat. A raincoat and thick wind pants went into the mesh behind the driver's seat. And dress clothes went onto a couple hangers that I hooked above the driver's-side backseat.

I tried to divide the car into neighborhoods: There, on the right, with the cooler and the granola bars and the Honey Nut Cheerios, was Cereal Row. The plastic clothes crate spanned the width of the passenger seat. Plastic Plateau. I tried to leave room on the car's left side—though it was tough to fit anything between the extra clothes and the cooking supplies—and the ministove and the tent and the ski boots and the basketball and the football and the baseball gloves—for Golf Bag Boulevard, which I figured would hold my little red Titleist bag by day and could serve as a sleeping alley by night. Finally, the small gap between the pulled-up passenger's row and the back of the driver's seat: the Crevasse. Lots of things fell into the Crevasse. Few returned.

I hadn't even finished packing before these neighborhoods began collapsing into each other, which seemed like a bad sign. But I was tired of packing. I was tired of wondering exactly how I would figure out what I was doing. I was even tired of people asking why I was going. (No one wants to be asked a question for which they haven't yet figured a suitable answer.) I threw my golf bag in and slammed the trunk closed. I didn't know *how*. I was still a little hazy on *why*. But that was okay—I was going.

The next couple hours were an emotional blur. Mom crying. Dad, silent, choked up. Then I was crying, too, as I drove away, and I made my first wrong turn of the trip within miles of my house, and my second wrong turn soon after. But it didn't matter, because I had nowhere to go. Soon enough I'd left Massachusetts, speeding past Troy, New York, and then I was on I-90, where the first inkling of the trip was born months earlier. On a long drive back from a vacation with friends in Michigan, the idea had hit me during a three A.M. brainstorm with my brother. Most late-night ideas get brushed away the next morning, usually with good reason. But this one had stuck.

It brought me out of the haze, that realization. I was living out a dream—for myself, mostly, but also for the idea: It felt important that a kid could come up with a crazy plan and then just press pause on the rest of his life to go pursue it. I was breaking free, if only for a short while, from a modern world burdened by lofty expectations on a familiar path—grade school, high school, college, a good job. From my teenage eyes, it seemed like a lot of the people on that path forgot to do the one thing that matters most: live a little.

I knew as soon as I saw the sign for Alder Creek Golf Course and Country Inn that I had found what I was looking for. An eight-dollar opening round in Boonville, New York, was *exactly* what I had envisioned for my first round.

My background with golf had taught me that rounds like this were the best kind. I wanted my trip to glorify the Podunk two-buck municipal. Elite clubs seemed like another meaningless status symbol, kind of like Rolls-Royces, which I assumed people just bought so they could say, *Hey, here's something I own that you can never have.*

They didn't exactly roll out the red carpet at Alder Creek. As I pulled into the driveway, I noted a dilapidated practice green a few yards off the road, its mini-flagsticks leaning one way or the other as if to mimic the schizophrenic grass on the putting surface itself. Hundreds of golf balls, some yellow and some an old, coffee-stained shade of white, lay abandoned on the ground of the too-short driving range, which looked as if it would serve as their final resting place. Wild grass had conquered two wheels and part of the front cage of the range picker and seemed determined to envelop it entirely.

My tire flattened a Busch Light can as I pulled into a parking spot in front of a large-ish white house that might've been the beginning of the Country Inn. Wait, no—there was a sign on it. ALDER CREEK GOLF—COUNTRY INN. FOOD-BEV. LODGING.

It read like a classified ad that didn't want to pay for the next ten words. I ignored its accompanying arrow, which pointed unhelpfully skyward, and continued to the right, in search of GOLF and maybe FOOD-BEV.

Lots of courses have signs by the road to encourage drive-ins, like PUBLIC WELCOME or COME PLAY! I wondered what Alder Creek's would've said: JOIN US FOR A ROUND! OR DON'T! SERIOUSLY, WE DON'T GIVE A DAMN.

Alder Creek's complete absence of presentation reminded me distinctly of Stamford Valley Golf Course, the site of my first membership and just across the Vermont border from home. I was eleven, and it cost me sixty bucks. I'd experienced a lot of firsts there. I'd rented my first golf cart. I'd made my first eagle, on the 369-yard, quadruple dogleg par-5 fourth, where if you scooted over the rock wall but stayed under the trees you could save yourself two shots. I'd gotten the f-word directed at me for the first time, after I short-hopped some guy's thigh, still learning the power I wielded with a driver in my hand. Stamford was legendary, the home of the goose turd and the eight-year-old maintenance crew, and I did a lot of growing up there. Alder Creek brought me back: the driveway, the practice green, the flattened Busch Light. It felt like a good place to start my journey.

Beyond Alder Creek's practice area, the golf course stretched back into the trees. As I approached the inn from the parking lot, I paused to watch a man step up to his ball, eyeing the flagstick from a hundred yards out on what I would soon learn was the seventh green. There's something about watching complete strangers hit golf shots that has always fascinated me—an obsession fueled by the endless possibilities of flight and the near certainty of human failure. I guess it's the same reason people watch NASCAR—for the crashes. This guy, dressed in a T-shirt and cutoff jean shorts, didn't disappoint.

After a methodical—if uneasy—takeaway that curled his club directly over his head, all semblance of rhythm disappeared. He descended on his target, delivering a wood-splitting hack at the earth behind his ball. The welcome mat of a divot stuck to his iron through impact, while the ball tumbled ahead out of sheer terror, coming to a stop ten feet forward and twenty feet to the side. Was this fun for him? What made him decide that playing golf was a good idea?

Lots of people are bad at things. Some people even have the misfortune of being bad at lots of things. Golf, though, is one of those things that people tend to be really, particularly bad at—yet those are often the same people always calling around to arrange a foursome. This was interesting: the mysterious paradox of the Bad Golfer. I wished I had shown up an hour earlier; I would've had a compelling partner.

I stalled through several minutes' worth of practice swings on the first tee in the hopes that another local would show up to join me for an afternoon nine, but all traffic seemed to have moved the way of the parking lot or the bar. Eventually I snagged a Titleist from my golf bag and coaxed a tee into the soft earth, leaving the ball about half an inch above the ground—perfect for my 3-wood.

I took a deep breath. *The first tee shot.* I didn't know what it meant, exactly, but this drive seemed important. How many first tees would the next year hold? At what golf courses would they be? I hoped they wouldn't all be solitary rounds, that others would join me—people with stories and senses of humor and wisdom.

If anyone was watching me, they would have had no idea what this single swing signified. I didn't know, either, how I was supposed to feel at the start of something so big, something so crazy. I wasn't moving in to college, wasn't meeting new friends as I hung pictures of the old ones on my wall. I was doing something big, but it was hard to know *how* to feel as I stood over the ball that late summer day somewhere in upstate New York.

I had been emotional all afternoon, not happy-sad emotional, but in a way that made everything feel magnified, like the world was more alive than usual. The sun was brighter, the views more impressive, the attached modular garages more architecturally compelling. That was one of my hopes for the year, really—to take the time to find significance in the insignificant. But did that really make sense? Did driving aimlessly like this make sense? And what if I was wrong about golf, about golfers—what if every first tee remained empty?

First-tee ennui. Some of this unease must have translated into the shot. My whippy backswing joined in a panicked union with my downswing, and my club head hardly even nipped the top of the ball. I looked up sheepishly to see the Titleist skittering along the ground just yards in front of me. It didn't even make the fairway.

I glanced around to see if anyone had witnessed the embarrassing spectacle. The coast was mercifully clear, I thought, until I noticed someone walking by the edge of the clubhouse—my jean-shorted friend disappearing around the corner, heading for the eighth tee. I wondered if he'd watched my tee ball. I wondered if he'd told jokes about me in his head. It was a humbling moment as I walked several steps forward to hit my ball again and wondered if I really knew anything about golf after all.

In truth, Alder Creek was disappointingly well maintained. If I really wanted to slum it, this wasn't the place. The greens were so large that they accommodated two flags (white for the front nine, blue for the back), and they were smooth if not fast. Any imperfections in the fairways seemed to disappear in the low afternoon sun, as if the lengthening shadows had snuck around, filling in divots.

My golf swing improved from the first tee, and the course did as well—working its way back from the highway into the middle stretch of holes, pleasantly contained by the surrounding Adirondack forest and devoid of human life. The *ping!* of my driver was the only thing that interrupted the serenity of my surroundings, coated in late summer sun.

But as I putted out on the final green, maybe an hour after I'd started, some of the serenity faded. Our memories tend to form in two ways—from our first and last impressions. As I walked from the ninth green to my car, I was left with the impression that Alder Creek wasn't particularly strong on either side.

The enduring sights in our memory also develop in the remembering. There was a particular place at Alder Creek I would revisit often, the sight of which would grow more miserable in my mind's eye. Over the subsequent months I would remember a patch behind the inn's lodging that must have been intended to be a playground. A graveyard of miscellany was scattered across the ground, where a tornado had apparently gone through a tag sale a decade earlier. What had once been lawn chairs lay strewn across what had once been a lawn, a collage of plastic and metal and cloth. A faded-blue former trampoline had crumpled at the edge of the deep grass, a soggy taco of rust and neglect. Cracked Wiffle balls and broken Frisbees had succumbed to the decay of time like artifacts from a forgotten civilization. The centerpiece of misery, though, was a pink tricycle with two oversize back wheels and no front one at all. I imagined a little girl snapping her front axle in a midlawn crash, but the visual didn't quite work. Maybe it had been her brother, jealous that she had a real toy while he had to go hit on the driving range with Dad. Or a golfer coming off a tough double bogey on number nine, wielding an iron in maniacal vengeance. Maybe it was just nature taking back control, breaking down the new bike just to ensure that the lawn remained in a state of derelict equilibrium.

Every day we see *pieces* of the bigger puzzle, hints of the network of human lives we inhabit. People coming and going, fighting and making up. We see what they carry with them and what they leave behind, and we wonder why. People watching, some people call it. I fancied it more like detective work; I looked for little details and hints that might answer the question of why they were doing what they were doing. It's the same reason I love going to the airport. Everyone is going somewhere, with someone, for a different purpose, but time and opportunity have fated them to spend a few hours in the same tin can thirty thousand feet above the ground. It's a miracle of humanity, the way people's paths intersect, and watching these intersections became, for me, the greatest guessing game in the world—and one in which the real answers almost always remained a mystery.

I have a hard time letting go of these puzzles. I can't stop wondering how they fit together. Any resolutions I reach just make it worse—they drive the questions deeper. *How are those two related? Are they on a date? What number date? Have they had sex?* That urge to be an observer of humans and all their wacky behavior—that's part of what drove me on this trip. Over the next year I'd collect a lifetime of clues, an infinite number of puzzles that I couldn't solve. But I'd have the time, and the freedom, to figure out some for myself, to follow teenage curiosities.

I was still wondering how the tricycle had become a bicycle as I climbed onto a stool at the Lowville Diner some thirty miles down Route 12. The cook greeted me with a low grunt. He was wearing a blue Eli Manning T-shirt, and from the looks of it outweighed most of the Giants' offensive line. I glanced down at the Red Sox tee I had just thrown on, realizing it might not have been the wisest choice. On the surface, then, he and I had little in common. I never got past the surface. I would have to work on that: navigating local customs.

I finished a burger, which was good, and followed it up with a slice of blueberry pie, which wasn't. The sun was beginning to disappear over the hills to my left as I got back on the road, pointing Subi northwest. As I drove through the outskirts of Watertown a half hour later, it was almost completely dark, but I pressed onward to Sackets Harbor, a small town jutting from a peninsula into northern Lake Ontario. I pulled Subi to a stop in a park and walked around some before settling into a bench over-looking the water's edge. I watched as the last orange reflections disappeared beneath the evening's swells. It had been just twelve hours since I left Williamstown.

I stayed on that bench for a while, just thinking. Most of my friends were settling into college right now, completing orientation trips or decorating dorm rooms. And here I was, alone in Sackets Harbor, watching the sun set. There were no professors cramping my schedule, no classes to attend (or skip), no practices to get to. Hell, nobody even knew for sure where I was, never mind where I was going. I didn't even know myself, exactly. I knew one thing: Tomorrow was another golf day. I had gotten a text from a friend of a friend in Rochester: 1:30 tee time the next afternoon at Irondequoit Country Club. A family friend's "Oh, maybe I could help" had come through. I took it as a good sign. From there? Subi and I would keep heading west.

For now, though, I was my own master, counting stars on a cloudless night over Lake Ontario. I understood that this freedom put me in a pretty unique situation. Anyone with as few restrictions as I had was probably unemployed, retired, or homeless. Yet here I was—sure, sort of homeless, but with no desire for or pressure to gain employment—and retirement wasn't exactly on my horizon.

But despite all this freedom, I still didn't really know *why* I was doing what I was doing. I had explanations, sure, answers I could recite when concerned parents had pushed for them in the preceding months. For whatever reason, my own parents had never quite asked for the why, although they had every reason to. I was smart and athletic. I had friends. I had liked high school and was excited for college. I had never wanted for anything, never gotten in trouble, had never made any enemies. I was on a path to likely success. What was it about me that needed to mess that up?

Why would come when it had to, I guessed. All I had to do the first night was find somewhere to sleep.

From growing up in Williamstown, I knew it would be easy to find a quiet place in a quiet town. Somewhere to read, maybe, or to go make out. Not that making out seemed likely to be in the cards anytime soon.

Finding somewhere to spend an entire night, though, quickly

proved a much more difficult task. I drove along the shore, looking for campsites or pullouts. I cruised through back roads, sure there would be a park or a turnaround. Nothing. One street abruptly concluded in a dead end, and as I slowed to make a three-point turn I saw a woman peering out her kitchen window. I could tell from her look: I was an intruder. I didn't like the feeling.

I'd thought about all the places you could sleep undisturbed in Williamstown—there were a million—and figured that everywhere else would be the same. Most of the time I'd get there in time to pitch a tent, I figured, and other times I'd just clear out room in the backseat. I hadn't considered until now that you can't exactly discover these places in a day. Hmm. This was going to be harder than I'd thought.

I got on the highway heading south, hoping to catch some bit of inspiration from a road sign. A few minutes passed and I saw a sign for a state park. *Perfect.* State parks were quiet. They had camping. Nobody would be around. There might even be a shower I could use in the morning.

I pulled in through the gates and followed the left turn for parking. The park road was well back from the highway and just a few dozen feet from Lake Ontario. I saw a sign that read, in large red letters, NO CAMPING ON THE BEACH, but this didn't worry me. It was too late to set up my tent, and besides, the radio had told me it was supposed to rain. I pulled around a corner and entered a parking lot so massive I figured it couldn't fill up on even the hottest July day. In fairness, there *was* a sign by the entrance, again in bold red lettering, that said, NO OVERNIGHT PARKING.

But it was well after ten o'clock on a September weeknight. Who would care?

I would come to learn that, in any state park, at any time in the day, someone is always there whose job it is to care. I pulled to the far corner of the lot and got out, opening the trunk to survey things. If I was going to sleep in this thing, I needed to do some serious rearranging—which was pretty bad considering I had packed the car that very morning. As I stood scratching my head, headlights swooped across the parking lot and made a bee-line in my direction. Uh-oh.

The park ranger slammed to a halt next to me, his window already down, gray goatee glinting in the moonlight.

"What're you doing out here?" His voice was gruff, low, humorless.

I had no answer ready. "Hanging out?" *Nice one.*

"You know you can't spend the night here."

It wasn't a question. "Uh, yeah," I responded. "Just leaving." He rolled his window back up. I fiddled around with some bags for another minute, waiting for him to drive off. He didn't.

I was defeated, again. The ranger followed me most of the way to the exit before turning off, presumably to protect another besieged parking lot.

This was supposed to be the easy part. But I had been trying to park my car for a few hours now. Anywhere. And I couldn't figure that out? What the hell was I going to do for the next year?

I would do a lot of nighttime thinking over the next year, and a lot of nighttime driving. And the thing I kept learning was that whatever feelings you brought into the car with you—frustration or contentment, anger or hope—would get magnified on the lit road in front of you. Maybe it's what happens when you can't see too far ahead.

I was frustrated as hell. Helpless and frustrated. It got worse as I got lost while heading back to the highway. "Lost" isn't quite right, I guess, because I had no idea where I wanted to end up.

It had started to drizzle. Lightly, so that I didn't have to turn my windshield wipers on, but the rain was visible as I drove on, like static in the headlights. I made a turn that put me on a smaller road. And then another one, onto a different, bigger road. It was the same thing I had been doing for hours. How many hours had it been? One? Five? And was that the same intersection I had already been to? That looked like the same stop sign. Perfect. I was going in circles.

But as I kept driving on that same road, the one that might have connected the towns of Adams and Rodman, a pullout appeared on the left.

It was no more than a hundred feet long, but it ducked behind a low hill that gave it some protection from the road. It was mostly gravel and somewhat hidden—the type of roadside nook where police hide when they're looking to catch speeders. I had been looking for a place like this for nearly two hours, and now one had found me.

But as I surveyed the night around me, I had a little burst of anxiety. Who else used these spots? What if someone else came into the turnaround and ran into me? What if the cops found me there?

It would have to do. I shut the lights and turned off the engine. I clambered into the backseat as best I could, shimmying around the driver's seat and over the CD case. I grabbed my golf bag and shoved it up onto a couple duffels to the side. I unpacked my sleeping bag and an extra liner, which was basically like a giant pillowcase for my body. It was too hot to zip everything up all the way, so I left the windows cracked to keep some air moving through.

The narrow sleeping alley I had tunneled out was far from perfect. My golf clubs were a nudge away from crashing, driver first, onto my chest. The section of car I had cleared seemed like it could fit my head—pressed against the driver's seat—*or* my feet—crunched into the rear door—but not both; if I adjusted one, the other cried out in discomfort. Worst of all was the clothes container that dug into my ribs, the big plastic thing that spanned the width of the backseat, forcing me to lie sideways on a step. And as I lay there, wondering how I was ever going to fall asleep, I couldn't stop grinning.

Why was I doing it? Why was I going? Hell, I didn't know. But I was seventeen, and I had a car, and I had a year, and I had a big, vague plan.

This was going to be the best adventure ever.

CHAPTER 2

Exposure

B lack people do play golf.

It wasn't a revolutionary idea. Not in 2009. Tiger Woods, the best golfer in the world, was African-American, of course, and he'd given the face of the American game a new skin tone. But when I hit a red light at a busy South Buffalo intersection, stopped, and looked to my left, I was a little surprised by what I saw.

I'd seen African-Americans on the course before, but rural western Massachusetts was a very white place, and as far as I'd *seen*, so was the golfing world. Here, though, foursomes of black men and women trekked flat fairways in downtown South Buffalo. I felt naïve for thinking that it looked different. But I liked that I was here to see it.

I'd slept for a few hours that first night, waking up several times to imagined noises coming in through the windows. Soon after the sun rose, I was up for good. I finished off my bag of minibagels, brushed my teeth, rinsed with my water bottle, peed behind Subi, and found my way back onto I-81 south. By noon I'd made it to Irondequoit Country Club in Rochester for a sunny afternoon round with Joe, a friend of a friend from home.

The second day had been easy, really. And I was feeling good.

Now, on day three, I was flying solo again through South Buffalo. I pulled into a driveway next to a sign proclaiming, GROVER CLEVELAND GOLF COURSE, SITE OF THE 1912 U.S. OPEN.

This seemed like a dubious claim. Grover Cleveland looked like an ordinary municipal course, a "muni," the kind with a simple one-story clubhouse and white plastic chairs scattered across the patio out front.

I paid the junior rate—fourteen dollars—and teed off alone. It was a warm afternoon, the kind of day when the ball flies far and bounces farther, and I quickly caught up to the group in front of me. I played through them, and the foursome in front of them, too, and then I caught up to another single on the fifth tee—a man named Gerald. I could see him taking his time as I got off the fourth green, waiting hopefully.

"Mind if I join you?" I called ahead.

His face crinkled into a warm smile. "That would be wonderful."

No more than five foot seven with a bit of a stomach, the seventy-six-year-old had soft blue eyes, a cautious smile, and spoke with a quiet pride. He was delighted that I was an out-of-towner, and even more so that I was interested in his home course, and he was eager to tell me about it. To Gerald, Grover Cleveland was home, where he spent five to six days a week—including Mondays with his wife.

Though it was originally a private country club, the county had long since taken control of the course, and it hadn't flourished under new ownership. They'd sold sections of land to the adjacent hospital, shortening and diminishing the layout. What was left was a par 69, at just 5,700 yards—longer eighteens frequently top 7,000—and a course that was entirely defenseless. The terrain was flat, hard, and fast, so balls bounced extra long on fairways already much too short. A smattering of diminutive pine trees did little to block the sun from the ground, never mind a player from his target.

The course was dotted with the occasional bunker, and these actually *were* essential to avoid. Not so much because they'd be hard to hit from—the traps were flat and shallow—but because

I cringed at the thought of cleaning that gray dirt-and-goose-dropping sludge from between my spikes.

Still, at least you could stay away from these hard-packed litter boxes. Forget filling water hazards (there were none); it wasn't clear that Grover Cleveland used any water at all. The greens, which were brown, had been recently aerated and were so slow and bumpy that most putts didn't break but instead bounced from side to side in an incalculable vacillation that, with some luck, ended in the general vicinity of the hole.

Most courses have gotten longer and greener over the last century. Mowing has gotten more efficient. Strategies of aeration (where they take a hole puncher to the greens, basically, to get oxygen to the grass roots) have evolved into a careful science, and fairways are flusher, greens smoother. Every surface is more controlled now than it was a decade ago. Grover Cleveland was moving in the other direction, defying every advance in technology and maintenance. If this place had been good enough to host the U.S. Open, that meant that in the previous century it had accomplished something rare: This course was significantly *worse* than it had been in 1912.

But Gerald didn't like to think of it that way. "It's a nice course," he insisted. "The greens don't roll the quickest, but they're true." Gerald's pride in the course was part of a larger affection for his hometown. "Oh, I'm Buffalo born and raised," he declared. "I went to high school right over there. Buffalo's got good people. All around. I've been to a few cities in my day, but this is where I belong."

It struck me as odd that *this* was what anyone would choose. I had no doubt that Grover Cleveland was a friendly, convenient, welcoming place to play golf. But the course, like the city, smacked of decline.

We hit our tee shots and walked up the fairway while Gerald continued to muse and advise, generally thinking out loud. He told me about his sons, Richard and Eric, of whom Eric was larger—"stronger'n hell"—but Richard was the better golfer—"he's got those hands, y'know? Those soft hands." He told me of his hole in one, told me how you never do know about such things. He told me how, if I tied a string from my golf bag to my head cover, I would never lose it, and how, if I just watched him a little more carefully, I could hit the fairway every time too. When I said I was headed to Cleveland, he told me the route. When I said I was headed out West, he told me about a campground in Colorado that I *had* to see.

Gerald told me freakin' *everything*. And he spoke with no ambiguity, instead with irrefutable fact—as though his sentences were answers to questions I had not asked.

"I must say, I am excited for you," he told me. "But a little concerned. There are a few things you'll struggle with as you go along . . ."

One of the grandiose claims people make about golf is that it's a lot like life. It's the same claim that baseball fans make about baseball, or tennis players about tennis. The game's nuances as proverbs for life. Most of the time I wasn't so sure with my sport. Golf seemed as if it was probably just a game whose players are the type of big talkers given to thoughts like "Wow, golf is really a lot like life." Still, as I listened to Gerald talk about his golf game I noticed a lot more coming through than just swing tips.

The way Gerald talked about life, he seemed to think mostly about surviving, about keeping his head above water. If golf was like life, then life was a lot simpler than I had come to believe. In golf, you figure out the right answer eighteen times a round. In life, how do you ever know you have it? It made sense that he never missed a fairway—any unknown, to Gerald, was a danger. Any golfer will tell you that you might score worse, but you *learn* more playing from the rough. I liked Gerald a lot. He was kind, caring, and pleasant to play with. But I worried that maybe he himself had given up on learning.

He was really trying to help, I think. But the idea of such a big trip seemed to scare him, and escaped him even while he tried to keep the idea within his control, as if he were tying a balloon around his wrist. There was just such a stark contrast between us, the man whose world seemed like it was shrinking while mine was expanding to parts unknown.

Whatever certainty and stability he had in his golf game, Gerald betrayed all of it in his body language. Comments were sometimes followed by a pause and a nervous chuckle, and more than once I looked over to see him staring sadly off to the east, into the cramped confines of the city. The stories, the advice, the statements of fact, I realized, were Gerald's attempt to stay relevant as a retired man starting to get lost in Buffalo's chaos. Grover Cleveland Golf Course was his sphere of control. Anyone who threatened that sphere was an enemy. As we teed off on the twelfth hole, the twosome behind us, a young man and his wife, drove their golf cart up beside the putting surface—too close for Gerald.

"Why don't you just park on the green?" he growled. "Asshole."

But with me, he was thrilled to have a companion, someone with whom he could share his ideas and his memories. Our handshake on the eighteenth green was earnest, an acknowledgment that we had found something in common, the seventeen-year-old watching the world open up and the seventy-six-year-old trying to hold on to his fair share.

Playing with Gerald was a momentous occasion—my first full round with a complete stranger. I was fascinated by this friendly old man and by his eagerness to tell me his story, and even more by the closeness I felt after just a few hours with him. He was encouraging, and kind of sad, and if everyone I met over the next year was as interesting to me as Gerald was, I knew my trip would be a success. I knew because I was sorry to leave Gerald.

"Really, you know, this is why I play golf," he said gruffly, looking at the ground. "I like to meet people like you."

Likewise.

• • •

Having checked New York off the list—three times over—I crossed the border into northwest Pennsylvania later that night. The gates to Presque Isle State Park had shut at eleven, but Subi and I could stay awake no longer. There was a small restaurant just outside the park gates with a mostly empty parking lot. Good enough.

But I slept fitfully, uncomfortable in my sleeping nook and not fully at ease on the edge of this parking lot. By five A.M., I had rolled around enough. I made my way around the gate and walked into the park as the sun emerged, staining Lake Erie a dull orange as it rose, covering one swell at a time, cutting the morning's chill.

The whole day was ahead of me, but I had already decided that Pennsylvania could wait for the return journey. My plan was to head counterclockwise around the lower forty-eight: Snow was coming, soon, to the northern United States. I may have had total freedom, but I also had a big goal—and a brain that kept factors like Mother Nature in mind. With nearly a week of September already behind me, I couldn't dawdle on my way to Washington.

Of course, that wasn't actually true. If there had been *real* urgency, I could have driven to Seattle in a matter of days rather than a couple months. But I wanted to make *some* progress— checking off states and rounds and experiences—and find some balance between having a plan and maintaining my total freedom. For now, though, the plan was pretty simple: Dawdle. Explore. Drive on.

I lingered in Ohio for a couple days. I played with David, an acquaintance and Williams alum, at Mayfield–Sand Ridge Country Club, where there were pretzel sticks and lemonade every third tee box. And I played at Shawnee Hills, a public course, with Drew and Tom, whom I sort of knew, and Art, whom none of us knew but who was eager to converse, and to help if he could.

"You got a weapon?" It was the first thing he asked me once he heard what I was doing. "You could use a gun. Gimme the afternoon, I'd get you a gun." Things were going well. People were looking out for me already. I laughed off Art's offer as absurd— what would I want with a gun?

I didn't think about the gun until later that night as I lay wrapped in my sleeping bag in the back of Subi and remembered, as I did every night, that I was very much alone—the type of thinking that made me just a little bit anxious.

I knew the financial crisis had hit eastern Michigan hard. I knew it because I had read it in newspapers and magazines and on the Internet, and because people liked to make fun of Detroit, which was funny until you thought about it too much, and then it felt cruel and kind of depressing. What I didn't know, though, was what the collapsed economy would look or sound like. And I was curious. I hoped that was okay, to be curious about suffering.

Where I grew up, after all, a factory was just an old brick building down by the Little League field—the one with weeds growing through the windows. None of them had been operational in my lifetime, that was for sure. And unemployment? Wherever *that* existed, it was wrapped in hushed conversation under layers of euphemism. So I entered the city limits of Flint, Michigan, with particular anticipation, knowing how this town—for decades an auto-industry titan—had fallen on hard times.

I thought I was braced for desolation, but Flint exceeded expectation. The ENTERING FLINT road sign bore another inscription, scrawled diagonally in black spray paint: GET OUT *NOW*, the last three letters enlarged—in case the message wasn't absolutely clear. As I pulled up to a stoplight, I noticed the emptiness of the broad road's four other lanes. A single car sputtered up next to me. I tried to picture the same stoplight a decade ago—or was it two decades, or three?—and wondered if all five lanes would've been filled, thousands of proud Michiganders on their way to work. In the skyline ahead I could see factories, ghostly outlines in the morning haze.

Red turned to green, Subi lurched forward, and I entered a

residential area. Rows of houses appeared down side streets, bas-ketball hoops hanging into the road and the occasional garbage can left at the end of a driveway. A neighborhood. But where were all the neighbors? All I could see were houses. Some sat in disrepair, with chipping paint and missing shingles.

Others were boarded up entirely and had been for a long time—even the slats nailed over the windows were weathered or broken. Their rectangular front yards were overgrown. Shin-length grass had worked its way down driveways and into the cracks in the sidewalks. One fence sagged miserably over the curb, every gust of wind threatening to dispatch it into the road. Each dilapidated property seemed to blur into the next.

The residential sector bled into the remnants of a commercial district where closed businesses and abandoned lots lined the street. One parking lot served as an open grave for broken-down cars, although a faded sign claiming AUTO REPAIR hung limply above the adjacent garage.

Over the next few blocks, roadside desolation gave way to des-perate sales pitches. CHEAP CARS!!! LOWEST PRICES EVER! WORRIED ABOUT THAT CREDIT SCORE? WORRY NO MORE! GOOD CREDIT? BAD CREDIT? NO CREDIT? NO PROBLEM! Car lots bordered repair shops that bordered more car lots, lots that offered new cars for cheap and used cars for cheaper. A mangled Pontiac sports car sat in an open parking area bearing a flat tire, a cracked windshield, and a sign reading, optimistically, $1000 OR BEST OFFER.

This didn't look like a place that would have a golf course, or anything so bright and mowed and playful. But I had checked my laptop at the Holiday Inn Express in Fenton that morning and, sure enough, several were still listed within the city limits. So which should I choose? I entered and exited the parking lots of two courses—one looked too expensive, the other looked too abandoned—before settling on Swartz Creek, a municipal just southwest of the city that overlooked several old auto factories. I paid the fourteen-dollar greens fee and was heading for the first hole when a man in a sun-stained black polo shirt and khaki shorts entered the pro shop. I asked him if he wanted a playing partner. He chuckled.

"Ah, no," he said. "I'm just practicing for now. Wouldn't want you to have to spend the whole round in the woods looking for my ball."

I continued to the tee alone. The opening drive was straight out, and I could see a distant line of red stakes denoting a water hazard. 265 YARDS TO THE CREEK, read a sign next to the tee box. I made a few aggressive practice swings, trying to loosen up a crick in my neck that I'd acquired from my previous night's stay outside a town called Holly, where I had found a dirt turn-around down a quiet-enough back road. The crick wasn't going away, though, so I cozied my driver up behind the Titleist 4, took a hard cut at the ball, and felt the satisfaction of impact as it jumped off the center of the clubface. I watched the ball soar out over the creek, drawing gently from the middle of the fairway to the left side as it landed safely on the far side of the water and bounded forward on the dry surface.

Satisfied, I turned to pick up my tee. "You're gonna kill some-one with that swing," called a voice from the edge of the practice green. The man with the black polo was smiling in my direction. "You in that junior PGA event this weekend?"

"No," I answered. "Just traveling through, trying to get a feel for the area."

"Traveling through here?" He was confused. "Your parents with you?"

"Nah, just me."

"Just you? Do you know where you're staying?"

"Haven't figured it out yet."

His expression shifted to one of worry. "Well, be careful around here. Keep your head about you, y'know? I was a fire-man in this city for twenty-seven years, and it's as bad now as ever. If I were you, son, I'd play your round and then get the hell out of Flint by the time it gets dark."

He bid me good luck and safe travels, and I set off onto the

front nine, his words seared into my mind. *By the time it gets dark.*
He made it sound lawless, violent—an urban Wild West.

Whatever Flint lacked in ambience, Swartz Creek was a fine,
cheap, friendly golf course. It measured out to a midlength from
the back tees, at 6,700 yards. Tall fescue grasses lined some holes,
while the woods and the creek lined several others. Still, the
broad fairways allowed for a fair margin of error, and it wasn't
a particularly challenging layout. I made it through the front
nine in a brisk one over, playing through one twosome before
catching up to another at the turn. Two African-American men
were waiting on the tenth tee when I approached from the ninth
green. "Go ahead, young man, we don't want to hold you up,"
said the older of the two.

"You guys want a third?" I asked. The older man looked at his
partner, visibly surprised, but after a moment told me sure, that
would be fine. The younger one introduced himself as Lamar,
his partner as Randy.

Randy teed off first, his swing slow but on a steady plane, and
his ball tracked down the left side of the fairway before skittering into the edge of the rough. Lamar slapped a 3-wood that shot
out low but rose into a high, soft cut that dropped in the center
of the fairway. I hit last and worst, snapping my 3-wood well left
of Randy's ball into the shadow of a short tree. I tried to project
nonchalance as I picked up my tee and slung the 3-wood back in
my bag. Nobody likes playing with an angry kid.

I walked with Randy toward our balls until he broke the
silence.

"Haven't seen you around here." I couldn't tell if he was curious or just didn't like the awkward quiet.

"No, I'm not even from Michigan, actually," I told him. "I'm
from Massachusetts, just traveling through the area."

He raised an eyebrow. "Traveling through?" Again the same
skeptical—suspicious, even—tone as the fireman. I was guessing
people didn't "travel through" Flint very often.

"Well, sort of. I'm trying to go to every state this year, playing golf and talking to people. I finished high school this spring and—"

"Well, congratulations."

"What?"

"Congratulations. Graduation, that's a fine accomplishment."

"Oh—thanks." I was taken aback. In Williamstown, graduating high school was just something you did. I didn't expect to be really, genuinely congratulated for it any more than I did for brushing my teeth. But then this *really* wasn't Williamstown.

"So you're going everywhere?" he continued. "For how long?"

"Until next June. That's the plan, at least."

He gave a low whistle. "Damn. Now that's pretty cool."

I noticed Lamar had heard the last part. "Let me get this straight," he yelled over to us. "You're going to see the whole damn country, and you came to Flint?"

"I heard you can't see Michigan without seeing Flint," I offered, not sure if I was telling a joke. "So here I am."

"Well, shit, you could have," he exclaimed, grinning for a moment. "Ain't no reason to come see this goddamn place." We walked on. "That is pretty cool, though," he added. "When I graduated, it was, 'Get your ass to work.'"

As I soon learned, both Randy, who was fifty-nine, and Lamar, ten years younger, had worked at General Motors their entire careers.

"See those towers?" Randy asked me on the twelfth hole, closest to the factories across the highway. "I remember when there was smoke pouring out of them all the time. Twenty-five thousand people working there every day. Now? Three, maybe four thousand. Way it used to be, you knew coming out of high school there was a place for you in the factory. Now what happens to you?" He directed the last question at me, suggesting that had I grown up in Flint, not Williamstown, things would be different. He wasn't accusing me of anything. He just sounded sad.

"Everyone's talking about the economy now, like we got some

new problem," Lamar added. "We've been in a recession here for nine years. Don't nobody hear nothing about it until now." I wondered if nine was right, or if it was ten, or twenty, or more.

"You've lived here your whole life?"

"Unfortunately," he responded, and lapsed into silence.

I was afraid to ask exactly why, at age forty-nine, he was "retired." Maybe it had been his choice; he had saved up enough in his twenty-five years there. Listening to them talk, though, it was hard to believe that I had stumbled upon the only two people in the area who had left their jobs voluntarily.

It can be hard to get a sense of someone's golf game from just a few shots, but these two were well versed in the layout of their home course. Not working—voluntarily or not—had afforded them plenty of time to get to know Swartz Creek. Randy ran off a string of pars while Lamar followed a bogey-double-bogey start by draining consecutive lengthy birdie putts. Their contrasting styles mirrored their personalities—Randy was strong but steady, Lamar volatile, a ball of potential with a chip firmly planted on his shoulder.

Lamar swung the club with the powerful, aggressive rhythm of someone who had grown up around golf. I was surprised to hear him say, then, that he had only taken up the game five years before. It wasn't until several holes later that I understood where the swing had come from. On the par-4 thirteenth, he launched his drive down the right side and it settled a few yards off-line in the edge of the rough.

"Crushed it," I said. "Nice shot."

"Can still hit a curveball a damn sight better than a golf ball," he remarked, the sort of throwaway line people drop when they're too proud to say thanks.

But he had opened up a whole new line of questioning. I coaxed out of Lamar that he had played Division I baseball for Mississippi's Jackson State and had an impressive baseball heritage. His father and uncle had played in the Negro Leagues, and he had three first cousins who played pro ball.

"You ever heard of Dennis Boyd?" he asked. "He pitched for your Red Sox."

"Oil Can Boyd—of course," I said. Oil Can was an eighties legend, a walking quote machine who was famous for the way he reportedly combined his loves of baseball, booze, and blow. This was great. "That's your cousin? No way!"

Lamar wasn't so starstruck. "Dude can't let go of the game," Lamar said of his most famous relative, who was still pitching in a league in Las Vegas at age fifty. "He's always trying to get me to go watch him. I tell him, I don't wanna watch your old ass pitch! I ain't going to see no senior citizens play baseball."

Lamar did his best to undersell his own baseball career, too, but reading between the lines led me to believe his college career had included some star power of its own. He had even spent a few years bouncing around low-level pro ball. Even as I prodded him to tell me more, though, he made sure to distance himself, to make it clear: *He* wasn't the kid who had spent summers on buses so far away from here. Or if that kid *was* him, those rides only ever had one destination; all the stops were just little detours on his way back to Flint. I didn't get the sense that he was glad he had stopped, glad that he'd made it back. I got the sense that he had wondered, "What if?" ever since.

It was a power of possibility that he had lost in the decades since. From hearing him tell it, his city had lost some of its sense of what was possible, too. But golf has a sneaky way of introducing some new hope back into people's minds. Famous people take up the game when they need a new challenge—Michael Jordan, having beaten the game of basketball into submission, tried to conquer golf; Justin Timberlake became a golf fanatic once topping the music charts became routine; Bill Murray and Bing Crosby and Bob Hope sought out golf to stay entertained once they'd entertained everyone else.

Maybe Oil Can should've taken up golf. Maybe Lamar should've kept playing baseball. Or perhaps, by this point, it didn't matter. Lamar, like anyone who plays the game, seemed driven by the pursuit of a well-struck 5-iron, the type that drew without hooking and went high without ballooning and, most important, felt good in his hands—like it was hit right on the barrel of the bat.

"Golf keeps you chasing, man. You go all day trying to make that good swing, but just 'cause you've done it once don't mean you can do it again."

It struck me that the way he thought about the next shot, the next hole, the next round kept him looking forward in a city that seemed stuck on rewind. He didn't look like Gerald back in Buffalo, and he didn't sound much like him, either. But I felt that the way the two played the game had something in common. The chase.

I wanted to know if I was reading too far into it, if he felt the same way. But we were out of holes—the back nine was over. "Well, good luck to you," Lamar said as we putted out on the closing par-5, and added, half joking, "I hope for your sake you never have to come back here."

"I dunno," I replied. "I think I like it here."

He studied me, holding our handshake for an extra second before he shook his head. "Whatever you say, man."

I smiled. It seemed as close to a compliment as I was going to get. I started walking toward the parking lot, bag slung over my right shoulder as I noticed my shadow stretching out some thirty feet in front of me. It was beginning to get dark in Flint.

It felt too easy, heading to my car, leaving Flint the same day I had entered. If I'd been from the city, I'd be driving home, down the road, to join my family and friends in facing an uncertain future. Was there anything for me to learn from Flint? Was there anything to hope for?

"Hey, Dylan," Lamar called from behind me. "Buy you a Coke?"

I guess if everyone left when it got dark, there would be nobody around when things got lighter. I could stay a while longer.

CHAPTER 3

Solitude

My days in the Midwest drifted by like clouds, passing slowly but disappearing quickly, moving at the whims of the wind.

I left Flint and drove west until I hit water, then pitched a tent on the eastern shore of Lake Michigan. Next I cut back south down the center of Indiana, wondering how many miles away I could spot headlights on the dead-flat, dead-straight county roads. I stayed with a friend's parents' friends, Mac and Sarah, in Indianapolis, which struck me as the quietest, most content collection of one million people I could have imagined. And when I mentioned that I wanted to experience rural Indiana firsthand, they told me to stay in their farmhouse for a night, deep in Amish country. I stayed three nights, by myself, in a house built in 1828 that got so dark that I couldn't even see my feet as they creaked along the centuries-old floorboards.

In what became my Friday-night tradition, I got into Subi and turned on the AM radio, scanned until I heard the unmistakable local call of a high school football game, and then I went and found the stadium, and I stood in the stands, and I watched the hopes of entire towns get put onto seventeen-year-old shoulders.

I toured the roads of small-town Indiana, where my license plate alone was enough to spark suspicion and confusion among the locals. I got queried at a gas station one morning by a flannel-shirted man with a Hoosier drawl so thick that I could barely tell where his sentences started and finished.

"Oh, drivin' you's up to where's how from Boston then?" I thought I heard.

"No, I'm not from near there," I said, guessing at his question. "The area where I live is more like it is here."

He gave a strange chuckle, as if forgiving my error in judgment. "Oh no, boy," he decided. "You've not been in Indiana, then."

Despite his misgivings, I felt like I really *was* in Indiana. I played golf, in Carmel and French Lick and Terre Haute and Seymour, mostly in the evenings, just before dark, and I'd join people with names like Garth at places with names like Shadowood Golf Course. Garth, like most of these people, first wondered what a nice boy like myself would be doing so far from home, but by the time we shook hands on eighteen gave me his number and assured me that the next time I was in the area we'd get a real game together, and that Indiana was sure glad to have me.

Before I knew it, life had settled almost into a routine. These slow, magical days drifted to the end of September as I crossed into Illinois, up to Chicago, and back to the five-lane highway. I stayed with a family in the northern suburbs—cousins of my friend Luke—and relished the unbelievable comforts of having a bed, a family, and a hot shower. It rained for several days and I stayed put, listening to the woes of attending a huge, competitive public high school and its unpleasant realities, like the popular girl needing your history study guide the night before the test.

I spent another night in Chicago proper with a set of distant cousins who introduced me to their world—the beautiful lights and sights of a city by a lake and the seventeenth-story apartments and the forty-dollar parking and the places not to walk at night. I liked Chicago well enough. But after a few days I was eager to get back to open roads.

I left the city and continued north for a few days, crisscrossing southern Wisconsin, a quiet relief after noisy Chicago. I stopped one afternoon just outside Saukville, a couple miles from Lake

Michigan. Saukville felt sleepy, a well-to-do community far enough from the city, where the marsh met the interstate and the water met the woods. I pulled into a course called the Bog just as a group of dark clouds began to swallow up the day's light.

There was a different sort of chill in the late afternoon air. It was the feeling of an October back nine, when a thin 6-iron numbs your hand and the wind starts to get some real teeth. I shivered as I stepped out into the parking lot. Fall was just about here.

The pro shop, an elegant stone-and-glass lodge, was almost empty in the cool evening save for a middle-aged attendant who gave an obligatory nod from behind the front desk as I entered. I chose my words carefully—I was starting to grasp the strategy in these situations. Ask for a free round, and I was likely to get a cold stare. Make it seem like it was his idea, his generosity—that was the ticket. "What would it cost me," I began, glancing down at the wallet I had just slipped from my rear pocket, "if I wanted to get out and play a few holes before it gets dark?"

He glanced at the clock, then out the window, and then back at me. "Well, I don't suppose you'd get more'n a couple in before the storm hits anyway," he responded. "But you're welcome to a cart and the course. Won't cost you a thing."

He was right about the storm. It's one thing to play through the wind and the rain, but when the lightning hits, I'm gone. Before I left home, I had made a list of safety rules for the trip, a list that I quickly narrowed down to one: *Don't die.* Running around in a thunderstorm carrying a bag of eleven miniature lightning rods was in clear violation of this rule. So after seven soggy holes and a handful of menacing thunderclaps, I cut back past the clubhouse to my car, where I pushed my dripping golf bag as far into the corner as I could to avoid soaking my clothes or sleeping alley.

The rain went on for several hours, by which point I'd stopped for the night at the edge of a local park. The gravel lot seemed quiet enough, and a cluster of houses several hundred yards away provided the only light on a starless evening. Still damp, I tugged off my khakis and peeled a protesting red polo over my head before laying them out on the headrests in some unlikely hope that they would be dry by morning.

An hour or so later, I snapped awake to a light in the rear windshield so bright that everything else had disappeared, and for a moment I had no idea where I was. I had gotten used to this feeling—the waking up and not knowing—but it took me a little longer to grasp reality this time.

I propped myself up on my elbows and rubbed sleep from my eyes, recognizing that there were actually three separate lights—two headlights and another, the most intense, a sort of spotlight pointed at the back of my car. After a minute, a silhouette interrupted the light, and I caught the glint of a police badge as a tall, flashlight-wielding officer approached from the side.

He reached the passenger window, cupped one hand around his face, and peered in at my stacked clothes and bags before lifting the light to point directly into my eyes. He rapped on the window twice as I scrambled to open the door, still in a daze, to see what he wanted.

"What're you *doing* out here?" His question was accusatory, filled with self-importance.

"Just, uh, trying to get some sleep," I yawned, a mixture of apprehension and irritation. "I was, at least."

He stayed silent for a moment. I could sense that he was glowering back at me in the darkness. "Can I see your driver's license? And could you please step out of the car?"

"*Crap,*" I muttered under my breath as I tracked down my wallet from a pair of shorts on the floor and extracted myself from the sleeping bag. There was no easy way out from the backseat, so I wormed my way between the hanging dress clothes that guarded the passenger door and tumbled headfirst onto the gravel outside. I sprang to my feet and handed my Massachusetts ID to the cop. He surveyed it for a while, holding it at its very corner between his thumb and forefinger, the way a new father might hold a dirty diaper. He studied me, then the ID, then me again.

Under his glare, two sobering thoughts hit me at the same time. The first was that I had made it out of the car and into the scrutiny of the officer wearing only a pair of blue-striped boxers. I looked woefully through Subi's window at the khakis I had draped over the passenger-side headrest. *Now* I was awake.

The second realization, the more surprising one, was that I had apparently fallen afoul of the law. For a kid who had about as much experience breaking real, legal rules as he did playing for the Red Sox, it weirded me out.

I started to utter a request, an excuse, something, but the cop cut me off.

"So you're seventeen," he said with an accusatory sneer. "You're out here, by yourself, trying to *get some sleep*. You drove a car here from Massachusetts. I don't get it. Do your parents know you're out here?"

For the next forty-five minutes, any other late-night crimes that may have been going on in Port Washington, Wisconsin, took a backseat to my violation of park hours. I tried several times to explain to the officer exactly what it was I was doing there, but I couldn't make it past the second sentence. He didn't seem to want to understand. A few minutes later a second patrol car pulled into the lot, and two more officers joined the investigation. They called the station and ran my name through some huge, sluggish database. By the time the third car arrived, I asked if I could put on some pants.

It only got worse. After the police squadron concluded that I wasn't registered as a criminal, runaway, sex offender, or missing person, one officer decided that it was necessary to phone my house anyway—even though 12:30 A.M. in Wisconsin meant 1:30 A.M. at home. Nobody told me what they were doing, either—so I didn't realize what he was doing on his cell phone until I heard his first few words.

"Hello, this is Officer Dickerson of the Port Washington

P.D.," he began. "Do you have a son who was traveling by himself in the Wisconsin area?" he asked.

Why use the past tense? Those must have been the worst few seconds of Mom's life.

I could have punched Officer Dickerson right there. He didn't even attempt something reassuring—a "Your son is fine," or, "He's okay, we have him here." I could picture the thoughts running through her head for that split second, what she must have imagined was coming next. *We found his body.*

The cops seemed to lose interest after my mother confirmed that yes, now that you mention it, she had been sleeping, that her son was indeed traveling, and that Wisconsin sounded about right. And they put me on the phone just long enough to enthusiastically say, "Hey, I'm fine!" and, "Yeah, these men are so friendly and helpful."

Go to Walmart, the officers said, and sleep in the parking lot there. There are lights and people, so you'll be safe.

I chose not to make the point that I wanted to sleep where it *was* dark and there *weren't* people, or that the Walmart parking lot sounded like a good place to sleep if I wanted to wake up to a crazy woman standing over me holding something from the cutlery section. Instead I reassured them that I had driven by the store before, that I knew how to get back, thanks, and that I was *so* grateful for their checking up on me, three lies delivered so earnestly that I wanted to throw up just listening to myself.

I waited until the following afternoon to call Mom back, hoping that by lunchtime the previous night's incident would seem inconsequential. If she didn't think it was a big deal, then I could convince myself of the same thing. But in my naïve conceptions of right and wrong, something had gotten messed up. I was a good kid, and I had an entire police force on my case. Weren't they supposed to be on my side? *I didn't do anything wrong,* I told myself, a thought that quickly shifted to *screw 'em.*

Mom took a little more convincing to get to the screw-'em

stage—her fear that *she* might be doing something wrong clearly had deeper roots than mine.

"Dyl," she said. "He made me feel *so* guilty about letting you go. I don't know. I don't know what we're supposed to do. I didn't think this was all so *illegal*. I need to talk to Dad more, I think, and we'll figure out a plan."

I ground my teeth on the other end of the phone, trying not to sound frustrated. I knew I was safe. I knew I was doing what I should be doing. But having her *not* know was unsettling.

Living alone mostly meant that I could avoid things I didn't want to deal with—like bananas or calculus or eating dinner before ten—but when, every now and then, I did have to deal with things, I did so by myself. The Port Washington wake-up fundamentally threatened the way my parents saw my trip. They hadn't said so explicitly, but my mom had implied that maybe *all of this* wasn't such a good idea anymore. The thought of losing their support had never really entered my mind until I didn't know which idea I liked worse: putting an end to the trip or becoming a legitimate runaway.

The next two days were unseasonably warm, and I spent them outside, running and shooting hoops at a park by the shores of Lake Michigan. I even hopped in to cool off after a run—a short, chilly dip that I nonetheless decided made up for three days without a shower.

I spent much of my idle time over the next months in this same vein: finding pleasant places outside to while away the hours because I had nowhere to go inside, really, and because I was afraid that every extra minute I spent in Subi meant a greater chance that I'd be somehow poisoned by the stench of my laundry bag. And when it was dreary outside, I found public libraries so that I could read and use the Internet to write entries on a blog that I'd set up to chronicle my days so that I'd know, years after, just how the year had transpired. But these were already becoming hard to keep up with—doing stuff and then writing about what I'd done immediately afterward was already feeling redundant.

Most of the time I'd stare at maps, plot routes across the West, and write ahead to bigger, nicer courses, wondering if they would let me play for free—because these courses were a part of golf, too, the top of the game, and I wanted to play on the fairways I only knew from video games and see what kind of people played alongside me. But none had written back yet.

Before leaving Wisconsin, though, before the dust had even settled on my run-in with the cops, something else happened—something that changed the way I saw the nature of my trip.

I had pulled off the highway just west of Green Bay and into the back lot of a Holiday Inn and Suites that was filled but quiet—one in a row of near-identical hotels, restaurants, and convenience stores on the fluorescent strip. This was trucker America: a buffet of the quickest, cheapest ways to get fed, fueled, and rested, right off the interstate. It seemed like a safe enough place to walk around, find a quick dinner, and check my e-mail in the hotel lobby. But by the end of my Burger King to go and the conclusion of the football game I'd been watching on my computer in the lobby, when I began to wonder where I should go to sleep, it occurred to my tired mind that I didn't have to go anywhere—I could sleep where Subi was already parked.

It may be just a trick of my memory, or maybe the third Value Menu double cheeseburger, but I recall having particular trouble getting to sleep that night, my senses heightened to the sounds of the nearby road. A light evening rain had subsided, leaving Subi in a cool darkness. Tender currents of air breathed through the window's edge, tickling the tuft of hair that covered the tip of my left ear. The streetlight to my left kept flickering on and off before eventually settling into a dim sepia that bathed my knees in a warm glow. Every few minutes a lone truck pierced the calm as it rumbled across an adjacent overpass. My focus flitted from one to the next, from air to light to truck, spinning in some sort of sensory roulette as I lay there, not yet asleep—but not awake either.

My sleeping had gotten progressively lighter since I had left home. Rather than adapt to my surroundings, to sleeping anywhere, to not being afraid, I increasingly spent each night slipping in and out of consciousness. It became a routine of unease, a series of half-hour naps that left me about the same amount of tired at every hour of the day. I don't know what it was that kept me awake or what I was afraid of, but the less I knew about my surroundings, the less I could sleep.

Maybe it was compensation for Mom worrying about me, or maybe I just thought it was cool, but as a new measure of protection, I had started sleeping with a small ax—more like a big hatchet. It just felt like an object any traveling teen should have. It looked good, too, the way it lay across Cereal Row, blade glinting in the streetlight, sharp enough for—well, I didn't think about it that way.

I don't remember my eyes closing or drifting out of consciousness. But I remember jerking awake, my subconscious screaming so loudly that as I shot up I slammed my head into the ceiling, knocking the blur from my eyes. Without thinking, I grabbed the ax from my left and whirled my head around to a sound in the front seat. I guess it was unreasonable to hope that the ax would help me sleep or deal with the not knowing, but as I turned to look, I was glad I had *something* in my hands.

I'd left the passenger-side window cracked open to allow fresh airflow into Subi's stuffy interior. Now a forearm was draped through that same window, and a bony hand and the hand's dirty tendrils were feeling up the inside of the door, searching for a lock they couldn't quite reach. I froze, willing the fingers away from breaching the limits of the vehicle whose well-being was already so indistinguishable from my own. He—the hand—was getting closer, his arm now stretched to the door handle directly above the lock. I felt my mouth open wide in a silent call for help.

All the air had gone from my lungs, but a quiet yelp escaped me, like I was a dog and someone had stepped on my tail. The hand froze. An instant later the arm slithered out of the top of the window and into the night outside, where I finally saw the man to whom it connected. He was short and thin, with a scraggly salt-and-pepper beard that darkened his jagged jaw. A ripped black Nike Windbreaker hung loosely from his figure. But as I glanced up at his face, I saw neither anger nor aggression in his sunken eyes. This was the unmistakable look of a man caught in sheer, bone-chilling *terror*. We sized each other up for what seemed like forever but could have been no more than a split second, the scared aggressor and the scared victim, and already it was becoming hard to tell which of us was which. And then he was gone, sprinting as fast as he could away from the ax-brandishing lunatic in the rear of the Outback.

I stayed upright, my heart pumping and my breath ragged, and considered my options. Instinctively, I reached for my phone— to call the police, my parents, someone—but once I had it in my hands I paused. The police were certainly out of bounds. I know, even today, I could pick his face out of a hundred-man lineup, but I had no interest in pursuing the failed burglar. I thought of the trouble the cops would have given me, what laws I must have been breaking as a seventeen-year-old sleeping in a Holiday Inn parking lot fifteen hundred miles from home.

Calling my parents was even more out of the question. I could hear my mom's voice from the previous day: "You have to sleep in campgrounds, safe places," she told me.

"*America* is a safe place," I had implored. "We live in a safe country, with good people." Her reaction to a new three A.M. phone call would scare me as much as her—it would make this threat real.

I dropped my phone and turned to open the door instead. Barefoot, I stood outside the car, considering my reflection in its window. I was alone.

I walked around the side of the car and something caught my eye. In his haste to bolt, the thief had dropped what he had been holding. Three objects sat in a shallow puddle by the curb: a pair of black sunglasses, a CD, and a five-dollar bill, each presumably taken from the glove compartment of some less-present car owner.

I gingerly rescued them from the water, placing the sunglasses on the hood of the SUV parked in the next spot. "R.E.M.," the CD read, "*Live in Dublin.*" This seemed like a strange choice. I tried and failed to picture my night visitor kicking back to some alt rock. It was a funny image, and I started to laugh, but the laugh got stuck in my throat and stopped, and hurt. I'd never looked into eyes like those before. Was it because I'd never seen a criminal up close? That must have been part of it. But there was another part—I was away from home and its middle-class comforts, and I was hungry, and cold, and closer than ever to understanding the type of need that would make one man reach into another man's car to see what he could find.

Maybe, I thought as I placed the CD next to the sunglasses, we weren't so different after all. But then I had been holding an ax, which meant, theoretically, that I'd been thinking about using it. Which one was I—the victim or the aggressor? I tried to brush away the thought as I bent over to pick up the crumpled five-dollar bill.

I put it in my pocket.

Over the next six days, I disappeared into northern obscurity. I worked my way up the western shore of Lake Michigan as the trees began to turn colors familiar from Octobers in Williamstown. I wondered how the leaves looked at home now. Taylor's soccer team was undefeated, I knew, and he was starting to apply to colleges—I wondered if he'd still have time to talk to me in a few weeks, during playoffs, with deadlines looming. I wondered if Evan was looking at the same colors I was—maybe with that new girl he'd told me about on the phone. There was no denying it: life in Williamstown was continuing without me.

All I could do was continue north. Milwaukee had given way to Green Bay, then to Marinette and to Marquette and eventually to Upper Peninsula towns that only showed up on the map because, well, the mapmakers figured they should write *something*. Any remaining blue sky disappeared, and Mostly Sunny turned to Partly Cloudy turned to simple, definite Rain.

A wall had gone up between me and the world at home. The night intruder hadn't built it—he'd just helped me realize how alone I was. This realization didn't scare me, really—although for weeks afterward I would wake up panicked, seeing faces in the rear windshield.

No, what I felt was closer to sadness, but that wasn't right, either, because it felt so damn close to happiness, too. The strongest feelings came late at night, in the time between turning the car off and my eyes finally closing. Sometimes it was a few minutes, sometimes a few hours, as I lay on my back, awake, and imagined stars into the ceiling. That's when I felt it the most, a sorrow that nobody was there with me mixed with a gratefulness that I could be so alone, so exposed.

I wasn't just alone. I was free.

I woke one early October Upper Peninsula Saturday to the complaint of my cell phone, whose outlet-deprived battery rarely made it through a full day without crying for help. I let it die. For now, I thought, this new wall had made it *my* world. It was a wall that would never go down, and if I was sometimes unreachable to everyone back home, so be it.

But there were signs that another world might be opening its doors. I opened my laptop that same morning to find an e-mail from Kevin Manninen, the golf pro at the U.P.'s Marquette Golf Club, inviting me to come play eighteen on their dime. Already I had written to (and been ignored by) several of the Midwest's premier clubs, but I'd read rave reviews of Marquette's recent addition—the Greywalls course—which was being heralded as one of the best new courses in the country by the sorts of magazines that decide these things. I pictured it new and largely undiscovered, and once I'd seen pictures, this northern gem had climbed high on my wish list.

The Monday I was scheduled to play began the way the previous week had ended: cool and gray. I killed some time as I tried to wait out the morning rain at a coffee shop in downtown Marquette. But my mug of cocoa disappeared much more quickly than I anticipated, and I was left, half an hour later, around the corner at Hardee's—a staple in the world of Midwestern fast food—for an early lunch. I made my burger and fries last as long as possible, but eventually even heading back outside to face the elements seemed like a better option than lingering, especially when the kid the next booth over complained to his parents that he'd spotted some boogers on his bacon. *Blech.*

The sky looked lighter, I told myself as I walked out, resisting the urge to hurl on the way. The temperature had climbed to a balmy forty-four degrees, too, which seemed about as good as it was going to get. I decided to make my move up to the course.

Marquette Golf Club had two eighteen-hole layouts: the original Heritage course, which had been around since the 1920s, and the Greywalls course, which had only opened in 2005. The Heritage course looked nice, but Greywalls was truly special—the region's "crown jewel," my U.P. travel guide crowed.

I arrived to find a fairly empty parking lot. A small fleet of golf carts was parked alongside the modest pro shop, collecting drizzle and runoff from the gutter. The young shop attendant had a note granting me free rein, so I got eighteen with a cart for free—my first real complimentary round.

The VIP feeling didn't last long, though. I walked back out to load my bag onto one of a line of carts that had been wisely parked in the spot where they could gather the most runoff from the pro-shop roof. I surveyed my options and, finding nothing, selected one slightly less watery machine. After a futile attempt at toweling off the driver's seat, I gingerly settled into a small puddle that my pants did a much better job absorbing than the towel had.

A five-minute ride from the clubhouse to the first tee cut through parts of the course, and with no one around to play with,

I began the drive alone. A bedraggled foursome was returning as I set out, their heavy jackets and winter hats soaked through. They shot grins at me, a shivering teen in a short-sleeved shirt and khaki pants, and one shouted, "Hope you're ready!" as he passed, knowing all too well that I wasn't.

As I reached the first tee, the rain had stopped, allowing me a moment to admire my surroundings. The tee was elevated, and might have looked out over Lake Superior on a clearer day. On this afternoon, though, the trees below me had vanished so completely into the mist that they may as well have ceased to exist entirely, and the elevation served only to expose me to a vicious wind.

The opening hole was as impressive strategically as it was aesthetically, and as I took a couple hurried swings to get loose I surveyed what lay between the distant flagstick and myself. At nearly six hundred yards, the par-5 stretched from the top of the course down onto a broad landing area. Nearer the green, though, the fairway narrowed, requiring good position for an approach onto the tricky putting surface, which sloped off on both sides.

My drive seemed to linger forever over the ocean of fescue left of the fairway before the wind deposited it safely on the short grass—the rare shot aided by a sideways gust. Even though I made par from there, I began to feel the impossibility of the conditions on the very next tee. The blow-your-hat-off wind had at least been behind me on the opening hole. Now I was hitting dead into it. The 425-yard par-4 had turned into one much longer, and my drive got hoisted higher and higher into the air before dropping, disappointingly short, into the deep rough some thirty yards right of the fairway. From there, I was blocked out by trees and could only scoot a 4-iron layup down the fairway. But as it turned out, my punch flew farther than I had intended, ricocheted off a rock in the center, and flew fifty yards farther to land, improbably, on the left side of the green. Mother Nature was toying with me.

The surrounding scenery was a cross between seaside Scotland and the mines of Moria. The course proved a work of sculpture, hewn out of stone but shaped by the wind, leaving a rocky test created through a union of man and nature. Holes were set up with a deliberate emphasis on keeping an authentic Highland feel, and as a result huge rocks and trees remained in unpredictable spots all over the course. These natural features added dramatic visual effects as well as subtle difficulties to each hole. Even the straightest par-4s were turned crooked by the fairways, sloping monsters with steep drops, sudden valleys, and granite pillars at every turn that required each shot to be hit with specific intent.

These rock formations weren't just in the fairways but also lined the rough, perfectly framing several tee shots with the striking gray walls that had given the course its name. Nowhere were these more evident than on the par-3 sixth. The tee box gave way to an almost sheer drop-off to the valley floor many stories below. The green, which appeared inaccessible from the tee, was hewn from the wall on the far side of the gorge, nearly two hundred yards away. A mossy granite slab guarded the front of the green, and small cliffs flanked the other three sides. Any shot that didn't make the putting surface would roll down to a collection area—in the fairway, but still dozens of yards below the target.

It had begun to rain again, but I was so caught up in the dramatic layout on the green that I barely noticed. And if others were on the course, I didn't notice them either. I was playing in a strange solitude, a rugged, solo exposure to the elements. It felt like golf at its most basic: man against the course, against the weather, with no other people around to mess it up.

Through nine holes I was thoroughly enjoying the solitary struggle against Greywalls. The fear that I might lose the grip of my club on any given shot seemed to have actually helped my swing, and numbness had simplified my game, so I rolled off a string of pars. Protection from trees and cliffs even sheltered me from the wind on a few holes, and making the turn, I was a picture of soggy optimism.

Somewhere on the eleventh hole, the magic began to fade. Falling temperatures and increasing winds played a part, along with the fact that, after absorbing an hour of sideways drizzle, I was soaked through. Every turn of the cart was becoming torture; a cold ride in a vehicle that welcomed the wind and rain with open arms. I pressed on, determined to play the entire course, so practice swings disappeared altogether. It took me six shots to get through the par-4 fourteenth, and seven more on the par-4 sixteenth. When I splashed in a twenty-five-footer on the eighteenth green, it was with relief that I fished the ball from the bottom of the cup to wrap up a thirty-minute back nine.

Dripping wet, I ventured back to return my cart key, feeling like a victorious David returning home from his fight with the giant. I envisioned showers of praise, wide-eyed wonderment, maybe a parade for the conquering hero who returned holding the head of the beast. As I entered the pro shop, I shook off the outdoors proudly and blew a couple drops of water from the tip of my nose, delighting in the room's comparative warmth. I looked expectantly at the man behind the counter. He merely glanced up from his book, expressionless. "Like the course?" he asked matter-of-factly, a cruel dismissal of the trials I had just endured as a result of its very architecture.

You can't really blueprint the weather into a golf course. Architects design and implement, but at a certain point a project leaves their hands and gets turned over to the land and the elements. Marquette's design was bold and beautiful from the start, but there was something important about *where* the course had been built. Marquette was a city of cold and wind and rain. Golf, like most everything in the U.P., was a little more rugged. I would continue to find that out.

I felt I'd gained some ruggedness of my own as I shivered in Subi's front seat, stripping off one article of clothing at a time until I was completely naked in the corner of the parking lot. Was it this exposure to the elements? The pure solitude? I pulled on a pair of rain pants that I had cleverly left in the car as my khakis flooded during the preceding hours. I liked this feeling, living alone in the U.P. amid the storms of October. Completing a round of golf, finding a meal, and staying warm were real challenges, and completing each task felt like a huge accomplishment. My trip would get more complex as I drove on over the next months. But here in the U.P., I had found its essence: play golf and survive.

I could feel the weather getting worse still as I drove aimlessly out of Marquette. Although the rain had actually eased, the wind was getting downright scary. Trees on both sides of the road were bending unnaturally, some actually breaking, and fallen branches littered the roadside. I could feel the wind battering Subi from the side, and I drove on with a mixture of trepidation and excitement. I turned on the radio to hear the automated voice declare a "gale warning" for Marquette in effect through the next morning. *A gale warning?* "Gusts in excess of sixty miles per hour," warned the automated female voice. "Swells on Lake Superior are fifteen to twenty feet, and could grow to twenty-five to thirty feet." Thirty-foot swells? What *were* thirty-foot swells, and how could they possibly show up on a lake? "Swimming is strongly discouraged," she continued. *Thanks for that.*

As if on cue, I rounded a bend in the road and found Lake Superior in front of me. Massive waves crashed on top of each other as they roared toward the shore, except these had stopped acting like waves. There was none of the rhythm or the reliability of the seashore I knew back East. The water was filled instead with violent collisions as each swell wrecked itself on another before spraying and re-forming for another crash. As far as the eye could see, whitecaps crowned the lake's surface and haphazardly rose and fell. I pulled into a roadside parking area—these seemed to be about every half mile in the U.P.—and tried to open my door, which the wind was determined to keep shut. But I was in the U.P., dammit, and I was going to experience this firsthand, so I fought my way out of Subi's protection and, after I gained my footing, launched myself down a swaying flight of stairs to the beach, where I stood, shivering, in sheer awe of nature.

I felt every bit the buccaneer as I stared into the lake, my hair matted to my forehead by the gale. I ventured forward to feel the edge of the water (unseasonably warm) before retreating. But then something caught my eye farther down the shoreline. A middle-aged man was walking toward the water, a significant stomach bulging through his gray wet suit. Wait. This dude was going in? *No freaking way*. I began a sort of crouched jog along the beach toward him. He glanced over as I approached.

"The thing is, it's almost *too* windy!" he shouted at me, as if I somehow needed convincing not to join his battle with Poseidon. He strode into the water holding a small camera aloft and paused about waist-deep to snap a picture. Problem was, "about waist-deep" was a very temporary position, and as he turned to return his camera to shore a wave broke hard and awkwardly across his shoulder. As I watched in horror, he lost his footing and went down hard, arms flailing at the air, until his entire body had disappeared.

For a split second I thought he was under for good—that the riptide would do exactly what the lady on the radio had warned. Another wave crash-landed on the spot where his head had disappeared. I wasn't going in after him. Nobody could. I thought I saw his leg flail into the air as a third wave thrashed toward shore. Could that be the last of him that anyone would ever see? A disappearing limb?

A moment later, he sputtered to the surface and flailed his way back to the safety of the sand, where he choked out a mouthful of water and lay, panting, on the beach. "Don't worry," he shouted hoarsely, pointing to his camera. "It's waterproof." I wasn't the only rugged individualist in these parts.

I returned to Marquette to sleep the night. I settled for supermarket grub—a blueberry muffin and an orange—which I ate in the Safeway parking lot. All around me, pairs of people dashed through the diagonal downpour from the store to their cars. I watched them drive away, imagined them returning to the safety of their homes—away from the meddling flashlights of cops, the prying fingers of parking-lot thieves, and the mood swings of Mother Nature. In that moment I wanted so badly to be one of them, curling up to the crackle of a fire or the comfort of a blanket, the touch of another person. Instead I watched as they ran by, splashing and laughing while the wind rocked Subi back and forth and back and forth in a most lonesome lullaby.

CHAPTER 4

Survival

"**H**ello there, how are you this evening, sir?"

Too many of my nights were involving cars with flashing lights.

The park ranger beamed at me. He was tall but wholly unintimidating, with graying hair and a disarming smile. A day had passed since my round at Marquette, but I was still in the U.P.— I'd found a campground just off Route 41, in the woods between the road and Lake Superior.

"Hope I didn't alarm you with the lights. Just wanted to make sure everything was squared away with checking in."

"Oh, yeah, I had a question about that, actually," I said, grabbing a sheet of paper from the passenger seat. "*Keep this copy,*" it read. There had been nobody at the front gate, so I'd grabbed a registration form as I entered and filled it out for my evening's stay. "I didn't know what to put for 'campsite,'" I told him.

"Oh, that's no problem," he said. "There are plenty of open sites. I'd try taking your second right up ahead, there should be several there. Are you planning on pitching a tent, sir? Or . . ."

I checked the car's clock. 11:15. "It's pretty late, I think I may just stay in the car."

He nodded. "Hey, I know what it's like getting in late. I'll take care of it. Have a good night."

I rolled up my window, feeling a twinge of guilt. I hadn't lied to him—not technically—but I'd certainly led him to believe that I'd left the seventeen-dollar fee and the official half of the registration in the drop box at the gate.

As it happened, I didn't have any cash on me, even if I *had* intended to pay. And the other section of the form? I was sitting on it.

Where to sleep each night? The question was becoming harder to answer. I was trying to be safe, to stay overnight in places that weren't parking lots, where Subi and I could sleep responsibly and in something resembling peace. It wasn't a tangible fear that kept me from sleeping in rest stops or random pullouts. I wasn't scared of robbery or murder, not exactly. I was more scared by an uncertainty of my surroundings—a fear of fear. I couldn't get the face of my would-be intruder from Green Bay out of my head, and something in the darkness gave me pause.

Campgrounds seemed like my safest option, except campgrounds cost money, and I didn't have any to spend on lodging. Out of the $4,700 and change I'd started with a month earlier, I had already spent over $600. I'd need every cent I had left—and much more, probably—to complete the trip, and short of winning the lottery or looting one of my hosts, I had to keep a tight belt. I was still too smart to try the former, and still too principled to do the latter—even if I'd occasionally fill up my water bottle at the McDonald's soda machine without telling anyone.

I'd been tracking expenses to the penny, and I had divided my necessary expenses into three categories: food, golf, and gas. There was no way around that last one, I knew, so I'd have to do what I could to keep the other two low.

Over the first thirty days, I had spent $120.44 on food. Granted, I had spent some nights at dinner tables in private homes or dining out in restaurants on someone else's dime, but four dollars, one and a half cents per day is pretty hard to turn into good grub. Keeping such careful track was probably a bad idea. It became a game, the spending, that I played against myself. And I was competitive enough to make it an unpleasant one—definitely an unhealthy one.

I'd also constructed a list of food rules, including "Finish your meal," "Quantity *is* quality," and "Expiration dates are for rich people." Those Styrofoam pancakes. Those Snickers and pretzels—and only those—for five meals in a row. The tuna salad three days after purchase. Peanut butter. Oyster crackers. Ketchup packets. Nothing was off-limits. Whoever said there's no such thing as a free lunch, I realized, had obviously never been treated to a free lunch. I figured the list would only grow as my savings shrank.

It's not that I couldn't spend *any* money on food. But I wanted to make good investments. A meal at a country diner with a cute waitress and strong local flavor was worth something, so I was happy to spend for it. And shelling out money to play golf—well, that was kind of the whole point. So I kept my eyes peeled for bargains and tried not to do too much math. I'd make it work.

The rain still hadn't stopped in the Upper Peninsula, but as I awoke in the campground early the next morning, I felt my stomach rumble. I'd downed a box of Pop-Tarts the previous day, but they'd run out by dinnertime. I patted my stomach apologetically. But I felt something as I rose—a stroke of inspiration, perhaps, or just severe hunger—to act on a plan I'd been mulling over for several days.

A half hour later I marched through the main entrance of the Econo Lodge with feigned confidence, striding past the front desk and down the hallway to the left as my stomach growled in cautious anticipation. Left was a lucky guess. There was my prize—third door on the right—the continental breakfast room. I had been pillaging hotel Wi-Fi for weeks, but this was a new level of brilliance: the free hotel breakfast.

The continental breakfast plan was nearly foolproof. The staff at most chain hotels would turn over between the night and morning shifts, so they wouldn't know who had checked in—

and besides, I was young enough to be someone's kid. I couldn't make it painfully obvious that I was walking straight from my car to the Froot Loops, and I didn't want look too depraved—it's a bad look for any hotel to welcome homeless moochers in for breakfast. It makes the paying customers feel unappreciated. But I felt secure. One of the most awkward things for a person to do is to catch another person in a lie—so nobody ever tries to. I was golden.

All this ran through my head as I charged to the front of the line. I didn't blend in, exactly. The rest of the room was filled with leisure-traveling sixtysomethings. But my scrambled eggs, sausage, bacon, two waffles, three blueberry muffins, and bowl of Cinnamon Toast Crunch came with an extra side that morning: triumph. This was a game changer. I was a pioneer of survival, and the run-down Econo Lodge side room with the fuzzy TV was my Plymouth Rock. The discovery may not have made me a better person. But it likely saved my trip.

It was wrong, stealing food like this. I could try to justify it, tell myself they would've made the same amount of food anyway, that it didn't make a difference whether I ate some of it or not. (Anyone ever been to a continental breakfast that ran out of food? Didn't think so.) Did I *need* it? I'm not sure. It certainly felt that way. But I really wasn't hung up on these moral details. I was doing what I felt I had to do—and it was strangely satisfying.

The realities of the road had hardened me. It was fun figuring out how to survive—but it was hard, too. My needs were tough to meet on my budget, and I was making some compromises. Good meals and good morals weren't necessarily compatible.

We sat in silence, my new peers in breakfast if not age, watching the shaky Weather Channel feed on a twelve-inch screen mounted in the corner of the room. It was hard to say exactly what the descriptions under the weekend forecast were, but the sun, complete with spiky yellow mane and cool black shades, seemed to be a starring figure, a happy alternative to the flood warnings I had been hearing the last week. I had stayed silent, but I was near bursting with giddiness by this point.

"Well," I announced aloud, "anyone know where I can sell an ark?" Crickets. One jowly guy with a Vikings jersey glanced over at me with a look that made me stare back into the syrup-drenched half waffle sagging on the plate in front of me. Tough crowd.

Even though I had grown used to spending days on end by myself, I left the U.P. somewhat battered by the challenges of solitude. There were the physical hardships, like showering—which I had done exactly once in a week and a half, in the rest-room of a state park. Or shaving—an act I performed awkwardly in rest stops or even more awkwardly in my rearview mirror, using a commemorative dog bowl I had gotten at Dog Night at the Cincinnati Reds game a couple weeks before. But the emotional stuff was more challenging. Time spent alone offered plenty of rewarding insights, but during especially long stretches I missed the comforts of home, sitting down to dinner with the family or dropping by a buddy's house to watch TV and shoot the breeze.

Was I going to make it? I couldn't be sure. I had my bouts of homesickness, but the day-to-day challenges of eating and sur-viving and planning my next move kept me engaged. And some two weeks after leaving the U.P., the first time I played golf in the snow, I knew—finding ways to play golf wasn't going to stop me.

At home in Massachusetts, the year's first snowfall had always been something to celebrate. We'd break out the skis and the sleds and the shovels. Mornings spent digging forts into snow-banks would turn into afternoons gliding our way around Pros-pect Mountain. For Dad, it meant the long ski-free off-season was over. He was at home on cross-country skis, shushing his way through a fresh coat of powder whether there was a trail there or not. He had made Evan and me come with him at first, but pretty soon we followed at every opportunity. To me, the first snow meant family. It meant the first hot chocolate and the first great opportunity to fall asleep by the wood stove in the basement. Under fresh snowfall, our little wooden house felt just a little cozier, knowing that we were warm and dry while the land outside was transformed.

I felt some of that instinctive happiness as I peered out the window one mid-October Sunday morning to see that fall had disappeared beneath three inches of rogue central Minnesotan snow squall. I still had those skis bungeed to the roof, after all, even though I had started to wonder why. But I was due in North Dakota that evening, at the home of a couple named Beth and Kyle, for a late dinner some five or six hours away. I was three or four degrees of separation from knowing Beth and Kyle, but they'd volunteered to help a kid they'd never met, and the least I could do was show up.

The snow meant getting in a full eighteen holes in Minnesota was going to be tricky.

Even though it's counterintuitive to head north in search of warmer weather and, in this case, snow-free links, north was my only option. While the radio, the Internet, and my eyesight each suggested that I was doomed, I held out hope that milder conditions would appear somewhere along the road to Fargo. Large, wet flakes continued to fall as I brushed off my windows and set off onto I-94 from Andrew (another second cousin, I think) and his house in western Minneapolis. The highway cut diagonally northwest across the Land o' Lakes until it banked left in time to connect with Fargo and deposit me at my destination.

The fact that no reasonable golf course would be open in these conditions left me with two options. I could either find an unreasonable golf course that was inexplicably open, or I could sneak onto a closed course and hope nobody noticed. The evening prior, still snow-free, I'd driven to Chaska to find Hazeltine, the premier course in Minnesota and the site of the previous year's PGA Championship.

I'd recently spent enough time browsing lists of American

golf courses that I'd stumbled upon *Golf Digest*'s top 100 courses in the United States. Hazeltine was on there—not near the very top, with Augusta and Merion and a place called Pine Valley, but still, on there—which called for a visit, in my mind. I'd never been to any of these hundred. But to my surprise, Hazeltine was nearly empty, under construction and renovation, so I'd played the first two holes without anyone around to care.

For a second, I considered going back to Hazeltine in the snow—if you're going to sneak on, why not sneak onto the best? Then my instinct to stay out of jail kicked in. Instead, just after noon and just under thirty-two degrees, I put Minneapolis in my rearview mirror.

After a tense hour of driving, the snow on the side of the road *looked like* it was starting to thin out slightly. Three times I got off the highway to follow signs to a course. The first was completely covered in snow, fairway to bunker to green. Onward. The second was inexplicably packed with cars—for some sort of reception, maybe even a wedding—and I figured I didn't stand much of a chance of sneaking around a closed country club with hundreds of witnesses. At my third stop, several intrepid members of the grounds crew guarded the first fairway, working diligently on a half-done bunker that served as backdrop to the emphatic COURSE CLOSED notice posted out front. Things did not look good for Minnesota.

I got back on the highway and drove on, hoping for a sign from the golf gods. Looping back to Minnesota later in the trip made about as much sense as rerouting through Mexico City. What was I supposed to do?

Who would ever know?

The thought crossed my mind. I could dawdle for a few hours, tell people I'd played the day before. Nobody would ask— nobody would even know to ask. But even as the idea occurred to me, I knew that I couldn't miss Minnesota. I'd set out to play the lower forty-eight, with few other restrictions. I had created this goal so that I could wander with a purpose, so that I could travel America with a greater goal. I'd *made* it matter. It *had* to matter. If I lied about Minnesota, what was to stop me from lying about the rest of the trip?

There was hope for me yet. It was deep into the afternoon—although only a couple hours north of Minneapolis—when, sure enough, several parallel lines of trees appeared on my right, rows spaced some fifty yards apart—the unmistakable sign of a golf course. I slammed on the brakes, made an audacious swerve into the right lane, and turned sharply onto the exit ramp to track down these mystery fairways.

As I approached, I saw that most of the course was blanketed with wet, heavy snow an inch or two deep. The bunkers were now filled with an off-white sludge. Still, areas that had been exposed to the sun and wind, including large strips of fairway and green, were wet but snow-free. The whole appearance gave the impression of something missing, white speckled with green, as if a kid had started to draw a golf course on a blank sheet of paper but hadn't gotten very far.

It wasn't perfect, but it was nearly three o'clock and it would have to do. I pulled past the entrance to the pro shop, where a lone light still shone, and turned into the side lot of the adjacent retirement home. From there I laced up my golf shoes, grabbed my clubs, pulled on a sweatshirt, and sidled my way onto the tenth hole. Not a soul in sight. The air didn't feel as bad as I had expected. The wind was down, which was crucial, and Subi's heat hadn't really been working anyway, so thirty-seven degrees felt pretty reasonable.

The Albany Golf Club was a flat and uninteresting eighteen holes, the kind of side-of-the-highway course that gets golfers salivating over the idea rather than the reality. But it was straight and easy, and the price was right, too.

My opening tee shot actually found the fairway, but it disappeared into a clump of snow. I kicked around for a minute or two before it revealed itself—I made a note to pay close attention to where my balls landed. I took out an 8-iron for my second shot, gave a hard swing, and struck just behind the ball. This was only mildly successful. There was an explosion of snow, including some to my face, which I wiped away just in time to see the ball fall to the ground less than halfway to the target.

I employed a new technique for the third shot. The ball sat in a layer of snow no thicker than a folded road map, so I decided I could pick it clean, hitting the ball and avoiding the snow like it was in a fairway bunker. But this time I caught it *too* clean, making contact only with the blade of the club. The shot actually worked out—it was a low line drive that settled at the back of the green—but the shock waves ran up the shaft and into my hands, sending them into numb agony.

"Aghhhh!" I yelled to nobody, throwing the club to the ground. This was going to take some getting used to.

The next few tries were gradually more successful, and once I'd settled on a strategy (an extra club or two, depending on the lie, a little in the back of your stance, and catch it clean) I actually did okay. I proudly shot the temperature my first nine, including a chip-in and a thirty-footer, each for birdie, each one fluky and flaky and beautiful.

As the wind picked up, the novelty pretty quickly wore off. My shoes were soaked and my feet were beginning to freeze—and it was 4:30, with darkness fast approaching. I had lost the feeling in my hands. Plus some hearty dog walker out on the course kept giving me weird looks. I skipped the first hole, which started too close to the clubhouse for comfort, and quickened my pace as I began the front nine.

I switched to a yellow golf ball, hoping to minimize the time I was spending kicking through snow looking for my Titleist. And then I switched to ski gloves because I couldn't really grip the club anyway, and at least the gloves would keep me hypothermia-free.

I played the final three holes at a stiff jog, with little success, before putting out on the eighth and cutting back over toward Subi. Sixteen holes at Albany plus two at Hazeltine made a full

Minnesota round. As I climbed back into Subi, I was desperately hoping that North Dakota's autumn would be a little milder.

It wasn't the hardest day of the trip—far from it. It wasn't even the hardest round of golf. But I was learning, in my own way, things that hadn't made the curriculum of the Williamstown school district—how to survive, to improvise, and to get what I needed.

It was nearly nine by the time I got to Fargo. Beth, who worked for an insurance company, and Kyle, who worked for the Farm Service Agency, were a down-to-earth couple in their forties who seemed eager to have a fresh face around. They'd saved me a plate, too, of steak and rice and beans, which reheated to perfection. I wolfed it down as I told them about my afternoon at Albany Golf Club.

"No way, that little track by the interstate?" Kyle asked as I described it.

"Yeah!" I was excited that he knew where I meant. "You've played there?"

"Gosh, no," he told me. "Always seen it, though. Always makes you want to tee it up."

A faint pitter-patter was coming from the stairwell, and their youngest daughter, Kate, who couldn't have been more than eight years old, came tiptoeing downstairs in her pajamas.

"Oh, Kate has something for you," Beth beamed. "Go on, give it to him, sweetie."

Kate approached timidly and held out a piece of paper, making eye contact just for a second before she shuffled off to a safer distance.

She'd drawn me a picture. "From Kate," it read in bright crayon. "To dyllan." I grinned. There was a boy in the center wearing a bright-green-and-blue-striped shirt and a wide, simple smile, surrounded by rainbows—one in each corner. I reached out to give her a high five.

"Thanks a lot, Kate," I told her. "Really, thanks. This might be the nicest picture anyone has *ever* drawn for me."

"You're welcome," she replied with a shy smile.

Beth led her back up to bed a short while later, and Kyle and I settled into the couch in front of *Sunday Night Football*. I kept sneaking glimpses at the picture.

I felt older, looking at this crayon-drawn kid in the blue-and-green shirt. He was so simply happy, this imagined Dylan with the short, spiky hair and the fat neck and no nose. I settled farther into the couch, feeling my eyes start to get heavy. *Real-life Dylan is happy too,* I thought to myself. And I was. I was *so* happy. But I felt other things, too, other emotions that made picture Dylan's smile look too easy.

Eight states down, forty to go. I could make it. I'd always believed that. But for the first time I was wondering who I'd be on the other side. What was this trip going to do to me? I blinked awake a couple times, then gave up and closed my eyes. If I ended up anything like the guy Kate had imagined I'd be, well, then I'd be all right.

CHAPTER 5

Cowboys

S tates have distinct identities in our national psyche. It's weird
the way Americans think about America. We divide things up
along state borders and assign them reputations. Most states have
a buzzword or two, but we rarely go beyond these surface-level
impressions to actually learn much about the real character of a
place. Most of us just know enough to make some quick association, thinking "flat" (when we hear Kansas) or "old" (Florida) or
"guns" (Texas).

Many of the stereotypes are based in reality, of course, but I
expected that the better I got to know a place, the more I'd realize just how off base my original assessment was. This was sort
of true.

When I'd driven into Iowa the week before, I'd been expecting to see a lot of corn. But I also half expected to have my pre-
conceived notions of Iowa busted, my worldliness and empathy
expanded, my eyes suddenly opened to just how wrong I was.
Iowa would look and feel different than just stalks of vegetables
in neat rows.

What I found was a lot of corn. I found fields of happy, just-
out-of-season corn with happy, just-out-of-season farm stands
out front. I found cornfields cut into labyrinths, with awesome
signs that read CORN MAIZE, which I hoped pointed to a punny
Iowan self-awareness rather than an Iowan lack of education. I
found cornfields that caught the sunset just right so that every-

thing turned a rolling golden brown, like we were stuck in sepia tone. And I found creepy, whisper-to-you-at-night cornfields where stalks took a breath of wind and turned it into words, made the hair on the back of my neck stand up; corn that drew clouds over the moon and made wolves howl and got me from the eighth fairway to the sleeping bag in the back of my car before you could say "Dubuque." Iowa's reputation wasn't off base—it was just incomplete. And I was having fun filling in the blanks.

If the United States were a middle school, there would be a clique of popular kids—California, New York, Florida, Illinois—who would be the jocks, the starters on the football team. A state like Massachusetts would have some jock friends but would tend to hang out with the quieter types like Vermont, New Hampshire, and Maine. Texas, the kid who hit puberty early and was a head taller than all the other boys, might not have a lot of close pals but would at least command some physical respect from everyone, even the kids who were good at everything, like North Carolina or Colorado. Everyone would wonder how Virginia turned out so pretty when her brother, West Virginia, had that gross facial hair and always looked (and smelled) like he'd slept in a tent the night before. The Midwestern states would keep to themselves, but they'd be steady, and hey, they'd have each other. Alaska and Hawaii, meanwhile, would undoubtedly be the new kids—they might get invited to the movies and they'd have some fresh appeal, but at the end of the day they'd be outsiders, apart from the in crowd (though Hawaii would be the kid to introduce weed to everyone, so he'd quickly get his own circle of friends).

Where North Dakota sat in this metaphorical cafeteria, I wasn't so sure. North Dakota was the kid everyone sees at graduation and nobody recognizes. Unless you're from North Dakota, what do you actually know about the state? Maybe you learned the capital in fifth grade. Maybe you've seen *Fargo*. It's possible, but unlikely, that you've driven through it. But even if you did, chances are you never left the interstate, and at a speed limit of seventy-five (the subtext seemed to read "or as fast as you want . . .") it was all probably a blur. With proper alignment, you could sleep from Minnesota to Montana and wake up in the same lane.

Apart from its appearance on a map, the third-most boringly shaped state in the country (Colorado and Wyoming tie for first), I didn't have too much to go on. Nobody I talked to even cared to have an opinion about North Dakota if I mentioned I was going there. "Oh, that's random," they'd say, like I was the pretty girl telling my friend that I'd just been assigned to do a history project with Frank, that kid who always sat at the far corner table by himself, staging imaginary fights between his french fries. That kid wanted nothing to do with the rest of the cafeteria, and it nothing to do with him. He wasn't worse, he wasn't better. I'd heard it from my own teachers since preschool. North Dakota was just different.

After breakfast at Beth and Kyle's, I headed west in a mixture of rain and slush from Fargo through Valley City and James-town, toward Bismarck and beyond. Twice I left the interstate and drove north on state highways for thirty or forty minutes, side trips that made it expressly clear that there were two North Dakotas: the towns and cities along I-94, and everywhere else. As I neared Bismarck, I decided to explore the "other" part for dinner. Consulting my trusty Central States road map, which covered nearly twenty states, I spotted a town called Wilton some thirty miles north of the capital city. I liked the name—*Wilton*. Sounded like a good place to find some local flavor.

As I passed through the limits of Wilton, though, I discovered that this was no lively city. In addition to a few hundred residents, Wilton consisted of one gas station and one place to eat, the Fid-dlestix Café, housed in an unassuming—and nearly unmarked—single-story tan shed. This would *certainly* do. I pulled into the parking lot, buttoned my grubbiest plaid shirt most of the way, and entered through the tinkling front door.

Four or five tables of varying size filled the middle of the room, while several booths lined the far wall. About half the tables were taken. An elderly couple sat nearest to the entrance, while a family of four took up one of the booths. A group of twelve sat at the largest table, apparently celebrating someone's birthday. *Everyone* fell silent as I entered. Twenty-five pairs of eyes turned my way, each with the same questioning look. I felt like a salmon at a bear party.

One of the biggest giveaways that you're an outsider at a local eatery in rural America is waiting to be seated when you shouldn't. Sometimes there are helpful signs that tell you to seat yourself, but most of the time you're just supposed to *know*. All eyes on me, I had to make the decision on the fly, so I elected to move, sliding into a booth against the wall. Trying to blend in didn't matter by this point, I guess, but at least this way I wouldn't be surrounded.

I had nearly finished the architectural design for a short par-4 on my paper napkin—doodling always felt less awkward than staring at the other restaurant goers—by the time I received any sort of service. A woman in her forties, the lone waitress, came to take my order as she worked on eviscerating a large wad of gum with her left jaw.

"Yeah?"

"Uh, yeah, can I get a cheeseburger, medium rare, and a water?"

She nodded assent.

Rather than delivering my order to the kitchen, though, she moved on to the birthday party table. I couldn't blame her—they seemed to be having a great time. She spent a few minutes chatting with them, greeted an older couple that had just entered, and finally disappeared back into the kitchen. Ten minutes went by. I had moved on to sketching a risk-reward par-5 that resembled the eighteenth at Pebble Beach, at least the way I imagined the eighteenth at Pebble. The waitress reappeared, carrying the meals of the folks in the booth behind me. Then she stopped at my table.

Cowboys

"What'd you say you wanted?"

Damn. This was a tough realization. North Dakota may have been the weird kid in the U.S. states lunchroom, but at Fiddlestix there was no question—that weird kid was me.

In planning for my trip, I had written North Dakota off. It fell into the "hurry through" category of states—i.e., play a round and move the hell on. But now that I was here, I wanted more. What was it like, living in blue-highway America? North Dakota didn't have the aw-shucks charm of the Midwest, nor did it have the expansive ruggedness of the West. It was easy for America—myself included—to dismiss the place. But now I realized that being "in between" may be the most interesting spot of all. I just needed someone to help me crack the code.

As it turned out, the wife of my brother's college ski coach, a great lady named Barb, had grown up in Jamestown, a city of almost fifteen thousand people, making it the state's seventh largest. When she found out from Evan that I was visiting North Dakota (and willingly!), she was ecstatic to be able to set me up with some locals. I had stayed with Barb's sister, Beth, in Fargo. (If you're unfamiliar with North Dakota's geography, Fargo's in the east, Bismarck's in the middle, and that's kind of it.) But she didn't stop there. Barb offered me a range of contacts, including her father and her cousin and her college roommate and a friend who might be able to connect me with a certain special golf course. Bingo.

What I soon learned was how North Dakotans delighted in their removal from the rest of the country—the way they were happy to live in regional anonymity. The essence of North Dakota is, in fact, this sense of community. I am convinced that everyone in the state knows everyone else, which may seem unlikely except that *everyone* I came into contact with knew of everyone else I had met, from librarians to mayors to pro-shop managers.

The High Plains boasted no great landmarks or high-profile

national parks, nor scenery of particular note—as far as I knew. Situated between bleak northern Minnesota and bleaker eastern Montana, North Dakota isn't really on the way to or from *anywhere*. No professional sports teams or even major college programs are in the region. Even shopping sounded hard to come by, often requiring a lengthy drive to pick up anything specific. Those in eastern Montana and western North Dakota traveled to Dickinson for supplies, while Dickinsonians headed to Bismarck. If you lived in Bismarck, chances are you wanted to head still farther east, to Fargo, but anyone in Fargo who wanted to shop would trek down to Minneapolis. Everyone, it seems, liked access to a more populous place, but the self-contained nature of North Dakotans kept them in a world of their own, where *moving south* meant no farther than South Dakota, and *up north* was anything off the interstate.

What I really wanted was for someone to take me through *their* North Dakota. As I made it farther west, from the snow and slush and power outage in Jamestown to a calm, cool night in Bismarck, I got word that Barb's friend Judi and her husband, Larry, were game for just that.

There is perhaps no better spot from which to geographically divide the country into east and west than at the Missouri River in North Dakota. The High Plains meet the Mountain West in Bismarck, and immediately I could feel the change. Outcrops appeared that evoked the Rockies; little rivers suggested canyons. Even the travel seemed to have taken on a different, more rugged mood. Just two cities earned notice on the road sign as I left Bismarck:

DICKINSON	96
BILLINGS, MT	413

The sign made it clear: Here, at the edge of the frontier, things were about to get a lot bigger.

I met Larry and Judi at the Elks Club in Dickinson, where they were just sitting down to a pair of large steaks—they'd ordered one for me as well. From the moment I arrived, it was apparent that all you really need in North Dakota was an in. Larry and Judi knew the menu, knew the waitresses, knew everyone who walked by—and everyone knew them, too, and was delighted to stop and converse.

"And who could this be?" they all would ask, looking me over head to toe, sizing me up as if I were on display.

As an outsider, I was regarded with a mixture of excitement and wariness. Nearly everyone I met was thrilled that I was visiting their state, if a little suspicious of any kid who would stray so far from where he belonged. My declaration that I was from Massachusetts was met with the same reaction each time: Whoever I was talking to would tell me the name of someone they'd heard of who had moved "near there," then would be mildly surprised when I didn't immediately know the folks they were referring to.

"Welcome!" they'd all say. "You're just going to love it here."

Larry and Judi lived in a renovated farmhouse outside town, where we returned just as the sun was setting. Larry and I watched the World Series for a while and swapped stories. He ran a burgeoning livestock-auctioneer business that moved hundreds of thousands of animals every year, and therefore was the perfect guy to talk to about travel in the West. We tossed around ideas about places I could go, in Montana or Wyoming or Colorado, places he'd been to sell animals or had just heard tell of. He was a golf enthusiast, and because everyone knows everyone else in North Dakota, he'd already set up a round for us the next afternoon at Bully Pulpit Golf Course with his good friend Rick Thompson.

Bully Pulpit was in Medora, the type of tiny western town built on the stories of the Wild West. It had a listed population of 112 and was located in the heart of Teddy Roosevelt National Park, at the northern edge of the Badlands and less than an hour from Dickinson. As I trailed Larry's truck into the park, I couldn't help but wonder how on earth a golf course could exist within its boundaries. Any real color had long since disappeared from the landscape, which ran the spectrum from tan to brown. We rounded a corner and a view opened up before us, and what I saw was confounding: an endless sand-castle kingdom stretched into the distance, with cliffs and peaks like battlements and turrets, piled on top of one another as far as I could see. For her part, Subi seemed excited at the reintroduction of elevation into our travels and rattled along happily as the road wound into and out of these weird-looking craters and spires. She might've thought we were on the moon.

We'd driven separately, as I was characteristically uncertain whether, after the round, I'd return to Dickinson or head on to my next (unknown) stop. As we came over a ridge and got our first view of the valley below, I nearly forgot to brake, almost rear-ending Larry in astonishment. This wasn't just a golf course: It was bright, bottom-of-the-stoplight green, a startling contrast to the muted walls that tried to hold it in. The grass looked too vivid, too modern, as if somebody had Astroturfed the Badlands. But then Bully Pulpit was *built* as an enigma, a 2004 design that overran centuries-old wagon roads.

Even from my car, I wondered the same thing Mom would have: Was there a fight when something so visually and ecologically disruptive as a golf course was proposed next to the park? Maybe there would have been if there had been more than 112 citizens. Or maybe those 112 were supportive—any golf course in such a wild spot must be an economic boon for the area.

I wondered lots of things, but I'd forgotten all of them by the time I stood on the first tee. I was here to play North Dakota's finest.

The first thirteen holes at Bully Pulpit covered the sediment-rich floodplain of the Little Missouri River, which meandered past the south end of the course. Low evergreens swarmed the backs of some greens and teamed with scruffy rough to penalize drives that escaped the broad fairways. The seventh and eighth gave the confusing impression that we were playing into the woods, but every other hole felt totally unfamiliar. Medora provided a landscape that simply doesn't exist on any other course. The ninth doglegged back toward the clubhouse, a welcoming mountain ranch with dark wooden beams that provided strength and stability on a golf course built in the wilds of nature. Out front it had a great front porch, the kind of place I imagined you could get stuck for an entire afternoon, sitting and talking and drinking and, mostly, looking around at where you were.

I'd been playing reasonably well, with a birdie and a couple bogeys, and—with the exception of one enormous hook that landed on the edge of the Little Missouri—had kept my ball away from the surrounding scenery. Rick and Larry were great playing partners, too, with an enthusiasm for the course that was infectious. And they were eager to hear about the golf, and the life, that I'd run into thus far on my journey.

We stopped to grab a snack at the turn. It had turned into the nicest day I had seen in over a month: A bluebird sky had opened overhead and temperatures climbed into the midsixties. The woman who had been tending the front desk when we had checked in was now sitting outside. A man in a graphic T-shirt, ripped jeans, and dark cowboy boots sat alongside her. The golf pro.

"Loved that front nine," I said as we passed.

She laughed. "You loved the front nine? Course hasn't even started yet!"

She was right. I was about to feel totally, completely speechless on a golf course for the first time in my life. But I didn't know it yet. Twelve and thirteen brought our group close to the wall of a sandstone butte that had, until then, just been a cool feature of the background. I felt the temperature rising quickly as we neared the green, only thirty feet from the pistachio-colored wall, a cliff with different shades and textures of rock so cleanly layered that Dad would've wept with geology-professor joy. I was sure that this green was the highlight of the course; I even made sure to be properly impressed for Rick and Larry. But that was only because I had no idea what lay ahead as we drove off toward the fourteenth tee.

I had seen the distant strip of green from the first tee, a half mile off in the hills, but hadn't understood what it was. Now, as we began the extended cart ride, I started to get it.

"Hold on," I said to Larry. "That's the golf course up there?"

"Just wait," he told me.

We drove up for a few minutes—they left extra carts for walkers before the ascent—before reaching our tee, the fourteenth, the beginning of what they called Oh My God Corner.

The fairway had opened up in front of us between the steep walls of an honest-to-God canyon. There was no other word for it. And we were supposed to hit our drives down the chute to the canyon floor. It felt like we were pilots flying in to land on a thin green runway—miss your spot and you were dead. The wind, no more than a breeze in the lowlands, had picked up significantly, too.

I was playing from the back tees, so I got the dubious honor of hitting first. My drive pinged off the clubface, soaring over the hills and valleys that separated us from the fairway. But it had gone left at impact and kept going lefter as it traveled, tumbling even farther off-line in the right-to-left wind. I could feel my enthusiasm dive with the ball, which seemed desperate to reach the ground as quickly as possible. It felt—and looked—like clear failure. *Crash*.

The ball had stuck decisively in a patch of scrub on the side slope. Everyone stayed silent for a second, paying our respects to the fallen. But Larry cut in. "Don't worry, that's actually a free drop," he said. Oh. I was almost disappointed—that kind of took the claws away from the hole. "They don't like people walking off the course up here. I'm not sure why—we could use weed whackers instead of irons and the stuff that grows there wouldn't care."

Livestock, after all, was Larry's business—land conservation for its own sake didn't really concern him. "I guess it's good that they protect some of this stuff, but the land's useless. Can't grow anything here. You wouldn't even get animals to feed."

"Gotta keep that space clear for them prairie dogs to do their business," Rick added. It's probably good they weren't in charge—for the prairie dogs, at least. I dropped in the rough and looked ahead to the green, which was tucked neatly at the base of a cliff ahead to the left. I looked along the cliff. Was that a cart path? I traced the line up and up, back and forth. Where did it end? Did it end?

I made a distracted bogey on fourteen, missing long and left with my second shot and barely two-putting for my 5. I was pissed, because I was always pissed when I made bogey, but I was curious, too. I tapped the flagstick impatiently on the ground as I waited for Larry to finish out a five-footer.

Anticipation had replaced anger altogether as I got into the cart. We climbed several steep switchbacks, the cart sputtering in objection up what must have been another hundred vertical feet to the next tee. Then we parked and got out. Rick pointed up, so we continued to climb on foot.

We'd made it up to *the* Bully Pulpit, the fifteenth, the highest tee, and now, as I turned, I realized: We were overlooking *everything*. We had worked our way out of the valley altogether, and now, all of a sudden, we were on top of North Dakota.

I had come to see the Badlands and here I was, playing in their midst, *above* their midst. I swiveled slowly, admiring as dull-colored towers cascaded out in all directions. The land was bizarre. It looked like the Rockies had died and left the skeletons of their peaks to rot, and crumble, and perhaps morph into something different altogether. And golf, of all things, had brought me here. How awesome was that? I wiped a tear from my face—the wind was making my eyes water. I think.

"God's country," Rick breathed.

My eyes finally settled on our target, an island green some stories below that looked about as large as a parking space and about as easy to hold with a 9-iron. The area around the hole dropped off sharply into the brush to the left, right, and long. A gale was whipping across the hole.

"It's perfect if you land it just short and let it run on," Larry said. I looked at him quizzically. This was a 161-yard bungee jump onto a glorified mouse pad. There was *no way* I was hitting the green.

I've never been so content, or resigned, watching my golf ball float tens of yards off-line into a hazard. The shot started well left of the green, and assuming I hadn't hit some sort of vicious nature-inspired slice, it was the wind that had grabbed the ball and shoved it farther and farther right, where it landed somewhere in the Badlands. We left it for the prairie dogs.

A short while later Larry and Rick bade me farewell, sending me off to stay with Rick's brother Jim in Spearfish, South Dakota. Rick would be there in a couple days, he told me, if I was still around. But I was sorry to see them go. This was the type of place I'd hoped to find—weird, and alien, and beautiful. Just like I'd hoped golf could always be.

There was so much I'd left without seeing. I hadn't been to one of Larry's auctions, or seen Judi's horses, or joined them at a Dickinson State volleyball game. They'd welcomed me into their home, into their High Plains network. North Dakota felt like a place I maybe shouldn't leave, but I did.

The drive to South Dakota, Larry told me, would be pretty straight and pretty light on traffic. He was right. I'd imagine that Mars is similarly light on traffic. And the road was so straight that the dashed lines in the middle—the only kind that North Dakota needed—made me forget whether I was on a one- or two-way road.

In the late afternoon I drove into Spearfish, a city of ten thousand tucked into the Black Hills on the western edge of the state. I was there to meet up with Jim Thompson, who was gamely becoming my host through about eight degrees of separation.

Any uncertainty I felt at the randomness of our connection didn't last long.

I was supposed to meet Jim at his studio, the address of which seemed to confound my GPS. So I drove down the main street, then decided I'd gone too far, so I turned to drive the other way. Then I decided I'd driven too far again—maybe I hadn't gone far enough the first time. I was turning around for a third time when I noticed my cell phone buzzing from the cup holder. I picked up.

"Any chance that you're the confused individual doing laps past my studio like it's a darn racetrack?" he asked, following it with a loud, long chuckle. "You're getting closer . . ."

Jim was a local legend. He'd been a longtime hall-of-fame-quality rodeo announcer—whatever that meant, exactly, I wasn't sure—and now hosted a radio show. I could see why people would want to tune in. Jim delivered amusing stories and anecdotes with clever, simple lessons. He had local news, from agricultural reports to rodeo results to football schedules, delivered with a quick wit and a pleasing chuckle. And he had a familiar way of talking, as if he were speaking to friends. I could see that people would listen to Jim because they'd feel instantly close to him. With his white cowboy hat, fine auburn mustache, and a voice that, even at a whisper, commanded the attention of the entire room, Jim was a larger-than-life embodiment of how the middle of America is different—and in many ways cooler than the attention-grabbing coasts.

Just listening to Jim talk about things in his life was mesmerizing—partly because of his voice, which lent instant importance to any story he told, and also because his life was so different from any I had ever been around. He knew lots of real cowboys, who not only wore hats and boots and rode horses but also went by names like Slim and Hawkeye and lived from rodeo to rodeo and did things like play real Russian roulette, which he said had recently claimed the life of one such friend.

Jim's wife was away for the night, so we defrosted chicken

nuggets—fast over fancy—and settled in front of the World Series until Jim announced his bedtime and showed me to the guest room. I lay in this cozy bed for a while, contemplating my strange surroundings. Jim had asked me to be a guest on his show the following afternoon. It didn't make much sense to me. I was certainly less interesting than even the most mundane Spearfishian seemed to be—or at least that's what Jim's stories made me believe. My impression of the town was that this was an outpost of sorts, a gathering place for the wandering souls of the Wild West. All of them had stories, probably all wilder than my own. Who was I to be giving an interview? I was a poor, homeless vagabond from the East. Sometimes I peed into empty Gatorade bottles in my car. Sitting at a microphone to tell people about it felt strange.

But the afternoon came: my very first piece of press. I met Jim at his studio, comprising a simple three-room office and the studio itself, which had several microphones and stereo equipment and was covered corner to corner in CDs, folders, and stacks of paper—no doubt the news reports and clever anecdotes from months past, and some unused material for shows to come. I sat down, tried on the headphones, and watched Jim operate. His voice was even smoother on the air, and I let his words wash over me, taking in the emotion of his voice rather than the information conveyed through his words. And then he introduced me, the day's featured guest.

I answered his questions pretty simply, talking about the favors I'd already received from folks along the way and how America had been good to me, particularly at a person-to-person level. I thought it went fine, besides hearing the echo of my own voice, which I didn't like. But Jim seemed to take more from the appearance. We came back from a commercial break to round up my bit.

"We've been visiting with Dylan Dethier," he said as the intro music died down, "a young traveler who's with us in the studio today. And sitting here with him, I'm reminded of two other young men who sat right where he is right now—Big Kenny and John Rich, or Big and Rich, country duo, as the world knows them now. And I can't tell you just what it is, but I have a strong feeling we'll be hearing a lot more from this fella Dylan as time goes on. Yessir, I think we'll keep an eye on him."

I sat across from him, grinning sheepishly. It was flattering, the way he welcomed me, the way he treated my story, made me feel cool. I was still an outsider, that was for sure, but I was starting to enjoy that role a little more. A warrior of the road. I thought of his cowboy friends, the ones who traveled from rodeo to rodeo, who returned to Spearfish with their own stories from the road.

Whatever nomadic titles I could claim, I knew that cowboy wasn't one of them. But I wasn't just a wanderer, either. And I wasn't just passing through these states, adding them to my list.

I was leaving tracks.

CHAPTER 6

Rule Number One

The head pro, Bryan, stopped me as I began to walk from the clubhouse to the first tee. "Dylan, right?" he asked. "I gotta show you something before you head out." I'm not sure he wanted to show *me,* specifically—but there weren't many other options around.

Before I'd left South Dakota, Jim Thompson had called his friend John, who lives in Sundance, Wyoming, and after a quick stop by Mount Rushmore—a wholly unimpressive sight up close—I wound my way to the far side of the Black Hills in time for dinner. John had not only hosted me at his house overnight but had taken the liberty of calling the pro shop on my behalf. Now I was playing this spectacular unknown course for free. A few houses dotted the front nine at Devil's Tower, and a smattering of others were in the early stages of construction. Those that were occupied looked enviable, raised ranch houses with strong wood beams and welcoming front porches. It wasn't clear if the houses were the early signs of a successful development or the manifestation of a stunted golf course/real estate project that had been launched in the wrong economic climate. I guessed the latter.

It was now late October in eastern Wyoming, which meant that golf season was coming to a close—and that hunting season was in full swing. Even on a sunny morning at the Golf Club at Devil's Tower, a scenic masterpiece with a new design, clubhouse, and back nine, I was the only one on the course.

"Hell, I'd be out hunting too if I didn't have to work," Bryan told me wistfully as we walked outside, past four women playing bridge in the corner of the clubhouse. I liked these Western golf pros, who didn't take themselves too seriously, saw the golf course as an extension of the scenery, and who, like Bryan, wore work outfits that were three parts denim. We approached his red pickup, where a crowd of flies had gathered above the bed. With a proud little wave of his arm, he lowered the tailgate, revealing the antlered head that had been attached, at some point, to an enormous moose.

I felt a look of mixed wonder and disgust creeping over my face, but I did my best to turn a gag into a smile, and moved in for a closer look. Wow. This was *huge*. And it smelled something powerful. Some foul reddish-brown liquid had pooled by the base of the neck. I made a noise that I hoped sounded like an approving grunt.

Nobody I'd met had ever heard of this course, not for lack of a good product but rather because it was in tiny Hulett, Wyoming— one of those towns I kept running into that felt as if they were straight out of an old Western. It held a bank, a trading post, a courthouse, a run-down motel, a few hundred people, and now, for some reason, a really cool golf course.

Golf means something different everywhere, but in Hulett I felt as if I could embrace it completely. Maybe my clean conscience meant I didn't care enough about the moose. But I think it meant more that I liked how golf, like everything, was open in the West, to people and animals alike. If this included some blood and guts in the parking lot, if it meant that "Beware of wildlife" and "No hunting" both made it onto the same score-card, well, I was okay with it. Because I felt as if this was golf that even Dad would get excited about—the game felt freer out here.

My golf game was comfortable in the West, both with Wyoming's greens fees (negotiable) and its unassuming T-shirt-and-jeans approach to the sport. Subi seemed to like the wide-open spaces too, the jagged mountains and impressive overlooks and absence of stoplights. The geographic emptiness I had traveled through in the previous month had been inspiring and thought-provoking, and I hadn't had any trouble filling the space with considerations and observations of my own. Since Minneapolis I had been in no city with more than a hundred thousand people, and most of the land I saw bore scant evidence of human interference. The road itself wound its way through endless plains, along roaring rivers, and over treacherous passes, but it belonged to the land no more than a scar belongs to the skin. In the valleys there were towns, and on the outskirts there were ranches, but these were just interruptions in the unblemished landscape of the West.

The day after my round at Devil's Tower, though, I wondered if maybe I wasn't getting *too* comfortable in my new environment. I remember precisely where I was standing when this thought crossed my mind—in the Big Horn Mountains atop a rocky ledge, looking down at Subi, eighty feet below me. How, exactly, had I gotten myself into this predicament?

One of the biggest problems facing a rogue seventeen-year-old on a journey across America is that he has nobody with him to keep his own stupidity in check, so it was difficult to track exactly where my trail of bad decisions had begun. I had left Devil's Tower after my round and reached Buffalo, Wyoming, tucked into the foothills of the Big Horns, at around 5:30 P.M. From there I had three options: Highway 16 would take me directly over the mountains, 90 ran north, and 25 headed south. At this point in the afternoon, 16 really shouldn't have been a choice. Storm clouds loomed in the direction of Powder River Pass, a treacherous section of road some five thousand feet above Buffalo. But I was in no mood to follow reason or play it safe—not when there was the chance for adventure.

One thing I forgot: Just because you can get up doesn't mean you can get down. It was the law of the mountains—the inspiration behind the CHAINS REQUIRED signs that I passed en route to the ascent. I made it up without any headaches—although it was beginning to flurry as I neared the top of the pass. What I'd ignored, though, is that from the top, everything is downhill.

Subi screamed out as we began the first descent. It was dark now, and we'd been down to one headlight for nearly a month. The remaining headlight served mainly to illuminate the fresh snow as it blew across my windshield. Now and then I'd catch glimpses of ice on the roadway, but more often I'd *feel* it as Subi's treadless tires slipped and slipped and slipped into freefall, sliding along the ice as I frantically turned the wheel—to no avail—and began to brace for impact until we'd hit pavement again and then the brakes would mercifully catch at last and slow my pounding heart. In good conditions, the drive shouldn't have taken more than ninety minutes. I had already clocked well over two hours and we were barely halfway. As I inched down the far slope, Subi's thermostat continued to plummet. Fifty degrees had turned to forty, and then thirty, and all of a sudden it was seventeen degrees and I was the only car on the road.

I hadn't realized that I had already made it through the worst when I admitted defeat for the night. A dirt road appeared on the left and I pulled into the parking lot for Meadowlark Lake. I bet this lake is a good spot to cool off after a summertime hike. But oh, Lord, was it cold now. And, I imagined, still getting colder. I had gotten pretty good at the cold, I thought, over the past few weeks. But being "good at the cold" had meant golfing in the forties, maybe even—gasp!—with shorts on.

I was still holding on to summer, but now Wyoming was doing its best to skip fall. I put on my thickest jacket and warmest sweatpants and curled up in my sleeping bag, even though it was only eight thirty, and tried to read myself to sleep. This actually worked well for a few hours before I woke up, for good, just after two. I should have just left then. Instead I rolled around as more and more frozen air crept in through the driver's-side door, slapping at my exposed face.

One thing you should know about sleeping in your car is that when it's below freezing, the outsides of your windows stay clear while the insides form a layer of resilient super-ice. I spent the hour from five to six A.M. trying to figure out how my crappy plastic scraper—a freebie from a lame auto-parts store—could clear off what seemed to be an inch-thick coating of the strongest ice of all time. It was like scraping a windshield off the windshield. Plus, the more successful I was, the more ice chips ended up in the driver's seat. I turned on the heat, which somehow cooled things down even further so that the temperature outside, which, Subi whined, had dropped all the way to six degrees, now felt warmer than the air-conditioned interior.

I thinned out the ice enough to see through a corner of the windshield—think flying a plane from an aisle seat in coach. It would have to do. I crept back onto the main road. Luckily, few drivers were making a six A.M. trek in middle-of-nowhere Wyoming, so I was able to descend in a low gear as Subi finally shifted from A/C to defrost and the sun began to shine through my front windshield.

Maybe my car windshield had defrosted before my brain had. Maybe I wanted to get some victory against the mountains that had already beaten me. Maybe it just really looked like it would be a dynamite picture. Just twenty minutes after I'd set out, I felt inspired to pull over next to a near cliff. I shimmied, clawed, scrambled, and willed my way up some eighty feet by grabbing onto jutting roots and unstable little trees that grew straight out of the soft rock. What a beautiful view! I snapped a photo of the early morning sun as it pressed over the more defined ridges that framed the road from either side. I checked the result on my camera. Hmm. Not half bad. Then I looked down.

Just because you can get up doesn't mean you can get down. I may have survived their arctic nocturnal temperature, but the Big Horns weren't done proving their point. Now I was staring down into what was essentially a sheer drop-off. My heart dove like a snap hook.

If I proceeded slowly and with extreme caution, I thought,

maybe, just maybe, I could make it down the same way I came up. Don't think about it, I told myself, feeling my chest start to tighten. Just go for it and you'll be fine. Wrong. I began the treacherous descent, sliding in the direction of the first checkpoint, a miniature tree sticking out from a crack in the cliff. I stumbled slightly, sending my momentum forward, but managed to grab hold of the tree, counting on it to slow me down. Holy hell—this was no strong pine. As my hands closed around its thin trunk, I felt the unmistakable sensation that the fish had escaped the line. The tree came out in my right hand.

It was October 23, 2009. On October 25, I would turn eighteen. In this moment, then, the prior seventeen years, three hundred sixty-three days, and seven hours began to flash before my eyes, and I didn't feel sad but instead a quick sharp anger. If I wasn't going to make it to eighteen, why was I *here* of all places? As my body turned, still hanging on to the tree, my weight swung backward, I lost my balance, and I began to fall. My left arm flailed around desperately for something to grab onto—but then, somehow, the tree held. One last root stuck out of the ridge, strained but unbroken.

Whoa. I adjusted my balance; I grabbed a rock and clambered back up to the ridge. Then I looked back down. Had that tree broken, I would have slipped backward and gone into freefall. I imagined myself bouncing down the mountainside, a lanky, red-T-shirted boulder. Death amid such spectacular natural beauty. How poetic.

Now what was I supposed to do? Going straight down was out—if I missed a foothold or chose the wrong tree, I was toast. I couldn't climb farther up, either—the handholds disappeared on the rock up to the ridge above me.

The thought of traversing around, into the shadows and around the dark corner of the V-shaped ridge, was the most terrifying possibility of all. Still, I could imagine that there would be a way out—maybe the slope would dip down there, at the crotch of the ridge.

At this altitude I was presumably free from snakes, by far my greatest fear, but the top of this ridge looked like the setting for a Discovery Channel special on mountain lion feeding habits. If I came around the corner face-to-face with a cougar, I would probably leap. I started seeing dens in the shaded recesses of the mountainside. I could hear my heartbeat.

Around the ridge was my only choice. I began a cautious traverse. The footing was less sure than I'd hoped, and soon I was crossing a narrow ledge, twenty feet long and no more than two feet wide. I shuffled along, leaning into the wall for support. And then . . . was that a paw print in the sand? I kept shuffling, kept my eyes on the wall, not daring to look back. It was better not to know.

I crept around corners like a kid sneaking for the cookie jar, determined to spot trouble before it could spot me. Panicking wasn't my thing. But I had no idea how this was going to resolve itself. A chilling thought came across my mind: *Nobody knew I was here*. This was often true during my travels, of course, but I'd never thought about it in a they-won't-even-know-where-to-find-the-body sort of way. I was visualizing a scenario involving mountain lions, my corpse, and several months of decay. Maybe I *was* panicking a little.

Step by careful step, however, I was moving ever so slightly downhill—marginally closer to the level of the road, to safety. Maybe this would be easier than I thought. Heck, if I got *really* lucky, there'd still be time to get to continental breakfast in Ten Sleep.

I reached the corner of the ridge at last, and what I saw injected me with a tiny shot of encouragement. There was a bowl-shaped nook eight or ten feet below, but if I could get down *that,* the next slide down looked doable. Once I made the first jump, though, I knew I'd be committed. The bowl's walls were steep and smooth, and so I'd be like a bug in a bathtub: no way out but the drain.

I blew a bead of sweat off the tip of my nose. *Okay*. I turned and crouched, finding handholds as I began to reverse-scale the wall. My left foot led the descent, searching the rock before it found a seam. But as the right foot came to join, the left suddenly slipped out and I fell backward, landing partly on one foot before doing an awkward sort of roll. My camera, which I had slung over my shoulder, whipped around and clocked me in the jaw.

I rubbed my gums as I stood up, my dignity bruised but the rest of me fine. Brushing a leaf off my elbow, I edged forward to survey what was left of the descent. From the bowl it was hard to tell exactly what lay below, but that was where I was headed, so I inched my way down the chute. I made it just ten feet before the view opened up.

More bad news. There was a reasonable route down the next several feet of rock, which was rough enough to hold my hands and feet. Below that, however, an old rockslide had smoothed the edges of the chute just as it turned into a sheer drop—some twenty-five feet to the level of the road.

I looked back. No chance. I looked down. Broken leg, at least. But in that moment I wasn't scared so much as I was pissed off at myself. *You're such a moron.* Rule number one drifted into my mind: *Don't die.* If there was any situation in which I had ignored that rule, it was here. I was beat, ready to cry uncle.

Wait. Didn't they make cell phones for scenarios just like this? *You're such a moron.* I moved to grab my phone from the zipper pocket on my jacket, sliding the rectangular shape out as I said a silent prayer for cell service. Crap. That wasn't my phone . . . it was a Snickers bar.

I scrambled back to the base of the bowl to take stock of my predicament. At the rear of the bowl was a nasty thicket where even the brambles grew brambles, surviving out of pure spite in this little death hole. The wall *did* seem to dip a little back there. I walked to the edge of the thorns to take a closer look.

And there, in the rear of my rocky coffin, was the answer.

At the base of the wall, nearly invisible beneath brush and bramble, was the trunk of one sorry tree that had toppled into this place and, like me, couldn't find a way out.

The tree was long enough that if I could get it standing up on its side, it could reach out of this jail and onto the upper ledge. To get it, though, I'd have to crawl through a gauntlet of pure pain. Nobody's ever cheese-gratered my arms and legs, but that was about how I felt forty-five minutes later, loping around the next section of cliff. Angry webs of red crisscrossed my shins and forearms, and my socks were stained with the rusty color of dried blood. My thighs complained, too; I'd shimmed up the tree and wounds had opened up through my shorts. I hadn't even spared my face, which had suffered from my headfirst charge to extract the trunk. But I'd made it out of the bowl.

It was another forty-five minutes from when I left the bowl before I reached the road. I had traversed about a mile farther up the canyon before a grassy slope opened up to my right, steep but still passable. I descended on my butt, inching my way down as little rocks skittered past me and down onto the road, alarming the passing cars. I wondered how it would look if I rode a rock-slide into the middle of the highway.

The roadway felt so secure beneath my feet. I was still a half mile from my car and must have cut a strange figure as I limped down the breakdown lane. I was exhausted as I collapsed into the driver's seat, my nerves completely shot. I realized that nobody would know what I'd just been through—the stupidity of the dilemma or the heroics of the survival.

"We must never speak of this," I told Subi, patting her reassuringly on the dashboard.

It was a large victory and yet such a small one. All that I'd really succeeded in doing was taking an average picture and walking back to the car. All I'd done was stay at even par. But here I guess the scorecard didn't tell the whole story.

By the time I was back inside Subi's windless warmth, I had been gone for nearly three hours. All the continental breakfasts would be closed by now.

I reached into my pocket and unwrapped my Snickers.

• • •

After spending the night in Thermopolis, I finished my drive across Wyoming the next afternoon, pushing through to my aunt and uncle's house in Hyrum, Utah. Hyrum was just outside Logan, in Utah's northeastern corner. Uncle Brock was my father's younger brother and, like my father, a college professor—of English, at Utah State University.

There was something different about being with a family—even more so because it was my family. Every home I had entered thus far in the trip had been new to me, every host a stranger. I'd never been away from home for my birthday, either, so it was nice that here, twenty-two hundred miles from Williamstown, I could ring in the big day with a group of Dethiers. (And do my laundry!)

I stayed in bed for a while that morning, lounging in my basement guest room before finally arising for a late cereal breakfast. Brock proposed a birthday hike, so the two of us set off just before noon. We drove up Logan Canyon before parking at a trailhead and continuing on foot, crisscrossing back through the trees and out onto cliffs overlooking the canyon. It was nice to be on an *intentional* hike. It was likely the most time Brock and I had spent together, just the two of us. There was an ease and a depth in the conversation that was reassuring—Brock knew something about me, and about the way I had grown up.

"Did it ever bother you, being a younger brother?" Brock asked. "I know that was always a big thing for me, figuring out a way to live up to your dad, who was so good at everything."

I thought about it. I'd dealt with similar things—getting called "little Evan" through elementary school, mistaken for Evan by my teachers, always comparing myself to him. "He was always better at some stuff," I told Brock. "A lot of stuff, I guess. He was smarter than me, sharper, better at school, better at skiing—even taller. But it never really bothered me. I always wanted him to be good at all that stuff. I liked getting mistaken for him—because that meant I must be doing *something* right."

I wasn't lying—this was all true. I had grown up in my brother's shadow, and if I did something well, there was a good chance that he had already done it—and had done it even better. It was a large reason I had joined the golf team instead of the running team in ninth grade. Maybe it was a large reason that I was out here right now. Stepping out of the shadow.

It occurred to me that here we were, the younger brothers, hiking together in Utah, while the older pair, my father and Evan, were together in Williamstown. I kept thinking about them as we made our descent. I missed them.

When we got back to the house, I saw that Aunt Melody had laid out an assortment of colorful bags, boxes, and envelopes. Presents! I had expected a couple phone calls—but I guessed this was the work of Mom, to coordinate a drop-off for my birthday. The gifts were a combination of useful and entertaining. There was a mini "survival kit" from my aunt, complete with space blanket and matches. There was a Subway gift card, twenty-five dollars, from Laurie and Keith, family friends. Luke, who lived down the road and had always been a younger-brother figure to me, had sent delicious fudge brownies that had somehow survived the journey fresh and intact. There were cards, too, from my grandparents and a couple friends, passing along well wishes. And there was an audio recorder from my parents—to record my thoughts on the road. It was a strange thing, that recorder. I must have looked at it a hundred times, flipped switches, changed batteries, pressed buttons. But I never got it to turn on.

Turning eighteen meant something legally, I knew. No more runaway hotlines. No more cops calling home. And now, if I decided I could afford it, I could even get a hotel room.

But turning eighteen this way meant much more. I was glad that I wasn't in the back of Subi, that I was with family instead. I was *really* glad that I wasn't at the base of a cliff with two broken legs and half a spine. I thought of Mom and Dad and how they'd love to see this, the presents and the family and the two-candled coffee cake. I thought of how far I'd come from the five-year-old who went to the golf course to run around after his brother.

And I thought about how I was growing up on the wide-open fairways of the West, and how—in more ways than one—I was now playing eighteen in America.

CHAPTER 7

Privilege

My first few weeks as an eighteen-year-old took me through Utah, up the western edge of Wyoming into Montana, down across Idaho, then up to Washington and down into Oregon. It rained most days and it snowed some others, and I squeezed in rounds of golf in between the two. It was early winter in these places, and once my golf requirement was satisfied, I spent dry moments hiking in Yellowstone, or exploring in the Tetons, or skiing in northern Oregon.

It was all feeling easier, simpler, finding places I could sleep and spending nights alone and exploiting cheap food deals. I'd streamlined Subi's setup, too. I shipped home a large canvas bag of excess clothing from Utah. I ditched my juice-stained cooler in a Dumpster in Montana. I'd found uses for every space in the car—and even discovered new ones. Clean socks got stuffed in with the tire jack. Shorts were crammed beneath the backseat. There was a funny amount of space if you lifted up the floor of the trunk, too—so sweatshirts went under there, and spare food went one more layer down, tucked in with the spare tire. I almost had room to sleep. Life was feeling easier fifteen states into the trip—and now I'd reached the Pacific Ocean.

Night was falling as Subi and I sputtered through the outer gates of Bandon Dunes, a golf resort in southwest Oregon.

I had written to my friend Taylor's great-uncle, who worked with the New Jersey Golf Association, and he wrote to his friend in Portland, who thought I sounded interesting and wrote to his friend at Bandon, who passed the task along to Laura, the assistant to the general manager and my eventual point of contact. I had gotten pretty good at wrangling such far-flung connections. "We'll get a round set up for you, and we look forward to your visit!" she wrote to me in an e-mail. It was weird—instead of me trying to weasel onto their facility without anyone noticing, I felt as though I was actually a guest, someone they wanted to show a good time. Laura, like most people who give you free things, made a great impression.

Bandon was a destination—a golf pilgrimage, really. The complex, a huge resort on Oregon's quiet seacoast, consists of four courses (the fourth hadn't yet opened when I was there), each ranked favorably among the country's top one hundred. I first heard about Bandon in a Michigan laundromat some weeks before when an article from the wrinkled remains of a magazine caught my eye: "Where Scotland meets Oregon," the caption read. *Where kilts meet weed,* I thought immediately. *Where bagpipes meet beavers. Where white people meet . . . white people.* But this was a golf magazine. A photo showed the carnage from a collision between wave and cliff, movement so violent that I almost didn't notice the flagstick emerging from the mist, and beyond that a ghostly collection of dunes trailing into the distance. I had been intrigued. And now I was there.

I had played a collection of unbelievable places in the preceding weeks and months, but as I got to the outskirts of the resort, a thought struck me: This wasn't Wyoming's best golf course or a cool find in northern Michigan. I had one of the most desired tee times in the world. How could that be?

Huge pines lined the driveway, masked sentries silhouetted against the dusk. I slowed down at a small booth labeled INFORMATION, which is exactly what I needed, but as I approached I saw that the window was dark and the house vacant. I continued on. A sign appeared pointing to "The Inn" in one direction and "The Lodge" in the other. Beyond that, more signs: "Grove Cottages" and "Chrome Lake Lofts" and "Lily Pond Rooms." It was too dark to really see the buildings, except that they kept looming out of the shadows, large and intimidating, as I drove around corners. I had agreed to a round of golf. Now I was choosing honeymoon suites. What was this place?

Show up Sunday evening, Laura had told me, and stay a couple nights, play a couple rounds. Fifty bucks a night for the room and no charge for the golf. I was getting a pair of days at a place that should have cost me a thousand dollars at about 90 percent off, and it had sounded perfect and easy when I read her e-mail. But in the dark, driving alone into America's premier golf resort, it didn't seem so simple. I didn't belong here. A nomadic eighteen-year-old with a carful of dirty clothes and an empty wallet—they might chase me out.

For one thing, I had no idea where to check my reservation—if I even had one. Was it for the inn? The lodge? The villas? Had Laura forgotten to make one? She must have forgotten. She hadn't even sent me a confirmation e-mail. I had been a ragged nomad for so long that the thought of navigating refined accommodations freaked me out. *Maybe I should just leave,* I thought as I wound my way to the pro shop, but instead I parked, squeezing Subi between a yellow Mercedes convertible and a large black Lexus.

One group's happiness can make an onlooker feel particularly isolated—it's a cruel trick of human emotion. As I opened my door, dozens of people were streaming from the golf course and the pro shop and into the pub or the inn, some dressed for fancy golf, others for fancy dinner, razzing each other about the rounds they had just been through on the course and the rounds they were about to get in the pub. Everyone was laughing, yelling, grinning. I grabbed my last clean collared shirt—a grubby maroon number that had spent the better part of three months underneath a crate of camping supplies—and pulled it over the unshowered brunette mop atop my head. Looking at my dark reflection in Subi's window, I ran my hand through my hair, where three days' worth of grease stuck to my palm.

Subi didn't look any more natural here than I did. We had spent the last several days driving through mud and slush in the Oregon mountains, and her salty brown coat stood in particularly stark contrast to the road-sign yellow of the Mercedes next to me. God, was I glad there was no valet parking. "I'm not sure we really fit in here," I whispered, patting Subi's rear window as I shut the door.

I knew it would be different if I had a group with me, too—four guys who could pile out of the car together—a united band of misfits. But as I walked toward the lodge, I felt as if everyone and everything were closing in around me: the sweater-vested CEOs, the high-profile lawyers, the rich politicians. Here, at night on the Oregon coast, had I found the dark side of golf?

The wishful smell of a salmon special I couldn't afford greeted me as I walked through the doors of what appeared to be the main lodge. A group brushed past me toward the restaurant, men with coats and ties and women with shoes that matched their dully metallic dresses.

I slunk into a short line of golfers waiting to claim their room reservations at the front desk. The guy in front of me was talking loudly on his BlackBerry.

"I told you," he bellowed. "I'm on vacation. You're in charge. How am I supposed to get rid of this slice if you're on my ass all the time? You own the company for a few days. Try to enjoy it."

Great, I thought. This was the kind of person I'd be stuck with for the next two days? After a minute or two, a squat brunette woman with a little gold nametag reading "Maureen" waved me over. I took a deep breath—the moment of truth.

"Hi," I told her. "My name's Dylan Dethier." *Stupid.* She gave me a withering look.

"Where's your reservation for?"

I had no idea. At this point, I was pretty convinced there was no reservation. I had no proof of it, nothing. Just a name. Where was Laura? "I can't remember, actually," I told her unconvincingly, pointing at the computer. "Do you have my name in there?"

She stared back at me for a second before giving a drawn-out, I-hate-my-job-and-all-these-people kind of sigh. "Spell it."

Through some miracle, Maureen had my name and my discount and even my room key. I could feel her eyes tracing me top to bottom—and not in a good way—as I signed my receipt and took a small envelope from her.

"Room's on the second floor. There's a side door that goes there from the parking lot, right next to the kitchen."

The side door—really? I looked that bad? That was the door for the kitchen trash bags, and the gross exhaust stuff that comes out of the sides of restaurants, and, apparently, jeans-wearing teenagers. God forbid the lodge's other patrons had to set eyes on me for another minute.

I relished the rush of indignation, but deep down I was glad to sneak in the side door of this place. I didn't want any part of the lobby. I stuffed some clothes and a toothbrush into a backpack, trudged past a Dumpster containing parts of the salmon that they couldn't serve to customers, and continued upstairs, where I found my door. I slid the key into its slot and removed it. The receiver flashed red and the lock gave a click to reinforce how, exactly, it *wasn't* going to open. I tried it again. *Please just let me in.* Red. Click. And again, and again, and again. It was all wrong. I wasn't supposed to be here and the key knew it and the door knew it and Maureen definitely knew it. I slunk back to the front desk to face her again.

A few minutes later, I finally gained entry into my first hotel room of the trip—nearly three months after I'd set out. I surveyed the room, mostly with relief in knowing that I could stay there in safety for about twelve hours. It was a small room, and understated. The walls were white. The television was tiny. The decor was sparse. Even the free stuff—two Bandon Dunes plastic water bottles—seemed pretty modest. *Maybe this is where they stick the poors.* Wait, poor people don't get to go to places like Bandon, I thought with a grimace. The window was open a bit and muffled laughter crept in, mixed with cigar smoke and maybe chocolate cake? No—I was probably imagining that part. Chocolate cake doesn't really smell like anything. I threw down my duffel and flopped spread-eagle onto my bed, wondering how I had gotten there.

Bandon felt like the golf I had been taught to resent since I had first picked up a club. The guests I saw in the lobby felt like the golfers who had made Dad cringe when I had told him I was going out for the high school team, that I was *pursuing* the game. It had always been easy to hate the kids who bragged about having played at a place like Bandon Dunes, and to reject the idea of going there myself. But now I was there, and I was the uncomfortable one. Who was rejecting whom?

I turned on the television and flicked through the channels, pausing as a Subway commercial caught my eye, one in which the sandwiches floated diagonally through the air like big steak-and-cheese blimps. It occurred to me that I hadn't eaten since midmorning. I was learning to suppress these urges. Everyone knows the feeling of being hungry in anticipation of your next meal, and eventually that sharp feeling in your stomach that doesn't hurt, exactly: It takes over. I couldn't decide which I liked less, the first few weeks—when I got so hungry that I'd lie in the back of Subi listening to my stomach growling as I tried to fall asleep—or those same pangs of hunger now that I was used to them.

When I resigned myself to the fact that a meal wasn't coming, like now, that I was spending fifty bucks just to sleep somewhere and couldn't spend a dollar more, the urges got duller. My mind was starting to ignore my body, I guess. I grabbed a couple saltines from my backpack, hoping to confuse my stomach long enough to fall asleep, and climbed under the covers. The noise coming up through my window was starting to die down, men's cigars extinguished, their whiskeys abandoned—or maybe my senses were just fading. There was no denying that it was nice to have a bed. *Maybe I can just stay here all day tomorrow.* It was a fuzzy thought, a tired thought.

• • •

Privilege

My eyes bolted open the next morning to several shocks of sunlight streaming into the room. And as my brain emerged from its sleepy fog, I heard the unmistakable sound of driver on golf ball.

"Good shot, Adam," a man called out.

Where was I? I rolled out of bed and toward the window to investigate. Directly below me, within spitting distance, several men were rolling putts across a practice green. Just to the right, I noticed the first tee. A small crowd was queued up around it, some holding coffees and taking in the scene, others swinging irons, loosening up. Several holes stretched out further to the left, and my eye worked backward from the eighteenth green down to the tee, then to the seventeenth, and then to sixteen and on. The fairways traced back a half mile into the distance, where the green of the grasses suddenly ended, replaced by the unmistakable blue and white of the Pacific Ocean. I could just make out a stretch of waves rolling in toward the shore, imagined I could hear them breaking on the base of Bandon's famous cliffs. I thought of the picture in the magazine and felt my first sense of real excitement since my arrival. The room may have been cheap, but this wasn't a low-rent view.

Everything looks different in the light of day. What had seemed imposing last night suddenly felt manageable. The sweater vests in the breakfast room now looked more worn, faded. The bodies beneath them looked as if they probably had some battle scars, too. Two groups of middle-aged men sitting near me didn't seem like CEOs, more like buddies on an adventure, a guys' weekend that they had set aside some money for. They were excited, almost giddy, in a way that grown men aren't supposed to be. Eating alone I was free to eavesdrop, to hear about Joe's long shot goal to break 90 and how Charlie *really* hoped that he had left his shanks at home and how, more than anything, they couldn't wait to get out there and *see it*. It was hard not to get carried along in their excitement a little bit, and I was feeling better as I began eviscerating the Belgian waffle in front of me. I could fit in at this place, couldn't I?

• • •

Grant Rogers was late for our tee time. Rather, he was late *according* to our tee time—I soon learned that trivial matters like tee times didn't worry him much. After spending much of the morning at Bandon's gargantuan practice facility, hoping to sharpen up a game that had gone dormant in the snow and rain of the previous two weeks, I had headed down to the first tee of the Bandon Dunes course to wait.

I putted for a few minutes, checking my cell phone nervously as our time approached, still somewhat skeptical that I'd be allowed onto the course. As 12:15 came and went, though, I went to talk to the starter. "Oh, Grant?" he said, breaking into a grin. "He'll be here. You've never met him?" I shook my head. "You're in for a treat."

Grant was Bandon's director of golf instruction, which would've meant "golf professional" except Bandon employed a small army of those. He was in his fifties, some gray in his hair and a hint of mischief in his eye. I'm not sure how I ended up paired with him, and I never asked—too much else about the man fascinated me.

Eventually, Grant sauntered in, bag slung over his right shoulder, wearing a faded navy pullover, a beige baseball cap, and a pair of worn khakis. The profession of teaching golf is usually nine tenths *looking* like you teach golf—either the hair-gel, tight-bright-polo, white-belt type who is good at golf but, well, not really *that* good, or the other stereotype: the older guy who thinks everyone spends their time watching the Golf Channel and exclusively wears one-size-too-big shirts from famous golf courses. Grant did not fit into either of those clichés, and I liked him from the start.

After a quick introduction, he gestured toward the practice green I had just come from. "Putting contest? We didn't want to be in front of those guys anyway," he whispered as we watched a foursome disappear down the first fairway. "Waiting kind of opens things up."

Putting contests are my thing. But Grant had something slightly different in mind than the holes laid out before us. As we approached, he surveyed the green the way an architect might look at a modular just off the flatbed, and then he went to work. I stood and watched as he went from hole to hole, taking each temporary pin and relocating it to the edge of a hill, or the middle of a slope, or the edge of the fringe. He returned to my side and joined me in admiring his handiwork. "Little better, don't you think?" he asked.

We played about nine holes, taking anywhere between three and ten strokes to navigate Grant's impossible new course. We each took seven tries at the final hole, two thirds of the way up a side slope that required making a twenty-footer or seeing the ball return to our feet, before Grant had seen enough. He flipped his ball into his right hand with the back of his putter and nodded toward the first tee.

"Ready?"

"Definitely." I reached down to grab my own ball as he started to walk away. "Are we going to leave the pins where they are?"

"Oh." He stopped and turned, but I could see a grin forming in his eyes. "It's always good to make people think a little extra, huh?" I liked this sentiment—and I was encouraged that I had met a relatively free spirit in such a conservative atmosphere.

Many top courses are so carefully monitored, manicured, and fertilized that the land essentially becomes an entirely new environment. Bandon, in contrast, looked, smelled, and felt natural.

The terrain wasn't shockingly green or overly landscaped, and the fairways wound naturally through expanses of dune grasses, fescues, and pockets of darker scrub. The greens were carpet smooth but not notably short or fast, maintained like the rest of the course to some standard of effortless perfection. There was no palace-style clubhouse or green-side real estate, and for somewhere so well-known in the golf world, I would have expected more distractions, more gratuitous amenities. But hell, they didn't even have golf carts. Maybe that was its own type of pretense, the way-it-was-meant-to-be-played gimmick. But I liked it. Here it was: links golf, where Scotland met Oregon indeed—the simple architecture that connected the sport to the land and the course to the sea. I had heard so much about it that I thought I understood. But I didn't. Not yet.

With Grant's help, I began to. We each made par on the first from the left-center fairway as I began to get a feel for Grant. He moved slowly and spoke quietly, as if talking to himself, which gave his commentary sage gravity. It seemed as though what I was hearing was inner monologue, that he spoke exactly as he thought, and part of me felt as though I was listening to secrets. Maybe that was his strategy: let the kid in, at least for a little bit. If he was trying to pique my curiosity, it worked.

"You ever hit a golf ball off a barge?" he asked on the second tee. I hadn't. "Well, just imagine. Think you could hit some water?"

"Yeah, that sounds pretty doable."

"Should be able to hit these fairways, then." He was matter-of-fact; I would hit all the fairways, and that was that. He was right to an extent—most of the fairways were wide, rolling expanses that didn't mind a little extra left or right in a tee shot. But the bunkers, which cropped up in the sight lines of every fairway, gave me pause. I mentioned it to him.

"Yeah, you're right, these are good bunkers 'cause they sorta look you in the eye," Grant said. He had a way of taking his own cool ideas and making it seem as though I'd thought of them. "I see what you mean about those. It's a little harder to hit driver straight when you're getting stared at."

I had to adjust to the tight lies in the sand-based fairways, which made the club bounce just a little before impact, just enough to avoid good contact. It made playing the ball along the ground useful and, as I soon learned, allowed players to test the limits of their putters. It was hard to tell where the greens started and stopped anyway, with closely cropped fairways and no real fringe, so after I had drop-kicked a couple wedges, I followed Grant's lead and started putting from twenty and thirty yards off the surface. Rolling the ball up and over hills, hoping the bumps evened out and the breaks fed the ball the right way, made it feel more like a game of backyard bocce than any golf I had played before. I guess that was the point.

If the modern golf game is all about the slam dunk—the high, stiff 6-iron to two feet—then links golf was something closer to the bounce pass. In every shot Grant hit, there was an element of assisting his next shot. He didn't go for the green or gun at the flag so much as he threaded through the defense, working his way into position for the next shot. This meant aiming for the correct trough, or playing away from a particular swale, or landing on the downslope of that little hill, to ensure that he would have a chance with his next look.

As Bandon and I began to get to know each other, my guide and I started to as well. Grant was largely inscrutable, but one thing I could tell as he began to talk more: He liked to push buttons. I asked him about Bandon's patrons, about dealing with the elite and the arrogant and the disillusioned. His stories began slowly, as though he was reluctant to tell them, but this must have been an act—he got too much enjoyment out of their resolutions.

"I like the way you said it, because, resort or no, it *is* still a golf course here," he told me. He had a way of turning sentences into hills, climbing slowly, exhaling one word at a time until he reached the top—and then he let the rest of his thought tumble out as if it were on wheels. "So there is a *certain* amount of betting that goes on from time to time. Most of the time, I *won't* take a man up on his first offer. But I don't like it too much when a guy is riding in a little high on his horse." He paused to hit his ball, a punched 7-iron that took two hops before settling on the front of the green. I hoped he would continue, and after a moment, he did.

"One time, this *big-time* banker was in for a lesson. I don't know why he was getting a lesson, though, 'cause this guy seemed to like giving orders a lot more than taking them. I told him it was a bad idea when he challenged me, that we shouldn't play for money, but if a guy's rude enough, I can't help but let him know a thing or two. So I let him pick the course, and he says the practice area course. You know how many times I've played that thing? So there I am, playing some ten-handicapper with a lousy attitude for a thousand bucks a hole." He gave a distant grin and a shake of his head, as though he still couldn't believe it.

On about the eighth hole I started to get the sense that Grant was trying to push *my* buttons, too.

"You know my favorite wager?" he asked as we walked down the fairway. "The pub here has these root beer floats that they bring out in huge mugs, about big enough for your whole dinner. So I'll play a lot of guys for one of those. There was a kid came in here a few weeks ago with his dad, actually—maybe a couple years younger'n you are. Dad keeps telling me how good a competitor his son is, how he rises to the challenge and all this stuff."

He trailed off into silence, and I couldn't tell whether he was continuing the story in his head or whether I was already supposed to know the ending. "Then what?" I prodded.

He held up two fingers. "One from the kid, one from the dad."

"You made the kid buy you one too?"

"You sound like his dad. If he didn't want to buy one then he shouldn't have played the match."

I had no idea if the story was true, but if he was looking to provoke me with a challenge, it worked. Or maybe he just knew that I was trying to understand him, and he was just pressing back a little.

"Okay," I told him on the tenth tee. "One root beer float each, paid for by the loser of the back nine, match play."

Things changed after that. We each tried to act as though they didn't, but men can't seem to help but attach a little piece of self-worth to any wager. We were still friendly, and he kept the stories coming, but when it came to the golf there was just a little extra edge in our banter.

The match itself was dramatic, but the result predictable. Grant went birdie-par to start two up and then turned himself into a spectator, running off a steady string of pars as he watched me try to catch him. I played well, for my part. I picked up one stroke with a sliding birdie putt on the thirteenth, and picked up another when he decided to tee off with his putter on the following par-3 and made a bogey. We were tied going to eighteen, a straightforward par-5 where we each stared at fifteen-foot birdie putts. I missed. He sank it.

Grant seemed like a guy who loved toying with his competition and then crushing it. When it came to gloating, though, he had some work to do. His stories all began eagerly and in great detail, setting up dramatic finishes, perfect climaxes. But then, right at the resolution, they'd lose steam. I'd have to coax him into explaining how he waited three hours before he told the banker he didn't have to pay up, or how he won an SUV off another poor schmuck and kept it—just for a night—before he dropped it back off in the morning. His triumphs ended with the same anticlimax as his stories. He'd forgive a debt or apologize to somebody, but in either case thoughts of his victories left a thin smile on his face, suggesting that this was a man who ran on self-satisfaction.

So as we sat down over a pair of root beer floats, my treat, he wasn't particularly triumphant. Instead all he would talk about was the 7-iron that I hacked from the fescue onto the edge of the green on the seventeenth hole. Then he ordered us dinner on his tab—an amazing gesture, because the root beer floats were damn expensive enough—and invited me to play the next day.

I played worse the next day, and so did Grant. At Bandon Dunes we had each shot about 75 and escaped his rule that if neither of us parred a hole, we would walk back and replay it from the tee. But Bandon Trails, which we played that second day, threw us a few curveballs. Rather than seaside links, the Trails course began in the dunes and wove into the pines, where the trees and granite replaced Scotland with New England. This was an idealized New England, though, where the huge, rolling greens were bathed in the low light of a winter afternoon, and where a scene created by man for man had been overshadowed by nature nonetheless. It was like the place I lived back in Massachusetts: a little wooden house at the edge of Hopkins Forest that certainly didn't threaten the trees for neighborhood domination. And it was the most powerful part of playing golf at Bandon: The golf was deferential to the land, as if the resort were on lease from God, who could pop in whenever he wanted just as a reminder that we were there at his permission.

By that third night, I started to feel as though I belonged at Bandon Dunes. Or at least part of me thought I did. Grant seemed to know an unreasonable number of people for a golf resort with a fluid patronage, and after that challenging second round, we spent the evening at the clubhouse conversing with Bandon's regulars, and its staff members, and its waitresses, all of whom took it as a given that I owed Grant another root beer float.

But at the end of the day, the sense of not belonging returned. I tried to fight it, to turn the sea of strangers in the lodge into faces, into individuals. After Grant bade me farewell, I went down to the Bunker Bar in the basement, hoping to find a card game or some guys shooting pool. But when the door opened I realized that I would much rather be back in my bed. I didn't even get out of the elevator. Instead I returned to my room and I thought about Grant, and I wondered what it was that made *him* fit in.

In some ways he reminded me of my own father, both in his wry humor and in the way he doled out wisdom in riddles, which would at first make me smile and then, minutes or hours or days afterward, would pop back into my head and make me stop and think.

But the comparison wasn't perfect. I couldn't imagine Dad here. Sure, *I* didn't feel comfortable, but I had made it through the gates; I hadn't left even after the first night. Dad would've appreciated the beauty—the cliffs, especially, and the dunes—but then he would've driven off down the road. Because he knew where he wanted to be. I didn't, so I stayed, happily but uneasily.

There was another similarity between Grant and my dad that made me smile. My father would return home from faculty meetings shaking his head, bewildered at the very idea of contract negotiations. "What's a few thousand dollars to these people?" he would wonder. He was skeptical of his coworkers, of his Wall Street–bound seniors, of the entire institution to which he belonged. And yet he was close enough to his students that they'd come over to play Wiffle ball, and he and Evan and I fanatically followed the careers of any athletes who happened to be geology majors. We went to their sporting events together, particularly soccer games, where we could stand by the corner flags and kick around a ball of our own. But Dad never went to football or basketball games, where it was impossible to watch without being part of a large purple-and-gold crowd. It seemed like an important distinction. I never doubted that Williams College was the place in the world that my father belonged, but he stayed comfortable by maintaining a slight—but definite—separation from the institution-at-large.

Grant had kept a little distance, too. He didn't seek the approval of Bandon's patrons, nor did he seem to change himself to please them. He was unimpressed by their wealth and amused by their priorities. Golf meant too much to them, and they spent too much money on getting better, and still they were no good. Here he was, living among them, facilitating their very actions, making a living on them even as he remained a separate force. It was a simple idea: the teacher who isn't himself defined by the institution employing him, whose kindness manifested itself in unusual ways. But it struck me as something to which I wanted to aspire. I wondered if I'd be able to walk the delicate line that my father and Grant seemed to manage with such ease.

There was still a contradiction to these men that I could not parse, but their roles seemed the more valuable for it. I couldn't picture myself as a golf pro, not even the kind like Grant. I didn't want to be him. But that element of his character that allowed him to live and love the game of golf without falling victim to its trappings was appealing and encouraging.

It was an exciting realization: Grant *was* golf—and I liked him tremendously. I thought of drafting Dad an e-mail, talking about what I was learning. He would've liked it, I'm sure. And he would've liked Grant, too. But something stopped me from finishing the message. Maybe I wasn't quite sure yet.

On my third day at Bandon, Grant had lessons to give, but he had set me up with a round at Pacific Dunes, the resort's third course. I got partnered with three other singles, which was a nice way to experience a new course—although it didn't quite come with the same pageantry as my rounds with Grant. I'd gotten used to the feeling of being a special guest, I suppose—but this was a fine consolation prize.

I'd caught the golf bug again at Bandon. As I drove out that afternoon, I couldn't wait to play my next round, to meet my next foursome, to practice every chance I could, to see if my game could get better. As I entered Northern California, I realized that Grant's mind-set and his golf game had *both* inspired me.

The late November weather I was used to back home—the first real snow, the major frosts, scraping the windshield every time we wanted to leave the house—didn't apply here. It was sixty still, often breezy and still rainy, sweatshirt-and-jeans weather. Ski season was starting in Massachusetts. I couldn't tell if I was jealous or not.

I woke up Thanksgiving morning in the redwoods. I hadn't been worried about the holiday, really: I had convinced myself it wouldn't be a big deal. I was spending another day alone. So what? I spent about half my days that way.

The place I'd spent the night, a pullout a minute off of Northern California's coast-hugging Route 101, was a cool spot. I opened Subi's door, put on a light sweatshirt, and headed off to explore the forest for about an hour before I continued my drive south. I stopped midmorning to take pictures at one beach where the fog hadn't quite lifted and the water glistened in the sun. A man in his twenties, perhaps mistaking me for some more credentialed photographer, asked if I could take a picture of him and his girlfriend. "I'll pay you for it," he told me. I took several, directing them to change angles as professionally as I could, all in the interest of catching the light better. Once I was satisfied with the product, he handed me his e-mail address and twenty dollars. I hesitated before taking the money—it would take all of a minute to e-mail this guy—but I took it anyway. His girlfriend was beaming. She must have been happy that he'd paid for a picture of them.

I continued to drive until I reached Arcata, where I drove to a downtown park with the idea of shooting hoops. I checked my phone. It was about this time that all our cousins would be sitting down to their Thanksgiving meal back in Ipswich, Massachusetts, at Uncle Chip and Aunt Mickey's. I took out a basketball and ran around the court for a while, holding several shooting competitions against myself. When I got tired of chasing rebounds, I went to the free-throw line and shot until I made ten in a row. That didn't take very long, so I decided to do it again. A father and his son, who looked about ten, rode up on their bikes and began tossing a Frisbee. The kid kept looking over.

"Dad, I wanna play basketball."

"I think he's playing by himself, Cal."

I intentionally missed a rebound and let it run off the court into the grass in their direction. Cal grabbed it.

"Thanks, buddy," I called to him, smiling. "You want to take a shot?"

His dad cut in. "I think we're just going to throw the Frisbee," he told me assertively. "Thank you, though."

I shrugged. A few minutes later I left. There was a missed call from Mom, so I called back. They'd just finished their meal. She handed me around to everyone, Kevin and Lindsay and Chris and Mark and Lauren and everyone else. They were all excited to say hello. And then I hung up.

I was all by myself on a day that you were supposed to spend with family and friends. I couldn't help but feel a little isolated. I was lucky to have them on the other end of the phone, I guess. I thought of all the Americans—the elderly and childless, the homeless, any lonely souls who didn't have someone to celebrate with on Thanksgiving. A sad thought.

I was hungry now. Everything was closed, so I stopped by the supermarket. I went to the deli and ordered a turkey sandwich with cheese and avocado. I ate it in my car, wishing for the day to be over.

I was back to my habit of stopping by public courses just before they'd close for the night, playing for twilight rates—usually a handful of dollars. I crisscrossed Northern California in this way, eventually reaching the Bay Area. I connected with another of my father's cousins, Kelsey, who put me up in her daughter's old room—my chance to catch up on sleep and blog posts and to explore more cheap golf.

It was late one of these afternoons on the tenth fairway of Tilden Park Golf Course, a public track in the woods above Berkeley. The wind was picking up and the sun was setting when I felt my phone vibrate from my left pocket. It was an unknown number. Usually I let these ring, let whoever was calling leave a voicemail. I decided to pick this one up.

"Hullo?"

"Hi, is this Dylan? Hope I'm not interrupting a round of golf or anything."

I gave a chuckle. "I'm on number ten right now, but that's fine, you're not interrupting."

"Great. It's Chad, from the pro shop at Pebble Beach. But we can talk later if this is inconvenient."

Pebble Beach? Holy hell. And they were calling me? Now he really had my attention. "No, no. Now's good."

As I hung up the phone several minutes later I felt a grin spread across my face. An innocent e-mail inquiry I'd sent the week before had miraculously made its way up the food chain to the CEO, who was from Massachusetts and "liked the sound of a kid like you," Chad had told me. "If you're interested, we'd love to have you out for a round on our bill."

Trying not to sound childishly eager, I assured him that I would be there any day, any time, with any playing partners— and that I'd wash dishes afterward if they needed me to.

This invitation felt different from any other I'd received. Bandon Dunes was big-time, but Pebble Beach was iconic. I'd be walking some of the most famous fairways in the world. The same fairways that Tiger, Jack, and Arnie had walked. The fairways I knew from watching the U.S. Open, from playing video games, and from gazing at golf course pictures over the preceding three months. The nicest public course on earth.

There was a lot I still didn't know about the round, of course. I didn't know that the second shot on eight was damn near golf course perfection. I didn't realize I'd make birdies on number six and number thirteen, or that they'd feel so good when I did. I didn't realize that I'd be paired with Chad and two other assistant pros, Matt and David, and that Matt and I would close out the other two on the sixteenth green, and that I'd be five dollars richer after playing a five-hundred-a-round golf course. I didn't realize that I'd feel so at home standing on the eighteenth tee as the sun hit the water and a mist fell gently out of the air, and I didn't realize that walking the cliffs of Pebble in the fading light was like falling headfirst into a postcard.

Even before I realized those things, though, I already knew something: I realized the second I hung up the phone with Chad the same thing I had begun to suspect as I drove out of Bandon Dunes that final day. These special golf courses, their fame and their beauty and the way people pursued them, well, *that* was part of what made golf so special, too. For the moment, I suppressed whatever qualms I had with a golf course charging five hundred dollars for a round and calling it "public."

After all, I'd *loved* my time at Bandon. The course had impressed my senses and inspired my imagination, and playing with Grant had helped me explore the role of golf in my life. I expected Pebble would awe me just as much. This was the top of the game, and it was some people's ultimate round of golf—it had to be part of the trip, too.

I hadn't set out seeking privilege or special attention—or if I had, I hadn't realized it. I'd set out to learn and explore and experience. But then, I'd learned from Bandon. I'd learn from Pebble, too. Was that okay, even if I needed to be a special guest to get there? What was wrong with a little privilege?

CHAPTER 8

In the Hole

I've always liked putting. It breaks the game down to its most essential elements: a club, a ball, and a hole. If you hit the ball at the right speed and you aim it in the right direction, it goes in. If you misjudge one of these two factors: failure. It's a binary system that was simpler than even the simplest issues in my life. Whenever I had something to think about in high school, whether it was college or baseball or girls, I liked to go to the practice green at night. I would bring a flashlight, set it up behind a hole, and putt at it for hours, learning the break by feel rather than sight. It didn't solve the problems, really—but hearing that ball hit the bottom of the cup always gave me some comfort, an assurance that everything would be all right. The thing about putting is that you always know where you're going—all that's left is how you get there.

I was in Palm Springs, putting alone in the pouring rain. The course, Indian Springs Country Club, was closed, as were all the courses in Palm Springs as well as many of the surrounding roads, thanks to the area's highest rainfall in years, or decades, or ever, depending on who I talked to. But the historical implications didn't matter much to me—I couldn't play golf and I didn't know anyone, and so here I was, hitting putts in the rain.

It was well into January now. I'd flown home from San Diego to Massachusetts for Christmas, a short reentry into my old life.

It was nice: the easy banter with my brother, Mom's simple joy at having the family under one roof, all the new places I could tell Dad about—even if he already knew about most of them anyway. Being home went smoothly and yet felt horribly jarring—journeys like mine aren't meant to be interrupted. After a few days of yuletide activities, I longed to get back on the road.

Since I'd returned to the West Coast, I'd accomplished very little. From summers on Martha's Vineyard—as a guest of Taylor's family—I knew Liza, a high school senior, who lived twenty-five miles north of San Diego in Rancho Santa Fe. I stayed in an apartment attached to her family's garage for nearly a week, packing up and planning—but mostly killing time. I'd finally left, driving the two hours to Palm Springs only to find it rainy. Bored and wet in a desert resort town? It was a cruel irony.

I had planned to zigzag back across America, northeast to southeast to northeast again. I had devised an efficient strategy whereby I could hit the corners of the bigger states to "collect" my round there. I would go to Nevada and Arizona, New Mexico and Utah, Colorado and Nebraska, Oklahoma and Texas, Missouri and Kentucky. Up and down and up and down. My plans had never been concrete, but this ambitious trajectory had always relied on my having two things: optimism and momentum. I had lost the former looking at the news. Icy roads closed in Colorado, snow all across Utah, even blizzards in Texas. As for momentum? I was losing that with every putt. I had no plans lined up, no golf courses to hit, no people to stay with, and nobody forcing me to decide when, exactly, I would figure any of it out. I sent another Titleist bounding across the green toward the hole, but this one didn't make it through—it splashed to a halt, a solitary ball in a too-big lake. Stuck in the rain in Palm Springs.

Palm Springs is a town of contrasts. Here I was, in the middle of the desert, yet at every turn I found a golf course with fairways greener than any eighteenth-century Scot could've imagined. The land in town was flat as a table, the valley's weather famously mild, and yet huge snowcapped mountains hung ubiquitously in the background. Cookie-cutter developments, identical condos gated off from the rest of town, bordered huge expanses of nothingness, miles of scrub and sand and cactus. Even the population, ostensibly old and conservative, was offset by a sizable younger gay contingent.

I drove around Palm Springs pondering these contrasts, what they said about our world, as the rain kept falling in one of the driest places in the country. Balance is nearly always a good thing. But this didn't quite feel like balance. People in Palm Springs seemed gated off from one another—many of them literally—and everything felt proscribed, sets of opposing forces failing to meet anywhere near the middle. It might've just been the mountains (what is it about distant mountains that offers comfort?), but I got the impression that Palm Springs was a good place to be if you knew what you were looking for. If you didn't? Well, then you could just get stuck.

There was a rest area off I-10 some fifteen minutes east of Palm Springs where I had taken up residence for the week. It was a simple place—bathrooms that were cleaned occasionally, parking spots with just enough lights overhead, and a red-roofed building in the back called the Whitewater Adobe Park, where pets did their business. I had gotten a rhythm down: I'd head to a hotel for breakfast—the Holiday Inn Express was the best and most crowded, so I had no problem blending in—then off to the library, where I read magazines and watched TV, killing time as the pitter-patter of rain continued to fall outdoors.

I saw the flyer for the Morongo at breakfast one morning, a sleek fluorescent thing. The lady featured on the cover appeared to be in a state of ecstasy—as if she'd just won a big hand and heard a hilarious joke at the same time.

Then my eyes drifted to the key caption: THE CASINO IS FOR THOSE 18 YEARS OF AGE AND OLDER.

Once I had absorbed this fact, it was only a matter of time. I had never before gambled in a serious way, yet I was instantly seduced by the same idea everyone is: the chance to strike it rich, to turn nothing into everything, to win big by playing a game. It was, in some ways, a very American idea. After all, wasn't the purpose of this trip to see America? And there wasn't any golfing to be had. But there's a real danger in falling in love with the *possibility* of things, particularly when the odds are carefully stacked against you.

Morongo was a cartoonishly large Indian resort casino just a sand wedge off the interstate in tiny Cabazon, California. In the flatlands along I-10, among towns of low-lying houses and fluorescent highway businesses utterly devoid of character, this three-hundred-foot behemoth stuck out like a desert lighthouse, beckoning drivers to its vast parking lot like a safe harbor for lost sailors.

It was dark enough for headlights on the mid-January Sunday when I first pulled into the Morongo. The parking lot—parking *lots*, I should say—were huge. And they were occupied, too—hundreds of cars, with many more pulling in alongside me. No one ever seemed to be walking *out* the exits, only walking *in*, drawn from all directions like moths to a flame.

I was nervous. I figured a solo teenager would stick out like a jockey at an NBA game. I didn't know *who* would be in there, or if I'd even be able to find my way around. I knew that if I'd asked nearly anyone, they'd tell me this was a bad idea. But I was mostly excited for two simple reasons: I'd be playing games, and I could win money doing it.

Still, I didn't expect to win. Not at first. I knew the percentages too well, had read about how unlikely it was to survive for long. At a golf course in Temecula the week before, a man at the snack shed had offered me a monologue about how the Indian casinos were a surefire way to drive the reservations deeper into poverty, how the stipends paid out to Native Americans didn't cost the casinos a thing because the money went straight back into the system and then some. Casinos were evil. Gambling was stupid. I wasn't an idiot.

Except then I made money the first night at a blackjack table. I bet conservatively at first, risking only the minimum five dollars per hand, trying not to screw up badly—but as time wore on and my chips were all still there, my confidence and comfort level rose. My final haul wasn't a lot—only about fifty bucks—but just by surviving on the table for a few hours I felt like I had come out way on top.

I had fought the monotony of these Palm Springs days by creating a routine. After I went to Morongo that first night, that routine had a new addition.

I fell hard for the casino. I loved that it wasn't driving, or golfing, or writing e-mails from Subi's front seat as I tried to pick up wireless Internet from outside a closed Panera Bread. It was a circus of sensory overload, a fantasyland of flashing lights and whirring, noisy machines and the slightly nauseating atmosphere of cigarette smoke and a Febreze-like cleaning product. Well, maybe I didn't love the smell. But I loved that there were people everywhere, more than I could possibly imagine would exist in a small town in the California desert—the old, pale Palm Springs retiree set and the teenagers from L.A. and the families from the reservation. I wondered where else on earth they could all coexist. Some sat alone at their slot machines while others traveled in packs, looking either eager or somber, depending on how long they'd been there and how many drinks deep they were. It was easy just standing in the midst of the action and watching this factory of human emotion. But eventually I would wind my way to the blackjack table, where I could settle in and let the rest of the carousel whirl around me.

In the middle of this money-changing zoo, blackjack was as complicated a game as I felt prepared to tackle. I had spent a couple hours in the library looking through basic strategy, learning when I should stay, when I should hit, and the stuff I shouldn't do, like touch my cards or check my phone at the table, lest I end up in a back room with some large, angry men in oversize suits.

At the casino table, the game was different than on the computer—the dealer was a blur with the cards and impatient as I mulled my move. (What was I supposed to do with ace-four when the dealer was showing three?) But as soon as I adjusted to the flow of the game, I was swept away in its current. After months of tracking expenses to the cent, how quickly and *easily* the chips seemed to stack up on the felt in front of me was intoxicating. Riding out a hot dealer was an unbelievable high, watching—my heart in my throat—as he would turn over a low card, and another low card, and another low card, and then—thank God!—that face card, sending him to twenty-two, or twenty-five, or a million.

There was an attractive fraternity to winning, too. When one person at the table was winning, it seemed like everyone was. We were all rooting for the same thing, really, and good for him usually meant good for me, too. During winning runs, the people at the other five seats became my best friends. We'd pound the table when one of us drew a first-card ace, rooting for a face card to follow. We'd high-five after a delicate hit worked out, yell compliments at the dealer, tell him he was gonna get laid tonight.

I had pushed golf far from my mind by the time I hit my first real hot streak. It was the second night, at a five-dollar-minimum table. I was sitting next to a guy named T.J. He was shorter than me and noticeably twitchy, with wiry, tattooed forearms that emerged from the rolled-up sleeves of a tight gray hoodie and rested on the table's edge, continuously tensed, suggesting that he was no pushover. I guessed he was forty, but his auburn-red buzzed hair contrasted with a goatee so ragged I wondered if he had lost some sort of wager on the side. T.J. spent the night half sitting, half leaning on the table, watching the cards the way a cat might watch a fishbowl. He knew he couldn't touch them, but that didn't mean he wasn't tempted.

"C'mon, c'mon, c'mon . . . yes!" he muttered under his breath as the dealer put a second jack on top of the one already sitting in front of him. I had nineteen and the dealer hit to seventeen, so my ten dollars turned to twenty and T.J.'s twenty became forty.

"Atta baby Adrian, attababykeepitup!" he told the dealer, a mousy man with spiked blond hair and red cheeks who smiled cautiously back. Adrian kept giving us face cards, and blackjacks, and fed us congratulations as he worked. T.J. was giddy. "Come on, Dyl-*on*," he shouted, torquing the second syllable of my name so that the phrase started to rhyme. Everything was working.

His shift ended, so Adrian yielded to Kim, a middle-aged Korean woman so tiny that I had trouble believing she could reach our cards. T.J. and I had each built up modest towers in front of us by this point—my fifty dollars had turned to three hundred, while his bolder bets had yielded more than twice as much. He had started betting forty, fifty, eighty bucks a hand, his stream of dugout chatter continuing unabated.

"Ooh, Kim, what's up girl? I like that name, ohsurereallydo like it," he babbled as she stood waiting for the decks to emerge from the automatic shuffler. She pretended not to hear and busied herself with the bank of chips before her, columns laid out of red and green and white and black. These stacks were a constant reminder; no matter how hot a streak you felt like you were on, Morongo sure as hell couldn't feel the difference.

"Feelin' good about this one, Kim, yup, think I am, think I am, know I am!" T.J. continued as she dealt out the first hand, giving T.J. nineteen as she showed a five of clubs. I stayed at fifteen and looked on as she flipped a queen, then turned an eight—twenty-three. Bust. "*Oww!*" T.J. yelped, bumping the table. "Oh Kim, me and you gonna have a *long* future together." As she dealt him a blackjack the very next hand, his voice shot into another register. "Ho-lee José! Baby girl baby girl, what should we name the kids?" Kim gave a faint giggle at this, her first sign of emotion. I thought she was joining our side, getting ready to ride out another heat wave with the table.

The next hand, Kim showed a jack, then flipped over an ace—blackjack—to some groans. T.J. stayed relatively composed, still glowing from his blackjack the hand before. "Okay, okay, no hard feelings, you got that one, sure tell ya what, I think this next one could be the big one, come on let's roll!" He pushed a stack of four twenty-five-dollar chips into his circle, the biggest bet I had seen at the low-money table. I added thirty of my own. With a slight nod of her head, Kim coolly dealt me and T.J. each twenty. Then she turned over another blackjack.

My face burned like I'd just been slapped. *That wasn't fair.*

It was the first time I had heard T.J. go silent, even if it was just for a few moments. He finally let out a low moan, the same sound a lawn mower makes when it runs out of gas. "*Ohhh,* Kim baby. I'm not sure it's going to work between us." This time she laughed out loud, a hollow, guttural sound that seemed to vanish the instant it hit the air, sucked into the ceiling with the cigarette smoke. It was a moment that stuck out in my mind later on, that loss, that laugh, the immediate sense that I'd been screwed.

But everything at the casino happens so damn *fast.* Not a second after I was gaping at our disappearing chips, I was back on the offensive, pushing thirty dollars into my betting circle. I had to make that money back.

Over the next half hour, our ascension quickly turned into a plunge. Kim was ruthless and efficient, and before I could stop to understand what was happening, I was in freefall. She was winning five hands for every one of mine. One of my stacks vanished. Then another. Soon I was reaching for the chips I had stashed away, zipped up in my jacket pocket to guarantee that I wouldn't lose money. When you're winning, the faces around you don't change much because they're winning too, trying to ride out that hot streak. But once things turn, stacks start dwindling, people stand up, the chips in front of them few or gone. That was the carousel—the losers rotated out one by one, the hopeful circled in. Win together, lose alone.

Off the floor, any seasoned gambler will tell you that once you realize you're losing, it's time to walk. My mom would've said the same thing, I suppose, although she would've scoffed at the idea of entering in the first place. But T.J. and I stayed. "Luck's gonna change soon," he kept saying. "Luck's gotta change."

I had lost any concept that I was betting a week's worth of meals, or a hundred miles of gas, or a new state's round of golf. I had been stretching my money so tight for so long, and now I was pissing it away like a jackass. But I hardly even felt like I was the one doing it. I was watching my own future get battered around at the whim of the table, like I was a balloon stuck in a ceiling fan. I'd either break free or I'd pop.

As my losses piled up, my bets grew more desperate. I had gone from five or ten to twenty and thirty bucks a hand. "Luck's gotta change," T.J. muttered feverishly, clawing at his goatee with one hand as he reached for his wallet with the other. I was glad he was voicing my own hopes—I had stopped talking entirely. But his luck didn't change, nor did mine, not until I had blown through three hundred dollars.

And it didn't change the next night, when I blew through three hundred more.

I couldn't stop doing the math in my head. At my peak, I'd been up over three fifty. Now I was down—some six hundred down. In my trip budget, six hundred dollars was supposed to last me close to two months. I burned through it in *twenty-four hours*.

My truck-stop parking lot seemed especially quiet those two nights. I could hear engines through my cracked windows, people stopping to go to the bathroom or walk their dog or pick up a vending-machine coffee. But their footfalls sounded softer, their voices subdued, as though they understood that I was in mourning and it was their duty to respect the grieving process. What a change from the frenzy of the casino floor.

I had always hated losing. I hated when I lost in Ping-Pong, or poker, or the stuffed-animal baseball game Evan and I played in the basement. This was worse, because in gambling, the losing was real—I wasn't just playing for pride—and it was dumb that I was playing to begin with. I understood all of this, and I hated myself for it. But I couldn't deny it—I loved it. Blackjack was thrilling in a new way, a high-stakes, real-life version of our

Tuesday-night poker games in high school. I didn't like that I liked it so much. I hated myself for going back.

I tried to tell myself that I could make it up, that I'd just have to spend less, that I could work it off somehow, that six hundred dollars was nothing. But on the second quiet night, it felt like a personal failure, like I had come up short, that I had sacrificed everything I wanted in the long term for what I had wanted at that second. The six hundred dollars felt like everything.

I wandered back to the red-roofed house, half hoping to step in a big pile of dog crap as I gazed into the edge of the Whitewater Adobe Park. It was cold and just beginning to drizzle. I stood in the rain and hoped it could wash away my failures, that I could ditch the hollow feeling that made me look in the rest-stop mirror and wonder what to think about the guy looking back. I listened to the rain fall all night, knowing that I wouldn't get comfortable in my sleeping bag when I wasn't comfortable with myself.

And yet I didn't leave town.

"Can I ask you something?" I said to T.J. the next night in between hands. We hadn't planned to meet up again. Morongo's gravity had done that on its own.

"What's on your mind?"

"How'd you get here?"

"What do you mean? I drove, same as you, man."

"Nah, I mean—*here*. This place."

He didn't answer. I thought he might just brush off the question; we were doing well tonight, after all. Why dampen the mood? But right now T.J. was the closest thing to a friend that I had. I needed to know what had made him this way. We played a couple more hands in silence.

"I always wanted to be a trucker," he began, speaking in a slower voice than the one I'd grown used to. "The travel. I'd get to travel around to all different places. See the mountains and the oceans—and the girls, man. I thought I'd have a different girl in every city, y'know, some kinda James Bond shit.

"Turns out, trucking's not like that. I was on the move all the time, yeah, but moving ain't travel, not like I wanted. Most of the time I was just bouncing from stop to stop, figuring out how much I had to sleep so's I wouldn't crash the next morning. As for the girls, man, they weren't hardly that at all." He lowered his voice here, looking around, self-conscious for the first time. "We called 'em lot lizards. They'd come up to your cab, middle of the night, tapping on your window telling you about how everyone needs company, how you don't wanna be alone.

"I thought I knew what it was like to be lonely, but you got no idea, not till you're paying one of these . . . and you're in your truck . . . and . . .

"But I started seeing a girl couple towns over from here. Friend of my cousin, and she was a pretty girl—nice, too. Better'n I deserved, man. So I started coming to Palm Springs every few weeks, couple days at a time. See the girl, play some poker, a little blackjack. Eventually I got a place of my own. And Morongo loved me, man, I'm telling ya—I had the hot hand. I would win hold 'em tournaments and bring my winnings to the blackjack tables out here and bet big, double or triple up. I kept it up a few times a week for four, five months."

I whistled. "How much did you make?

"Twenty, twenty-five grand. Man, I owned this place. Girlfriend wasn't the biggest fan of the gambling, but she didn't complain about the results, y'know? No girl I've met who's gonna turn down a fancy night out every Friday." He shook his head, jarring loose a memory. "I had fun with that girl." He trailed off, his eyes glazing over to a different time.

His use of the past tense bothered me. The dealer, who had been listening as she waited for a set of fresh cards, looked unsympathetic. That was the overwhelming feeling I got from the dealers: detachment. Never have I heard "Sorry" uttered with such a lack of sympathy as from dealer to disgraced gambler. "Better luck next time."

We got used to their detachment a lot more that night.

• • •

Hours later, I stormed out of Morongo's doors in an empty fury, my head ready to explode. I wanted to break something, hurt myself, do *something* with all this rage. The rain had started to fall again. *Holy shit holy shit holy shit.* What had I just done? I'd made it to the parking lot when I couldn't hold it in any longer.

"*Aghhhhhhhh!*" I roared at the sky so violently it hurt my throat. I knew people must be looking at me. I wanted them to be.

I sped out of the parking lot and down the road, splashing through the small rotary and onto I-10. The Morongo rose in my rearview like a giant, taunting middle finger—knowing that it could be as rude as it wanted, and suckers like me would keep coming back. I sped up to sixty, and then to eighty-five, and then to damn near a hundred, and still the casino stayed there in my rearview. I punched the steering wheel hard enough that the horn cried out in pain. I screamed with it.

The "empty" light had come lit on my dashboard. For a moment I considered just driving until it ran out. The idea was appealing—it was destructive and reckless. But I nixed the idea when I thought of Subi, my only constant companion, breaking down, all alone. *How could you?* A BP station appeared a few miles down the road, and I pulled in.

Gas stations have an especially desolate feel on rainy nights, especially when you're traveling far from home. Most people could put off filling their tanks to the next morning, or fuel up beneath an umbrella before they hurried home to the comfort of a hot shower and a wraparound couch. Not me.

My rage had dissipated, replaced by something worse, a fear that I had messed up everything. What was I going to do?

I slid my debit card in and out of the machine. AUTHORIZING SALE . . . read the screen. Then another message popped up. SEE CASHIER. Hmm. That was weird. I swiped again. Same message. *Perfect.* I went to see the cashier.

"I don't know, it just says you need to call your credit card company," she told me. "It seems like something's wrong."

I barely heard what the woman from Visa was saying. Her words washed over me like a bad dream: "Account frozen . . . negative eleven hundred dollars . . . need to call your bank."

I closed my phone and walked out into the rain. I wasn't completely broke; I knew that. My savings account *must* have almost two grand in it. But something was still wrong. I began to review the events of the previous six hours, and then of the previous days. Even if I had let my checking account run to zero without realizing, had it really been eleven hundred dollars? *Three hundred fifty that first night, then three hundred, then another four fifty*— yeah, actually, that sounded about right. It was pouring by now, but I couldn't move, thinking back to that last hand, that backbreaker.

It's basic psychology that we risk more when we're losing than we do when we're winning. And after winning for a while that final night, I'd begun losing for a while longer, enough so that I was down big—I had no real sense of how much, just that I'd reached into my pockets several times, which was a bad sign. So when I lost an improbable double down for a crack of forty dollars, I'd pushed two twenty-five-dollar chips into the betting ring—the biggest wager of my life.

My first card came—a six. The worst card in the deck. If you paired it with any ten, you'd be stuck at sixteen. I was sure that's where I'd be . . . But no! She had flipped another six in front of me, and for her, a five of clubs. I'd gone from terrified to thrilled in just a matter of seconds. It was instinct now—always split sixes against a five. I fumbled at my dwindling chip stack and slid out another fifty dollars.

She flipped another card beside the first one—another six. I pushed in my final fifty to split once again. Her next card was a four. Double down. Another fifty bucks. She flipped a king. *Twenty.* I sighed in relief. That was a sure thing against a five. She moved to my second six and deposited a five. I grabbed my wallet from my back pocket and slid out three of the four remaining twenty-dollar bills. Was this real? This was the dream scenario.

She put an eight on my eleven to get to nineteen, another made hand. She put a ten on my final six, and I stayed—her five was a bust card, I knew.

I looked down at my cards. A twenty, a nineteen, and a sixteen. Five stacks of fifty dollars lay neatly beside them, beyond my reach, yet almost certain to double up, to make it all back. The dealer flipped over her second card: a queen! I would have shouted in excitement if I hadn't been so nervous. Then came an ace. "Sixteen!" the woman next to me shouted, nudging me in anticipation. "Even better!"

Then the dealer flipped the final card, and it took me more than a moment to realize what the five diamonds meant.

Even once I understood, I couldn't move. She turned counterclockwise around the table, collecting the bets of each person in the hand, and I could feel everyone's eyes on me as I slid off my chair and began to back away, eyes glued to that last five. T.J. said something, reached out to pat me on the arm. But I didn't hear him, and I didn't feel his touch—the world was spinning around me, the lights swallowing me up. "Thanks for playing, better luck next time," the dealer said reflexively. Thanks for coming to the circus. Come again sometime.

Someone else was waiting to take my seat.

Now, standing by the gas pump, I had exactly twenty dollars to my name. No fuel, no food, and no bank account, at least not until the bank opened and I could figure out how to salvage any of this. I started to walk back into the station to fill up; I needed to be able to drive *somewhere*.

But I never made it inside. Ten minutes later, through some sort of gravity that I hope to never understand or experience again, I was back in Morongo, standing behind a ten-dollar blackjack table. I didn't sit, though. I watched, absentmindedly trying to keep the count of high versus low cards, which I'd practiced for a while at the library two days prior.

Was it my intention to play? I can't honestly say. But a portly woman with frizzy gray hair and a rest-station-gift-shop crew-neck noticed my arrival. And after losing two hands in a row, she pointed to me, patting the seat next to her emphatically.

"Come on in here! We're getting creamed. But it's about to turn around, I just know it."

I wanted to believe her, this woman in the bizarre purple pullover. I needed to believe her. Gambling is dangerous, I had started to realize, because people aren't betting dollars or drinks or cars. Not really, anyways. They're betting themselves, little pieces of themselves. I wasn't scared or sad or angry because Morongo had stolen my thousand dollars. I was scared because with every bet I lost, Morongo was stealing a little bit of me—leaving a weaker kid, a kid who didn't know his limits, a kid I wasn't happy to be. My trip was on the line, and the way I saw myself was there, too. These were big, big bets—and it's dangerous to make bets you can't afford to lose.

I couldn't afford to lose this twenty dollars. What was my Plan B now? Wash dishes in the casino kitchen? Pawn off Subi and continue on foot?

But I didn't lose it.

Over the next hour I hardly lost at all. I was betting wildly, risking half or more of my stack over and over. My odds of losing were the same whether I bet it all on one hand or a hundred, I figured. It was a dumb philosophy for playing anything, especially blackjack, but dumb luck was multiplying my twenty dollars quickly.

I had four hundred dollars stacked in front of me when the dealer changed. But Julia made a seamless transition to Marcus, who had a knack for flipping four or even five cards in front of him before finally turning a bust card.

But the real secret to my success was Cynthia, the woman who had waved me over in the first place. The most contentious part of casino blackjack is that the actions of the players—who hits and who stays—determine everyone else's cards. It doesn't matter, technically—it's still all random—but the regulars get pissed off when someone makes an unconventional play and messes up the predetermined order of the cards.

Cynthia was the opposite, though. She would hit on eighteen or stay on eight when she "had a feeling." For Cynthia, this didn't pan out particularly well. But for the rest of the table, it was infallible. If I needed a five, she would stay on eleven and, without fail, I would get the five, or the dealer would get the extra card and bust. The entire game felt as if it hinged on her hapless play, but as she managed to lose over and over, she course-corrected my cards to victory, like a weird fairy godmother of gambling.

The communal nature of the winning that I had felt earlier had disintegrated, I realized. I wasn't winning with Cynthia, I was winning *because* of her. Win together, lose alone? Bullshit. Nobody won together—nobody else cared how you did as long as they got theirs. I could feel it in myself, how Cynthia's losses meant nothing to me. I didn't like it. But I was still winning.

I had just won a hundred dollars on a nifty double-down when T.J. sauntered over, hands in his pockets. "Oh damn, check out this dolla man, the Dy-lon man," he called out. "I gotta get some of this magic. Luck's gotta change for this guy, right?"

I smiled as he sat down to my right. I had made up almost my entire debt. I was afraid to count up the stacks in front of me lest I jinx something, but I knew that I was circling in on a thousand dollars. Get to eleven hundred, I told myself, and I would walk, no permanent damage.

I tossed in fifty dollars, which I lost. So I threw in a hundred. I lost that, too. "C'mon Marcus, here we go baby," I chattered at the dealer, rocking forward on my chair and planting my elbows on the table as I tossed another hundred into the betting circle. "I'm-a give you another chance here buddy, c'mon Marcus, we're hitting it big tonight, gonna getcha a nice steak dinner when we're all done."

I looked over at T.J. and realized that I was mimicking his rocking motion, back and forth and back and forth, from my chair to my cards, waiting for the next deal to come. It was unsettling, seeing my action mirrored across the table. I hardly even flinched as Marcus dealt himself a twenty, which crushed my seventeen. I had already started to gather together my chips into more manageable stacks.

"I'll be right back," I told T.J. "I don't like how these chips are burning a hole in my pocket."

"All right, go get that cash and bring it back here!" he shouted back at me. "This is our night, man. Me and you!"

I walked to the cashier's desk, which was, by design, tucked into the drabbest corner of the casino—checking out was supposed to be hard—and dug the stack of chips from my pocket. Five black hundred-dollar chips, three green fifties, a blue twenty-five, and three red fives rounded out the stash. Six hundred ninety dollars from my last twenty. I was exhilarated and relieved, but I realized as I started to put the chips down that, more than anything, I was scared. I was scared that I could let myself get so low, scared of where a couple bad hands would have left me.

"Cash, please," I said to the attendant, a bored woman my mom's age, who looked up from her magazine. I tried to muster a smile.

"Looks like a good evening," she deadpanned. I reached out for the bouquet of hundred-dollar-bills she was offering and then stopped, put my arm down, tried again. My hand was trembling violently. She must have noticed, too, because she held the money an extra moment and looked up at my face. "Hey, good for you," she said, her voice softening. "A lot of young guys can't cash out like this."

I walked out the casino's front door without pausing to say farewell. T.J. would understand, I thought. Sometimes you've got to change your luck yourself.

That would be a tidy conclusion to my gambling story, but temptation doesn't slink away so easily. I didn't stay the night in Palm Springs—I wanted to outrun temptation altogether. The problem was that Nevada was the next state on my list, just three and a half hours away. Going to Las Vegas to kick an emerging gambling addiction was sort of like heading to Amsterdam in an effort to stop smoking weed.

"Get back to golf," part of my mind was telling me. But another part was ecstatic to see the Strip, the casinos, the nighttime debauchery. I had escaped the allure of Morongo and made it exactly as far as the fourth floor at the Luxor, whose rooms had bottomed out at forty dollars a night in a tanking national economy. They were just trying to fill the hotel, I guessed, and get their guests onto the casino floor. *Vegas is for suckers,* I thought. Suckers like me.

I felt relief and frustration in equal parts: Nevada's gambling age was twenty-one, so I could look but not touch—a theme throughout the city. The casino sprawled out like an airport—but with tables and slot machines instead of gates, cocktail waitresses instead of TSA agents, people checking nudie showtimes rather than flight departures. I'd spent most of the first day and a half in the hotel vomiting—my self-diagnosis was food poisoning. Finally back on my feet, I explored the city in a three A.M. trance, a strange scene, but then when is Vegas normal?

Gambling, like most other basic sins, wasn't far from the front of my mind when I arrived at the Painted Desert Golf Club. I hadn't played in nearly two weeks, but this seemed like a nice reintroduction to the game—a public course advertised as a bargain for Nevada residents (which I figured I was, for a few days) and junior golfers (I'd been seventeen recently enough).

I liked the name of the course. After all, what was Vegas but a huge painted desert? In gaudy colors, no less. Nothing was subtle about the place, and yet everything—and everyone—seemed to be wearing a disguise. If golf had been unnatural in the arid Coachella Valley, *everything* was unnatural in Vegas.

I was hitting some abandoned range balls as I waited for a spot to open on the first tee, but I was devoting most of my attention to checking out the characters in front of me. Like everywhere in Vegas, it was good people watching. One overweight balding guy—corporate golf trip, I guessed—was practicing with near-comical intensity. He wore a Carolina-blue golf shirt, his bulky stomach testing the shirt's stretchy fabric. Corporate-golf-trip guys tend to have the made-by-Budweiser body types that demand some extra stretchiness.

And there, two spots down from me, was Vegas Johnny.

Thickly bearded and clad in a yellow-and-black-checkered dress shirt, untucked from a pair of baggy khakis that featured a large dark stain down the left leg, his look was something like the Dude from *The Big Lebowski* or, perhaps, some sort of homeless Johnny Depp. He hit a low snap-hook, then a push-slice. Then a snap-hook again. Then a dead shank, straight off the hosel and 45 degrees right. This was impressively bad. I imagined he was some some kind of poker pro with cash to blow and a new competitive addiction to attend to—golf.

Mr. Corporate had finished his large bucket—though not before sweating through his entire shirt, gasping for breath, and grunting through his final swings as though he was playing the Wimbledon women's final. He was toweling off his irons, along with his head and neck, when Vegas Johnny approached him. I couldn't hear the exchange, but I watched as yellow shirt nodded in the direction of the first tee only for blue shirt to shake his head, *No thanks*. Yellow shirt moved back to snapping and shanking, and blue shirt waddled off in the direction of the parking lot.

My interest piqued, I sized up Vegas Johnny's swing. He took the club away just fine, tucked it behind his head just fine, but whoever had taught him the golf swing must have stopped halfway, because something different happened at the top of each swing, where he looked like he tried to scratch his neck with the club before beginning his descent to the golf ball.

He must have felt me watching, because he shot a glance over his left shoulder.

"I'm going out next," I said. "You looking for a game?"

He hit another grounder before responding. "Sounds good, brother." He had a soft, gravelly voice, which added a certain depth to the homeless look he had going on. Vegas Johnny smiled, showing a flash of tooth through his beard. "But I always like to play for a little something."

"Yeah, same. What kind of stakes you want?"

"Oh, let's say—fifty a hole, hundred a side, two hundred for the eighteen."

Holy shit. I tried to do the math in my head but only settled on there being a lot of money on the line. This was awesome. With my head whirring to estimate just how badly I could fleece him, I barely heard his last sentence: "I'd have to see some cash on hand, though," he said.

Normally this would've been a deal breaker, but in this case it was perfect timing. My winnings from Morongo were stashed in Subi's glove compartment, and I'd kept three hundred and fifty in my wallet. I took the wallet out of my back pocket and flashed a couple hundreds in his direction. He nodded.

On the first tee, Vegas Johnny lit a cigarette, took a long drag, and pumped driver into the trees well right of the fairway, where it hit a branch and fell straight down. Another puff.

I was practically giddy by this point. Vegas! Dollar signs in my eyes, I crushed driver down the left-center. From there I'd just have flip wedge into the short par-4. In my head, I checked off the hole. 1–0. Up fifty bucks.

It didn't work out that way. I hit my second to about fifteen feet, but Vegas Johnny punched from under the tree to a hundred yards, then hit a funky little wedge shot that bounced well short and rolled up to about ten feet. I two-putted for par before watching his ball race toward the cup, finding the back of the center of the hole. Par.

I managed to pick up the next hole when his punch-out from the right trees got caught in the vegetation and he made 6. And I birdied the par-5 third, with Vegas mustering another 6. Two up.

Then the fourth tee.

It could have been a different golfer. His posture changed suddenly, giving the impression that he'd grown several inches. The 6-iron that had seemed like such a burden now looked light in his hands. He stepped up to the ball and gave a confident waggle of the club behind the ball. And then, with a crisp, efficient swing that *really* grabbed my attention, he stuck it to eight feet.

I should've just walked off the course there. Even the shittiest golfers hit some stuff now and then, but this sequence of events—the perfect balance, the quick weight shift, the controlled shot shape, the backspin, even the held finish—wasn't the sort of thing that a hack just happened upon once in a while. I felt something rise in my chest. In Vegas, on the driving range, the most obvious of places, I had run into a hustle.

He won four of the next six and finished the front nine two up. I scraped out halves on six and seven, but I never had a chance on the others. I was playing scared and lost control of my swing, while he kept hitting putts that looked like they were going too hard until they vanished right into the hole. He wasn't wasting any time burying me.

Every round of golf has a unique mood. It's always interesting how the conversation and the competition combine. Often it leads to a game that's taken seriously but not gravely so. I always want to win, but in a normal day's round I would want my opponent to play well too, to stay happy so that we would have fun playing. Golf is a game, after all.

With Vegas Johnny, any pretense of conversation disappeared when his tee shot hit the fourth green. He was a snake and had stopped trying to hide it. The group in front of us was playing painfully slowly, so we had slowed too. It helped that Johnny walked like he was on a huge grassy tightrope, one foot right in front of the other, all while he rolled a cigarette from one side of his mouth to the other using his lips. It was a mesmerizing combination, the walking and the rolling, that I watched from a distance. I hated him, but with the weird admiration you have for anyone who's good at something in a particularly weird way.

And it wasn't just his golf that made Johnny strange. He took several phone calls as we waited, calls that he would stand fifty yards away to make and whisper anyway. If he was intimidating without the phone, well, it certainly wasn't easier staring him down once I started wondering if he was ordering hits from the eighth green.

I tried not to think about it, but I didn't need to do much math to reason that losing the back nine would put me more than five hundred bucks in the red. I bogeyed ten and eleven, and he gained another stroke. I was three down, seven to play. When he went to pee in the bushes by the green, I briefly weighed my chances of making a run for it. He'd been smoking like a chimney, after all. I didn't think Johnny would be much of a threat for more than a hundred yards. But this was Vegas, where running from your debts never worked in the movies and probably wouldn't work now.

The golf swing, like anything that requires trust, is much easier to lose than it is to find. You can't regain trust in a cheating lover overnight, and even if you eventually do, the relationship is never really the same. Or so I had heard from friends who lived through it. After my swing's front-nine infidelities, I had lost my faith as I came to the twelfth hole. But for better or worse, you can't break up with your golf game. You go to counseling, you put in a lot of quality time together, and you hope that something clicks and stays.

I tried to make an adjustment as I teed off. I extended my arms in my takeaway, keeping the clubhead farther from my body. And I tried to swing easily. Something clicked. It wasn't that I actually swung slowly—I didn't know how—but the ball jumped down the center, a slight left-to-right trajectory that turned a long par-4 into a short approach. I hit pitching wedge to ten feet and rolled in the putt. Easy. Two down. Then I birdied the par-5 thirteenth, and Johnny seemed to be losing steam a little. His swing, which had been airtight for most of the front nine, had grown shaky and his shoulders were starting to slump a little. Was the cool customer behind the rock-star shades getting nervous?

On the fourteenth tee, Johnny coughed loudly in my backswing. He started standing in the way as I began to address the ball so I'd have to step away and ask him to move. Then his ball, which looked like it had embedded deep in the lip of the bunker, all of a sudden wasn't plugged when I looked back to watch him hit. Meanwhile, he had stopped talking altogether.

I noticed a man dressed in dark clothing standing behind the green as we approached fifteen. He didn't acknowledge either of us as we walked up, nor as we putted out, but when Johnny walked off the green he immediately went to converse. His friend wore a dark-brown leather jacket and dark jeans, and even through the layers I could tell he had logs for arms. He looked like someone who would come in when his friend was starting to lose a bet and cut off the other guy's fingers. I looked at my hands. I liked my fingers—especially the way that there were ten of them.

The Finger Chopper smiled and gave a little wave to me as we walked to the next tee. Fortunately, he stayed behind.

Johnny had to scramble to roll in a par putt on fourteen, and we both bogeyed fifteen. He missed a short one for birdie on sixteen and nearly lost his tee shot on seventeen before making a bad bogey. All square.

Standing on eighteen I was thinking, for the first time since about the third hole, that I could win some money. A lot of money.

But I could still lose it, too. Eighteen was a short, straight par-4, and I hit a snap-hook 3-wood that dove left and settled in the sand behind a bush. He went down the middle. I was shaky-nervous walking down the fairway, thinking about my chances. Win the hole, win the back nine, the eighteenth hole, and the full match—up $250. Lose the hole, go down $250, and have to think about it by myself all night, all month, all trip. I hated losing.

I had landed in a desert-style bunker on the left, one of the course's favorite defenses. To get at the flag, I would have to hook an 8-iron some twenty-five yards around the two small palm trees in front of me. It was lucky, in a sense, that I had a hard shot. From the middle of the fairway I could've gotten really nervous, but here there was too much detail to focus on.

I pured it. I let my arms go loose at the top so the club would be able to turn over a little faster as it came through. I could feel just how cleanly the ball shot out of its lie and watched it hook in from the right, hitting just outside the green-side bunker as it landed and skittered to a stop on the front of the green, some fifteen feet below the hole. Perfect leave.

But I was playing Vegas Johnny, not some high school sophomore who would wilt at the first sign of an opponent's success. He had just sand wedged left and made another low, tight iron swing that landed at my ball and jumped forward. Eight feet for birdie.

My putt was easy. Uphill, the slightest right-to-left break. I knew I had to start just outside the hole and let it feed in. Right-to-lefters are easier for right-handed players because the ball breaks back toward your body as it approaches the hole. Left-to-righters, meanwhile, always feel like they're running away from you, like they're trying to escape. But this one fit my eye perfectly. *Remember, this is simple.* I could feel my heart beating. *Putting is simple. Right speed, right direction, it'll go in.* I stepped just behind the ball and took a couple practice swings, trying to keep my stroke smooth and aggressive—I had to make this one. My hands were shaking a little. My knees, too. *Just a club, a ball, and a hole.* But even with the nerves I could just *see* the putt so well that I knew it was going in right as I hit it.

Except then it didn't. It climbed the hill and turned toward the hole and then *just kept turning* a fraction more than I thought, so when it hit the left edge of the cup it spun out, finishing some eight inches past the hole.

"Nice try," Johnny said. It was the first time he had spoken in about four holes. I tapped in and went to stand by my bag, dreading his putt. He had the same line I had, except now he had seen mine, and he'd made everything he'd looked at all day.

He hit it with aggressive speed, like he'd hit all his putts, but

I knew right off the club that he had made the same mistake as I had, under-reading the break. His ball turned left and kept rolling out a little past the hole, some two and a half feet past.

He swore as the ball passed the hole, slapping the grip of his putter against the side of his shoe. Then he walked up to the ball, stood over it for just a moment, and hit it too hard at the left lip. It rimmed out and came shooting off to the right, where he immediately hit it back to himself with his putter, feigning nonchalance as he bent over to pick it up.

"Good match," he said, reaching out his hand.

"You too. Tough one there."

"What, you mean that thing? I figured that one was good."

To be fair, I had been giving him putts of a similar length all day. But I could see what he was doing and I was too pissed to let it happen. "You thought a three-footer for two hundred fifty bucks was a gimme?" I asked, my voice incredulous. "Look, man, I'm sorry, but I didn't say a word. You took your time over that putt anyway."

"You're freakin' kidding me, kid."

God, this was awkward. Until now Johnny had seemed mostly weird—kind of an asshole, like any hustler, but he had been quiet. Now he was angry. I glanced around, wanting someone else to be around. A few guys were on their way to the parking lot.

"Two hundred fifty." I was nervous now, but tried to be firm.

He grabbed his wallet, pulled out a bill, and pressed it against my chest. "Take it," he seethed. "And don't ask me for a goddamn thing more."

I had no intention to. I was still shaking from watching his first putt. My whole body was still bracing for disappointment. I hadn't been sure if I was going to survive the round with all my fingers, and now I was holding a hundred-dollar bill? Yeah, I was going to take it.

"Thanks!" I said, too enthusiastically. He was already walking away. I breathed out.

• • •

Enough, I told myself as I reached the car. Enough with the gambling. Enough with Morongo and Vegas, with T.J. and Johnny, with losing a lot and almost losing a lot more. I was satisfied, looking at the hundred dollars curled into the cup holder, but I knew: *Enough.*

I needed some other people around. I didn't want to share my gambling saga with anyone—I'd get chastised, told I was being stupid. I already knew that. But I needed someone, something, to guide me in the right direction. It wasn't healthy, gambling alone.

I drove mindlessly out of the city as it grew dark, cruising along Route 15, focused more on my rearview than on what lay in the road ahead. Momentum and optimism. That's what I needed. Arizona was fast approaching. Something occurred to me, so I reached for my GPS.

Only four hours to the Grand Canyon. It'd be nice, for a change, to see a big hole that someone *else* had dug. Onward.

CHAPTER 9

Ford

The rain lifted in the days following my departure from Vegas. Still, I couldn't shake the sense of isolation. Over the course of a month, from San Diego through Nevada, and then Utah and Arizona and New Mexico, I hadn't slept in a real bed. (The Luxor didn't count because I was throwing up the entire time.) The closest I got was a couch at Arizona State, courtesy of one of Dad's former students, now in grad school there.

As I began the drive east, I felt lost. Somehow, in the mountains and deserts and casino floors of the West, the meaning of the trip had gotten blurry. Even the Grand Canyon had been a momentary distraction. I took some pictures and continued on.

I wasn't bored. I never got bored—at least not in the way most of my friends talked about it. I was the kid who could sit and listen to ESPN Radio for eight hours in a row or decide to stop at a park and shoot free throws until I made twenty in a row. No part of the trip would've worked if I was the type to get bored easily. Still, I wanted the purity of golf, of human connection, of conversation to be the driving force behind my travels. And I knew that if I was going to move on, I needed something to reignite my interest. But I was having a hard time finding either competition or connection with other people. Without real connections with other humans, it was hard to keep *moving*. I had states to hit—but I didn't have grades, or sales targets, or performance reviews. But then, it was never about *collecting* states. Travel by collection is not really travel at all—humanity cannot be accumulated like rain in a bucket.

So as I entered New Mexico, I was looking for some sort of authenticity. The state had history, and not the variety I was used to in Massachusetts. I saw it in architecture and road signs and libraries—this was the home of gold rushes and shoot-outs and UFOs. I wanted to dive into the weird culture, an enticing combination of Western, Hispanic, and Native American, and discover something new—and return to the essence of my trip.

But nobody seemed to want to tell me about New Mexico—not the waitress who served me a Silver City burrito that burned through my insides, and not the librarian who answered my questions with "I think it's time for my lunch break," and not the barber somewhere off I-25 who hacked through my hair as if it had personally offended her.

I struggled to fill my days. Tourist attractions were sparse, the weather was uninspiring, and, with snow still blanketing the Midwest, I had no imminent dates to hit, no obligations to be anywhere at any time.

I should note that I *had* gained one weekly activity, though. My high school ski coach, Matt, ran a ski website—Fasterskier .com—and passed along the request from a college conference in the Midwest desperate for someone to handle their press.

I'm not sure these coaches knew that I was eighteen years old, or that I lived in my car, or that I wasn't going within a thousand miles of their ski meets. But just a week after applying, I'd become the new sports information director for the Central Collegiate Ski Association. The CCSA held races most weekends during the winter; over the subsequent weeks I'd scan the results pages, perhaps fire off a quick e-mail asking for quotes, and summarize what I'd read in a few paragraphs. I took some pride in the new title, and worked earnestly to produce coherent articles. But I did it for one reason: the money.

It was a good enough reason. I made more than a thousand dollars that winter filing press releases from hotel lobbies. It was hard to connect the rivalry between Northern Michigan University and Michigan Tech to my day-to-day actions, but the former enabled the latter. The CCSA held my budget together. And I'd need every cent I got.

Newfound job or not, golf still gave me a sense of purpose. I still relished that time of day when I would get into my car and type "golf course" into my GPS and drive to the nearest one that showed up. I didn't find big bets or glamour, but there was always a new course with a bit of character, and my own game to keep improving.

I had been seeing, over and over, how golf can step in when the rest of life comes up short—how the game has a way of filling in the divots in people's lives. I hadn't imagined that I would be one of those people.

Truth or Consequences is the only city I've ever heard of that got its name from a radio show. In 1950, a radio host named Ralph Edwards announced that he would air his program from the first city to name itself after his show, and for some bizarre reason the New Mexican township of Hot Springs quickly obliged. It wasn't quite a frontier town shoot-out, but I liked this odd historical nugget, and I was delighted to play a round at the T or C Golf Course with a Navajo man, Jim, even if he dodged my questions and didn't stay for the full round.

I remembered T.J.'s first words to me: "Glad to have a partner, and I don't care what you're like, either, man. Sometimes bad company's better'n no company. Gambling, drinking, sex. Shit, most things."

The next stop was Black Mesa Golf Club, just north of Santa Fe. I was excited from the pictures I'd seen on the Web. Even though it was in full hibernation mode—patches of snow skulked in the shadows, and the grass had turned that wintry brown that grass gets in January in New Mexico—the course exceeded expectations. Holes were tucked between arroyos and sandstone rock formations, some going uphill, others dropping steeply, the whole course set up like it was dug with a shovel on the beach. Black Mesa worked its way between ridgelines and into small valleys, isolating many holes from one another and messing up my sense of direction entirely. It was a labyrinthine setup that made the course feel discovered rather than constructed—the kind of course I like best.

But nothing seemed to quite work out for me in New Mexico. As I reached the sixteenth green, the pro appeared from the hill in front of me, behind the wheel of his red pickup—so that he could bring me back to the clubhouse before it got dark. "It's not the cougars I's worried about," he told me, "so much's it's the packs of feral dogs." It was a kind gesture, certainly, but it didn't make me feel any more secure, feeling that I was being hunted.

I left New Mexico and spent a couple days traveling in West Texas, through cities like Odessa and Lubbock but mostly through the farmland, along rural back roads. There was a particular kind of beauty to the place, where blue highways crisscrossed thousand-acre ranches. I imagined it must have been even bigger, more open, before the people had arrived and erected their trailers and shacks to divide up the land. There were no gun-totin' cowboys around, after all—but it seemed as though there were plenty of towns in need of heroes.

Small, insular communities cropped up every now and again, towns with water towers that bragged of decades-old state football titles. Huge oil derricks cropped up all over, their pump jacks bobbing gently up and down, large mechanical birds leaning over to drink from puddles in the desert.

Where was I going? What was I doing? Everything was up in the air.

"You don't know anyone in Texas, do you?" I asked Taylor one night during one of our regular check-ins.

"Texas? I don't think so." He paused, thinking. "Actually, wait a minute. I met this guy when I was at a soccer game in San

Antonio with my dad, and he was from near there—he was a Williams alum, too. I could e-mail him, I guess?"

So it was by pure chance that I got connected with Darryl— the man whose family would change everything.

Darryl Shaper was the kind of guy who got enthusiastic for no reason. Most people have triggers that evoke strong emotional responses to certain situations or issues. Passions, they're called. I kept hearing about them—and I was supposed to find mine. But Darryl's excitement required no particular cue, or, more likely, he just found excitement in everything that surrounded him, like a static balloon in a barbershop. Maybe it was just that Darryl had a passion for *everything*.

It takes a certain type of guy, after all, to take in a teenager whom he's only heard of over e-mail. I had considered not following up on Taylor's recommendation, but I was eager for human contact, to be in a home—I hadn't seen one in over a month. I sent Darryl a hopeful e-mail, saying that he should feel free to say no and that I wouldn't take offense, but here was my phone number and I could arrive Wednesday and be gone Thursday. Would that be all right?

I then shut my laptop and drove off, searching for a back road that wouldn't have traffic—or any citizen of the Republic with a six-shooter and a strict no-trespassing policy. I was still on the road, out of cell reception, when Darryl called me—within the hour. When I parked, I listened to his message on my voicemail telling me no, sorry, but that wouldn't work.

If I was going to visit, I had to commit to the weekend, too. "You can't see Texas in a day, man!" he said, a subtle twang dotting his exclamations. "P. Terry's! Sixth Street! Gruene Hall! The U of T! And that's all in our backyard! No way you can just stop by and just be on your way." After all, he said, any friend of Taylor's was a friend of his. It was a powerful sentiment, particularly given the fact that he had known Taylor—never mind me—for all of about two hours.

I suppose this all-encompassing enthusiasm was a requisite

for his then job, vice president of sales at the Scooter Store, or at least he made it seem like it should be, the way he tackled his role. As I arrived that Wednesday afternoon, Darryl emerged from the office building, his arms wide and his palms skyward, as I parked Subi and approached on foot. "And so the weary traveler returns!" he announced to the empty parking lot. "What in the heck's going on?" Darryl looked the part of the everyman—the blue dress shirt, the jeans, the dark goatee flecked with specks of gray—but it was his wide, youthful smile that made him stand out. I felt instantly at ease in his presence.

"We're gonna give you a little look at the real world!" he told me as we walked into his office, as though the Real World was an amusement park ride and his cubicle grid could turn into a kingdom where something magical lay within.

It was revealing, meeting someone in the context of the workplace rather than the golf course. Darryl was a super salesman, an inspirer of scooter salesmen, a guy who sold his employees on the idea that they needed to find passion in selling scooters. I wondered if a manager could be *too* enthusiastic—if the whole office could resent the man for being so damn cheery. This place was a calling center, after all. How inspired could anyone be at a job that consisted of making phone calls, especially when your demographic was *specifically* people so old that they couldn't walk? But whatever part of Darryl's desk wasn't filled with inspirational cards and sayings was covered in gifts from his employees—souvenirs and photos from faraway places that suggested people always had Darryl Shaper close to mind.

Darryl lived in a house between the woods and the river in a quiet neighborhood in New Braunfels, halfway between San Antonio and Austin, with his wife, Jeannie, and their kids, Helen and Ford. Helen, thirteen, was a sweet girl. Quiet and studious, she spent most of my time there at school, practice, or huddled over a homework assignment.

Ford, nine, was bright but less focused than his sister—happy to wander. He gave me a tour of the property my first after-noon there, which meant I tracked him like I would a deer as he darted through the trees in their backwoods. He was intent on showing me his world, the ways that he could sneak through his neighbors' properties like enemy territories and the way that sticks could turn into swords, brambles into opposing armies. Kids have a way of giving you an honest, unfiltered look at their lives—not really by choice, more because they haven't learned the ways that people keep secrets. It's refreshing, their openness. People lose it too soon.

Ford led the chase through the woods and I followed as best I could, although his size afforded him an easier path through the bushes than mine. He had gotten several steps ahead when I stepped on a dead branch, snapping it cleanly in two as I pressed through the brambles. Ford whipped his head around. "Shush!" he barked at me. "We can't let them hear us."

"Sorry!" I whispered back. "Who's 'them'?"

He pointed toward a particularly brambly patch of brambles ahead and to our left, half rolling his eyes at my dumb question. "Them!"

Ford had a mop of dirty blond hair and a way of staring off into the distance, at least until something nearer grabbed his attention. He was a nomad in both mind and body. He didn't like soccer practice because it was too restrictive, having all these people telling him just what to do. He didn't seem to love school, either, although I suppose not many third graders will say they like school. He was independent, and even if it was hard to fol-low his train of thought, which bounced around like a tennis ball in an elevator, I liked following him. After all, I used to run around the woods fighting invisible enemies with sticks, too. In some ways, maybe I still was.

Ford had another side to him, too—a side that reminded me distinctly of his father. We were sitting around that first night, talking about chasing down states, when Darryl suddenly thought of something.

"Oh! It's very good you're here, actually. We need an experienced traveler for some help with a pursuit of our own. Tell him, Ford."

"The quest for," Ford said, lowering his voice for dramatic effect, "the Choco Taco!"

Darryl jumped in. "For at least the last, I don't know, the last week or so, we've wiped New Braunfels dry looking for these little guys, but they're pretty elusive. And we're ready to take our search to the big time."

Ford grinned. He was a little self-conscious, but mostly excited. I couldn't blame him. What kid wouldn't want his dad to be so excited about tracking down a glorified ice cream sandwich?

"Can we go hunting for 'em tomorrow, Dad?"

"Definitely. I can barely wait that long."

Darryl called me from work at 7:45 the next morning, which, houseguest or not, I deemed too early to answer. But then he followed it with a text a couple minutes later:

"Gotta get some BREAKFAST BURRITOS! Call as soon as you wake up!!"

I wandered out to the kitchen, where I encountered Jeannie. "Morning, Dylan!" She greeted me enthusiastically. "Oh, Darryl wanted you to call him. Something about a breakfast burrito . . . ?" Jeannie had this great way of taking her husband seriously but not too seriously, a marriage of hugs and eye rolls in equal parts. It was perfect.

I smiled groggily. "I was just about to call him."

Half an hour later I found myself heavily involved with an egg-and-beef burrito as I watched Darryl launch into one of his own, his look of surprise and awe matching mine, as though he was a first-timer too.

"Man, I dunno what they put in these things! A little Texan lovin' and some good beef, I suppose. Gosh, it doesn't get much better than this right here."

Darryl got out of work early that Friday, and we spent the weekend exploring the area, Ford and Darryl and I, watching high school soccer and UT baseball and bouncing from New Braunfels to Austin and beyond—to trail systems where we could hike through lakes and forests. They'd wear me out during these days, from walking and talking and just from laughing, their enthusiasm never flagging. I hadn't done much laughing the previous few weeks, and it was a welcome feeling, laughing naturally, not because someone had told a joke and it was instinct but because my body was telling me that I was happy.

We stayed up late despite our long days, three guys dreaming about what our lives would be like down the road. Darryl told us about his goal to only drink water, which would help the environment, his health, and his wallet all at once. Ford declared his intention to own a river when he grew up—an ambitious, if not entirely reasonable, goal. Darryl called it a "capital idea."

They weren't golfers, but they were dreamers, and they were full of curiosity—so I told them all about why I loved golf and why I didn't and where I wanted to go. I told Ford that what I was doing wasn't so different from what he did, traipsing through the woods, hoping to find things that surprised me.

On my last night there, a Sunday, the whole family ended up on the couch in front of a movie. Eventually Darryl and Jeannie went to bed, and then Helen too, and so it was the two of us, Ford and me—too late for a school night, but we stayed up anyway.

At some point Ford's eyes closed, and then his head rolled over onto my shoulder. I let it rest there for a few minutes. His breathing grew heavier, his little chest swelling, and falling, and swelling out again. The whole scene felt safe, the couch and the movie and the little brother. I felt safe.

I could feel my own eyes closing. "All right, big guy," I murmured, picking him up as gently as I could. "Let's get you to your room." He was heavy, the full weight of slumber on my shoulder as I got up gingerly in the darkness. His eyes came half open as I set him down on his bed.

"Hey, Dylan," he whispered. "I hope that you don't leave tomorrow."

I smiled, but I could feel a lump rising in my throat. "Good night, my man."

Earlier that day, Darryl had mentioned, almost in passing, that I should write out some life advice to Ford. It had struck me as a difficult and quixotic task: How do you impart wisdom, or anything, to a nine-year-old in writing? I had been ready to let it drop, but, as I put Ford to bed, I remembered the odd request. And in the moment I felt something in the pull of family, in being depended on and appreciated and cared about, that I wanted to preserve, if not for Ford, then for myself.

"To Ford Shaper," I began. "Things to keep in mind and try."

I produced a list with two A.M. coherence, a list about games and chores and homework that both simplified and muddled the elementary-school lessons I was hoping to get down on paper. But number five was my favorite: "Appreciate what you have and what you can do," I said. "Every night when you're going to bed, think about what you did that day that was fun. Think about what you learned, or accomplished, and what felt good about it. If you can smile while you're going to bed, you'll smile when you wake up."

I slipped out early the next morning, the time of day that grounds crews sweep the dew off the greens, erasing the night air's artwork in favor of a blank grass slate.

I still hadn't quite figured out good-byes, and this one seemed too important to screw up. So I left, before Jeannie had arisen to drive the kids to school, before even Darryl had awakened from some motivational dream, all too ready to tackle another set of hardly mobile geriatric consumers.

I hoped I could follow my own advice. Smile while you're going to bed—that was good. If I could get through the day and end up in my sleeping bag, happy enough to grin, that was something worth pursuing. I hoped I would remember that.

CHAPTER 10

"Does this happen everywhere you go?"

O n February 25, I woke up in the back of Subi. We'd spent the night in a quiet parking lot in a quiet town off I-10 in eastern Louisiana. It was early, 7:15.

I rolled into the front seat and tugged on a T-shirt. It had been three days since I'd left New Braunfels, and I could feel three days' sweat in the way the shirt stuck to my chest, could smell it in the ripeness of the sleeping bag. *Maybe today I could find a laundromat,* I thought. *Or a shower.* I turned the key, Subi sputtered on, and we drove toward town. On the right was the big blue-and-green sign for a Holiday Inn Express that I'd scouted late the night before. I turned right.

I parked far away from the lobby, opened my glove compartment, and grabbed a Holiday Inn Express room key that someone had left on a table in Palm Springs. I walked along the sidewalk and turned in through the automatic glass doors, brandishing the card between the fingers of my right hand. I smiled at the receptionist and strode past the breakfast setup into the first floor hallway, where I turned right. I had planned it out, this turn right, because indecision was a suspicious look for a guest en route to the room in which he'd spent the night. But I had chosen luckily, and the men's public bathroom was looking right at me as I rounded the corner.

Out of sight, I slipped into the bathroom and removed several items from the baggy pockets of my Nike sweatpants: a tooth-brush, a tube of Crest, a razor, and a can of Gillette shaving cream. I brushed and spat and rinsed, and then did it again just for good measure. The blades of the razor felt good across my face, scrap-ing away a layer of dirt, sweat, and grease along with dark-brown stubble. I took my time. I soaked my face thoroughly before and after. I patted it down on my shirt before glancing to the mirror to admire the final result.

I didn't look transformed, but it was a big improvement. I splashed some more water into my hair and pushed it slightly over to one side, then, unsatisfied, back to the other. It was still short and choppy from my New Mexico cut a few weeks earlier, but matted down like this it was tough to notice much.

I stepped back into the hallway. I looked right. The carpet, a floral pattern in green and red, stretched down the hallway. Laid out on top of it at neat intervals, like table settings at a dinner for fifty, were crisply folded newspapers. *USA Today*. I grabbed one. Sorry, 103. Plenty more where that came from.

About four minutes later—a waffle, bacon and egg on a toasted bagel, two blueberry muffins, a bowl of Cinnamon Toast Crunch, a carton of milk, and an orange gathered before me—I opened the newspaper and flicked to the sports page.

And there, looking back at me, was a kid who looked weirdly familiar, standing on the cliffs at Pebble Beach, little red bag slung over his shoulder, smiling, beneath the headline: GOLFER HOPES SAGA LANDS HIM ON RIGHT COURSE.

It was a short article, but I had expected it to be. My mind flipped back to the e-mail I'd gotten maybe five, six weeks before, from the sports information director at Williams, telling me to look out for a call from a *USA Today* reporter. I remembered the feverish interview, which I'd given from my bed at the Luxor in between sessions of vomiting and delirious food-poisoned sleep. I'd been half dreading, half anticipating the story ever since.

I skimmed it with some trepidation. "Dethier has played 21

courses since September," it read. Twenty-one courses? Where'd they get that? I had played nearly that many in February. Tough start. The story continued in that vein, not so much bad as *wrong*. This was a story about a kid hoping to improve his golf game to make the Williams golf team. There was a quote from the Williams golf coach. Why had they interviewed him?

I sat back and closed the paper, not bothering to read it through. They'd missed it completely. I had been afraid of this, even though I hadn't fully comprehended that fact until just then. I was afraid that if someone else was allowed to tell me what I was doing, they'd change it, or they just wouldn't be able to get it right.

I turned back to my waffle, but I had lost my appetite. I wrapped the blueberry muffins in napkins and stood up. The paper, I noticed, was soaked through, the victim of a syrup container that had fallen off the edge of my plate. Now they matched, the soggy waffle and the soggy newspaper, and they both made me feel a little sick.

When I stopped to consider it, I realized that I was really proud of what I was doing—I wanted other people to know about it. I thought I had a message to spread about following dreams, doing what you love. And I was excited that something that had felt so unglamorous would end up in a newspaper in hotels and airports across the entire country—until I'd actually read it. Now I just wanted the story to go away. Maybe it would.

I drove east for a while along I-10 before I stopped, midmorning, at a public library in a small Louisiana town, just off the interstate somewhere between Lake Charles and Lafayette. I brought my laptop in and got the password from the front desk, and then I opened up my e-mail. And that was when I registered the change.

My inbox was inundated. People had responded. They had read the article, found my blog, and cared enough after reading it to send me an e-mail. I flicked through the messages. They were nice, incredibly generous, enthusiastic. What I had been seeing from America over several months—a spectrum of American golfers—was here, condensed, in my inbox: a blank scorecard to be filled in at the course of my choosing, and a skeleton key to every guest room on the Eastern Seaboard.

Room in New York. Bed and golf in Tennessee. Did I want to come back to California? Houston? Ohio? The refrain was the same in every one—"I love what you're doing. I wish I had thought of that."

Why? I sat there, dumbfounded, trying to figure out why the idea hit home so hard. It couldn't have just been the golf. There's a part of everyone that wants to hit the road. It's an American tradition, this wanderlust. The open highway, new people, unfamiliar sights—I imagine it appealed to anyone browsing *USA Today* who was stuck in one place as he dreamed of somewhere else. Maybe the specifics of my story didn't really matter—readers could just project their own desired journey in my place.

It wasn't just golfers. I had two separate messages from PR guys at PGA headquarters: Dave Lancer, director of information, and Joel Schuchmann, senior manager of communication. Did I want to play at any of their TPC venues? Did I! Tournament Players Clubs, a network of Tour-operated courses across the nation, are among the most elite courses in the country. Or, while I was at it, did I want any credentials to tour events? "We'd love for you to get some media coverage and meet some of our players," the e-mail said. *Damn.* I didn't know what to do with all of it. I closed my computer.

Was this what I wanted? A free pass, carte blanche access? Maybe this made it too easy.

I'd liked writing to individual golf courses and being accepted—convincing them that I was worthy of a free round at their course. I'd already written to TPC Sawgrass, the home base of the PGA Tour, weeks earlier. Sawgrass is one of the most famous courses in all of golf, host to the Players' Champion-ship, the so-called fifth major of the pro circuit. Located in Ponte Vedra Beach, Florida, a small, heavily gated town just south of Jacksonville, it was the new American home of golf. I'd spent countless hours on my couch watching PGA professionals walk-ing its swamp-lined fairways, and I'd watched the biggest names in golf win there—Tiger, Phil, Sergio, Davis Love III, Adam Scott. I'd watched dreams die in water surrounding the island green on the seventeenth.

When a Sawgrass pro had written back to me, telling me that I'd be allowed to play for free, I was ecstatic. Now the Tour itself was e-mailing me, inviting me to the same course, and I was almost disappointed. It had been a game, of sorts—I'd looked for courses to take me in for a free round the same way I had looked to families to take me off the streets for a warm meal and a bed. I'd made local connections, seeing who knew someone who might know someone at the golf course, accepting sugges-tions for where I should play next. It had been a gritty form of networking. The PGA's invitation to Sawgrass meant that I was closer to a guest of honor than I was to a wandering vagabond—which either meant that I had won the game or that I had lost it. I didn't respond to any of the e-mails—not right away—but I real-ized one chapter of this trip was coming to a close and another one was beginning.

I drove into New Orleans the next day, looking for a golf course. It was four and a half years since Hurricane Katrina, but there were still signs of it everywhere—temporary housing, abandoned homes, debris everywhere, especially in the neighborhoods near the water, where houses were being built on the ruins of houses that had collapsed.

I stopped to get gas and a sandwich and directions to a place to play public golf, and I got pointed in the general direction of Brechtel Park. It was a sunny day, so I sat on the hood of my car eating my turkey-and-provolone and thinking about Sawgrass.

"Nice license plate," someone said. I looked up to a man—a wiry, goateed guy with a ragged baseball cap and sunglasses, walking from the clubhouse to the parking lot, a small dog yapping at his heels. "I went to school in Massachusetts." He reached out his hand. "Peter. I'm the superintendent around here."

I returned his handshake and his introduction. He had gone to UMass Amherst, he said, and wondered how things were up in the Northeast. We talked New England news for a while.

During one lull in the conversation, I reached down to pat his dog. "Ouch!" I exclaimed, pulling away my hand. The little guy had chomped down on my middle finger, and after checking to see if he had drawn blood I looked back at the dog, still yapping, and made out the name on his little red collar: TROUBLE.

"Sorry," Peter told me. "I should have warned you. I pulled him out of the Katrina wreckage, he's been pretty mean ever since."

I pressed Peter for more New Orleans stories. "Only a few of us city employees stayed here. Once they told everyone to evacuate, I brung my kids to a shelter in Baton Rouge, then turned right around. That was the eeriest part," he told me. "The other side of the highway was jam-packed to a standstill. Some cars were stopped in the middle of lanes, some people who had run out of gas were walking along the side of the road. It was an exodus. It seemed like I was the only one driving back in." But even the terror of the actual storm wasn't as bad as the aftermath. "Certain areas I would drive around all tensed, because you never knew what was going to happen. Looters and hooligans were all over the place, stealing and worse. I never been more scared in my life. But then, I did have a shotgun strapped to my back and a .357 under the front seat, figured no one would try and mess with me then."

Peter had me fully engaged by this point. He made a move as if he had to leave—but I was too curious. What next?

"How about the golf course?" I asked.

"This one got ruined," Peter said. "The other one I run—the

city owns it too—was much worse. It was under twenty-two feet of water at the worst part. Within a couple months the water drained, so I started working with a couple guys to try and get 'em back into playing shape. I guess you could say it became kind of a symbol, to a few of us anyway," he continued. "If we could rebuild the golf course, maybe there was a chance for the city, too."

My own story was pushed from my mind as I made my way around the eighteen-hole design. The course was a combination of boring and frustrating—tee boxes, fairway, and rough were all the same coarse grass, uneven most places, dead in others. Still, it was golf. Peter's words popped up in my head again and again. Four years later, New Orleans still hadn't recovered from the most destructive hurricane in U.S. history. Funding was disappearing—so was national interest. Would the city ever recover? City officials could only do what money and personnel allowed, and so Peter was doing what he could—trying to bring back a little green to a city emerging from the dark.

I finished my round quickly—there wasn't much traffic on the course—and returned to the parking lot. Peter was loading something into the bed of his truck.

"Where you off to next?" he asked.

"East, still," I told him. "Mississippi, then Alabama, then Florida."

"Ooh, Florida. That's the place to go for golf, isn't it? Hell, you could spend about a year playing just golf courses there and not get through 'em all. And what's that one with the little par-three . . . the one with the island for a green?"

"You mean Sawgrass?"

"Yeah! You should play that one."

I could only grin. "Maybe so," I said.

"That would be pretty cool."

I felt a twinge of guilt that I was leaving without doing anything to help. I was glad that I'd been through the Big Easy, but it's impossible to pass through a place like New Orleans unaffected, to leave someone like Peter to continue his work alone. Still, Sawgrass beckoned. In a trip that shifted unceasingly between highs and lows, I knew this was one high I didn't want to miss.

Less than two weeks later I was in Ponte Vedra Beach, inside the offices at PGA headquarters, looking at the scenes of triumph covering the walls: Tiger fist-pumping, Phil grimacing, Sergio roaring. This was the office that set up those tournaments, allowed the players to become millionaires, allowed me to watch them play from home. There was the commissioner's office—there were his putter and his golf balls, because even the PGA commissioner practices putting on his office carpet. I was getting the behind-the-scenes tour of the production of pro golf.

This *was* cool.

I was crashing the night with Bart Robinson, a well-traveled golfer who spent his summers in Williamstown. I'd met his son once, a Williams alum who had heard about my trip and put us in touch. Bart and his wife, Ingela, lived adjacent to Sawgrass, just a couple minutes from the course. Bart would be my playing partner. We were due to tee off at ten, so we headed over a little before nine to warm up and admire the grounds.

The clubhouse was a palace, a Mediterranean-revival-style behemoth that measured nearly eighty thousand square feet. With stucco walls and auburn tiles covering the roof (and the turrets), it echoed the architecture of the surrounding houses, just scaled up by a factor of fifty or so.

We'll set up some media for you, too, if you don't mind. Dave Lancer, the Tour's director of information, had made this request as he toured me around the headquarters, and he was so friendly that I didn't have any thought of objecting. Plus, after the *USA Today* article, I was eager for a chance to get a more accurate picture of the trip out into the world. My first interview came at 9:30, when I stepped off the practice green to phone in to Jacksonville's morning sports-talk show.

I looked at my phone: less than a single bar of cell reception.

Crap. I pressed the phone to my ear as a producer explained the procedure—I had never phoned in for a radio interview before. Meanwhile a nearby groundskeeper, perhaps determined to protect the area from cell phone usage, had adjusted his lawn-mowing pattern to provide a drowning hum of background noise. To top it all off, I felt the low-battery buzz on my phone just as the call connected. This meant that every minute the phone would beep for about five seconds, blocking out sound and ruining any reasonable conversation. One pause came right as I was supposed to start talking, so I didn't know if they could hear me or not. I certainly couldn't hear them. We endured about a minute and a half of halting, awkward back-and-forth (word of advice: never answer a live interview question with, "Wait, what?") before the battery gave up and the phone turned off midanswer, which must have been a relief for any listeners who hadn't already tuned out.

The uneasiness of the interview seemed to spill into my golf round. I had seen the course on TV countless times and played it on Tiger Woods PGA Tour 2005. On my Mac, I could drive the 370 or so yards to the front of the first green. In real life, not so much. I pull-hooked my tee shot some thirty yards left of the fairway and into the woods en route to a double bogey. The rest of the front nine went about the same way. Sawgrass is a tough course no matter what, and if you're hitting it crooked, you have no chance. I bounced from the woods to the water to the sand, alternating pars and double bogeys. Sometimes when I hit what I thought was a good shot—like my drive on the par-5 ninth—my ball would find a hazard, in this case water that I didn't even know was there. On my old computer, I would have blasted right over it.

I could see why Sawgrass carried such a weighty reputation. More than anything, I found it to be *impressive*. Most golf courses are designed to fit with their geographic region and its particular landscape constraints. When Pete Dye designed Sawgrass, he sought the exact opposite effect. He wanted to build *on* the existing site—from the swamp up. This was crazy—the site lay just four feet above sea level in the midst of the Florida "death-lands," land so seemingly worthless that when the PGA Tour had bought the property in 1978, it did so for just one dollar.

But crazy determination produced a shocking result. After the exploration of the grounds from a rowboat and the draining of the surrounding area, the design and construction began. Unfathom-able amounts of dirt were shipped in (ten miles of filled dump trucks lined up one after another, a caddie told us) and, in the end, a championship golf course emerged. Still, signs of the swamp remained everywhere, from the wildlife—alligators, turtles, and birds of every kind—to the water, snaking alongside what felt like every hole.

Sawgrass wasn't subtle. The clubhouse wasn't subtle. The targets weren't subtle. You executed your shot and you were fine, or you missed it and you were dead. That's why the pros, after years of struggling to figure out how to find "fine," are finally going low on the course. It's also why I hit five balls in the water.

Bart and I played with a randomly assigned twosome—Mike and Darren, work associates from Atlanta, and their caddie, Paul. They were each decent players, single-digit handicaps who took their games seriously, and Paul was the ideal caddie—confident but detached. He made every club selection or putt read thought-fully but still casually, as if he knew he was right but in the end didn't really care if you could hit the shot the way you were sup-posed to. He had done his job, after all.

I followed my dismal front nine with a particularly awful 6 on the par-4 tenth, hitting from fairway bunker to greenside bun-ker to three-putt. I was trying to stay positive—this was a once-in-a-lifetime chance to play one of the country's most famous courses—but they could build a golf course on Mars and about two thirds of the first-time players would get damn frustrated. There was really no getting around it.

Approaching the eleventh, I noticed a cameraman behind the

green. The guys from the PGA had also gotten in touch with a local TV station, apparently. *Great, now I can suck on camera,* I thought. The press was going to be covering a hacker's best work on one of America's most iconic courses.

I snipe-hooked my drive, which barely stayed in play. But all hope was not lost. Eleven was a par 5, and I punched out to 150 yards—an easy 9-iron distance. Finally I hit one smooth, a little right-to-left on the ball until it settled fifteen feet short of the pin. I left my putt a rotation short, directly in the center of the hole, but I felt a lift—the kick-in par felt like a sigh of relief. It sparked some momentum—I smoked a 3-wood down the twelfth fairway, leaving just a sand wedge approach that I stuck to three feet. I rolled in the birdie putt just as a second camera crew pulled in behind the green. I did put another ball in the water on the par-3 thirteenth and missed a short par putt on 14, but I was at least hitting it better. By this point there was a small group looking on—we had been joined by a reporter and his photographer as well as Joel from the Tour's communications department. As my media entourage looked on, I blasted a touchy sand shot to a foot for an up-and-down par on the fifteenth, then grabbed my ball before going to stand with Mike as Bart finished putting. Mike grinned at me incredulously. "Does this happen everywhere you go?" he asked in a low voice. I returned his grin and shook my head. "Well," he said, "it's pretty cool."

Holes sixteen through eighteen at Sawgrass are among the most famous finishing holes in all of golf. They counter risk with reward—birdie is there, and so is double bogey. I did my best to entertain by going for the sixteenth green, which stuck out just slightly into the lake, and elicited a good groan from my newly devoted masses as my ball landed on the back fringe and skipped into the water.

But it was really all about the seventeenth. The signature hole at Sawgrass doubled as probably the most recognizable golf hole in the world. At just under 130 yards, the shot itself would normally be a cupcake for professional golfers—a clear birdie opportunity. The catch is that the green is an island, connected to the mainland only by a thin walkway, leaving only about seventy-five feet of landing area from front to back. It's an intimidating shot for anyone, but for tour pros with the tournament title and hundreds of thousands of dollars on the line, it's downright terrifying, especially with the wind howling the way it often does.

Our group had swollen still further. Bart's wife, Ingela, had walked out to join us, as had a reporter from the *Florida Sun-Times*. Some members of the grounds crew working the previous green had stopped what they were doing, too, in order to watch. The TV cameras were still trained on me for their local news stories; maybe they were hoping I would dunk one in the water to become another victim of the famed seventeenth. It wasn't unlikely, I figured. I'd been dunking balls like Oreos in milk all afternoon, and I'd been anticipating this shot since I had crossed the state line. Mike and Bart didn't exactly ease the tension: Mike flew it into the lake beyond the green and Bart missed short. "We left it wide open for you," he told me.

I realized that I was terrified. I was scared that I would fail with all these extra people watching. It was the same reason I was scared that I had been in *USA Today*. I was scared that if something happened, if the trip failed, I would be failing in front of everyone. Or else I was afraid that the trip already had failed, because instead of playing the seventeenth and figuring out what it did to people, other people were watching and figuring out what it would do to me. What did that even mean? I was starting to lose sight of the implications of my trip, and I could feel my hands shaking.

Deep down I knew it was a meaningless shot. I wasn't going to shoot a good number. We weren't playing a match, even. But as I clutched my pitching wedge, it felt like this shot meant everything. I drew the club away unsteadily, a little outside. *Any big shot, always take a little less club—that'll account for adrenaline.* I'd heard Tiger say it—I wasn't sure when. Why was I thinking about that? I stopped my swing short, some three quarters of the way back, and my heart skipped a beat as I made contact, the ball soaring out over the water. It wasn't terribly high, but it was headed directly at the flag. *Go!* I thought instinctively, rooting for the ball to reach the green, but before I knew it, the ball had flown over the flag and then past it. *Stop!* It hit—on land!—took a hop, and spun to a stop at the back part of the green, some twenty-five feet past the pin. "Good ball," Paul told me with a smile, reaching out a closed hand for a fist bump. I was so relieved that I three-putted to celebrate.

I wondered if there had ever been so much attention paid to a round of 84. I putted out on eighteen and went to the area that's right outside the scorer's house, where the pros usually do their postround interviews.

They filmed a brief bit, for Channel 30 or something. I was too nonchalant, I could tell, too off the cuff for them to want to use the footage. But the camera guy was cracking up. I liked that. They asked me where I stayed, usually, what types of places I liked.

"Well, I never really know where I'm going to stay. I mean, hell, I'm on like four TV stations and I don't even know where I'm gonna be *tonight*." I glanced in the direction of Bart and the rest of the group. "My stuff's still at their house, but I didn't get the invite back to stay tonight. Awkward, right? So I dunno. I'll find somewhere to park my car and go from there."

Had I failed Public Relations 101? To the professional communicators of America, I probably looked like a kid in desperate need of media training. I felt bad if the Tour guys had expected me to be more polished, a better advertisement. For me, though, it felt good, saying things like I did. The *not-knowing* was still there. Even TPC Sawgrass couldn't erase all traces of the rough wandering vagabond. After all, I wouldn't even be able to watch myself on the six o'clock news because Subi didn't get the six o'clock news. Instead I'd make do with a fast food dinner and a quick prayer that the seven inches of rain in the forecast wouldn't fall directly on me, at least for the night. Maybe I'd even get to those other e-mails. Or maybe the next day. Adventures don't have prescribed work hours.

CHAPTER 11

Temporary Son

The furniture in the Fox house was *comfortable.*

By this point in the trip—seven months in—I had figured out some best practices for being a houseguest. Wash the dishes. Compliment my hostess on her home decor. Leave my golf shoes in the car. If you're at ease, your host is at ease. Some places just never felt quite right. Sometimes I'd walk into a home and it would feel strange and stilted, and part of me couldn't wait to leave. That was not the case at the Foxes'. There, I could sink into an armchair and feel like I'd never have to get up—and that's the kind of place where it was worth staying.

Jay Fox, a tall, beefy guy with oversize eyeglasses and a teddy bear smile, did things right from the start. He emerged from his suburban Little Rock home to greet me with a big handshake. He had a glass of ice water ready and a college basketball game on TV. Some social situations are tough to navigate. This one wasn't. Or maybe that's just how you feel when you've found the right place.

I had driven to Little Rock straight from Tampa. I had told Jay and his wife, Kim, that I would be there for dinner, and, as I'd learned, in the South dinnertime is taken seriously. The drive was something like sixteen hours, and I had done it in about nineteen—stopping only for an hour or two of sleep in the parking lot of a Quality Inn near Calera, Alabama, at about four A.M.

It had taken a few phone calls to get connected with someone in Arkansas, but Taylor had come through once again. His great-uncle Steve had been friends with Jay for years and was excited at the prospect of someone he knew visiting Arkansas—and because Jay was the director of the Arkansas State Golf Association, the connection was useful on a number of levels.

That first night Jay must have spied me dozing off in my armchair in the living room. He pointed out my bedroom and the adjoining bathroom. Freshen up a little. I took the hint. Walking down the hall and into my room, I dropped my backpack onto the ground and opened my mouth for what started as a sigh but turned to a deep, throaty yawn that just about unhinged my jaw. I could have fallen asleep right there, standing up—except that I was always tired these days and could never really sleep.

We were supposed to go to dinner as soon as Kim got home from her job in the communications department at the University of Arkansas–Little Rock. I stepped into the bathroom, where, as if in a trance, I shaved and drifted into the steam of the shower. I could feel my eyes closing again, felt my hand press against the wall to steady myself. I tried to blink awake. Reaching for the faucet, I turned it all the way to the right, turning hot to icy. My body jolted, every muscle tense, crying for the shower to be over. I stood under the frigid water for about a minute. I went from cold to numb and all the way back to cold before finally, mercifully, reaching for the towel hanging on the door.

As I looked into the mirror, I was shocked by the person looking back. I was . . . different. It wasn't so much a change in my body; cycles of hunger interrupted by fast food binges had settled into an equilibrium that left my frame approximately where it had started—maybe just a touch thicker around the middle. My neck looked a little different. It was broader—stronger. Holding up my head must have been a piece of cake by this point.

My face and arms bore dangerous tans, dark and appealing, but that transitioned crudely into a torso that had, in the preceding months, seen about as much sunshine as the windowless bathroom I was standing in. My hair was finally recovering from the demon barber of Truth or Consequences. It was hard to even see the uneven parts anymore. But then, I hadn't used a comb since fourth grade and wasn't about to start now. I ran my hand back over my forehead and let my fingers enter near the roots, feeling the water on my scalp as I mussed it up, hoping that the wind would do a better styling job than I.

It was my eyes that really scared me. They looked distant, as though they had been forced to retreat into the dark sockets by the puffy bags that were threatening to become permanent features on my face. It was the look of someone who hadn't been at ease in a long time. I didn't like this at all.

"Hey, Dylan, you alive in there?" It was Jay. "Don't drown in the shower, insurance would be a mess."

I felt a smile drift over my face and watched the person in the mirror transform. The kid was still there.

We went to a steakhouse called Doe's Eat Place for dinner, a Little Rock institution housed in a decrepit building on a run-down corner of the capital city. It had been one of Bill Clinton's favorite hangouts, so they told me. Mementos and pictures covered the walls—all were related to the restaurant, except for the ones that weren't. The neighborhood, the walls, the dirty kitchen in the middle of the restaurant sent a pretty strong message that the food and atmosphere would speak for themselves.

"So, we've gotta get you some *better* publicity," Kim was saying. We had been talking about the *USA Today* article. "Get this story out there. It's cool, what you're doing," she continued. "But it'll be cooler to hear *you*, you know, so people get the full experience."

Jay chuckled. "Watch out, Kim'll make you famous. She's taking UALR big-time as we speak, and you'll be next, if she puts her mind to it."

"Oh, Dylan, you'd be the perfect side project. I'm ready for this. I'll be your number-one fan. We'll turn this thing into millions, just you wait."

I thought it was a good fit, Kim and communications: She was quick-witted and warm and seemed to me to be an excellent communicator. I liked that she was excited for me just because I was there, because I was trying something and she wanted young people to be encouraged to try things.

Our server brought out the food midsentence, and I could feel my eyes widening even as I laughed at Kim's enthusiasm. The steak, a huge slab served family-style to the center of the table, may have been the best meat I've ever tasted. It melted under my knife and then melted even more on my tongue in a way that even Dad's best never had. If this was Arkansas living, I thought, I could get used to more of this. What a great place to arrive. Though the steak was mouthwateringly distractive, I was enjoying the presence of the Foxes even more. They made me laugh.

"Who could we get to play you in the movie?" Kim wondered aloud.

I spent my third morning in Little Rock at the Arkansas State Golf Association headquarters. The ASGA runs educational programs, tournaments, and other events; keeps handicaps; and generally promotes golf across the state. I was sitting on the edge of Jay's office desk, shooting the breeze with Jay, who was the director, and his colleague Mac, who dealt explicitly with handicapping but seemed to be able to do everything or nothing around the office, depending on his mood. I had a map up on my laptop—I pretty much always did at this point—and watched as Mac traced his finger across a possible route. It occurred to me how much my route was shaped by people like Mac—people who wanted me to go places they'd been, or *wished* they could go.

"You heard of this place Sand Hills?" he asked. "Unbeliev-able course, sounds like, stuck in the corner of a tiny town in Nebraska. Five hundred people live there, but they've got an airport for these cats to jet in for a day trip." He gave a half shake of his head, like he had just surfaced and was trying to get the water

out of his ear. It was a look I recognized from every municipal I had played, a public-course awe of the game's more elite
domains—part jealousy, part disgust. In my house, the disgust
won in a landslide—but with most golfers it was harder to tell.

I wondered if Mac was picturing what I was: sand spraying
everywhere as the *whomp* of the chopper blades got closer and
closer to the ground. Helicopter doors opening, four men with
matching argyle sweater-vests and graying hair emerging—each
of them candidates to play the U.S. president in a made-for-TV
movie if they weren't busy closing business deals over twenty-
footers somewhere in the dune grasses of northern Nebraska.
Or maybe it was just me.

"Jay, you know anyone there?" Mac asked, snapping me back
into the present moment. "Think we could get Dylan on?"

Jay started to respond as the phone rang.

"Jay Fox speaking. Yeah, I've got him right here." He looked
up at me. "Sure, we'll be there this afternoon. All right. Look
forward to it!"

He grinned as he hung up the phone. "We're gonna go see
Channel Seven this afternoon. Mac, guess who they're bringing
in to do the story?"

A schoolboy smirk flashed across Mac's face. "Holly?"

Holly Sonders, fresh out of Michigan State, had only been in
Little Rock for a few months but she was fast becoming a local
celebrity. In a region that cherishes its local news, any change in
personnel would've caused a stir. But Holly wasn't just a new
face. There was no way around it. Holly was *hot*.

Jay and I arrived in the Rebsamen Golf Course parking lot a few
minutes early for the interview. The premise was simple—we
would go to the range and hit some balls with Holly, get some
B-roll, a quick interview, and done. After all, it was Channel 7 in
Little Rock—nothing to get anxious over. But then she walked
out of the clubhouse.

Holly's outfit would have been preposterous for any average

woman to wear anywhere. She looked like she had gotten lost on the way to a country club highlighter party. But then, Holly was no average woman.

I was hitting 8-irons at a tree on the side of the range when I heard a collective "Ohhh" whispered from the group of men behind me as Holly emerged. A hot-pink sweater clung so tightly to the curves of her upper body—oh God, the *curves*—that it could have been Saran-wrapped on. The sweater transitioned seamlessly into a magenta miniskirt that only covered the beginning of two tender thighs, so toned and tanned and natural that they seemed to stay still even as the rest of her body walked.

My mind had gone blank watching. I stood over my bucket of range balls as she shook hands with Jay, and two employees whose names I had just forgotten, and waited for her to approach. I had spent most of my young life pursuing girls in exactly this way—waiting for them to approach. It hadn't worked very well.

Luckily, I had the good fortune of being the object of her story. She *had* to talk to me. I just had to make sure I wouldn't be speechless when she did.

We smiled, shook hands, and said each other's names. I started babbling about Michigan State, where she had just graduated, and Big Ten football, and she talked about how she had become a sideline reporter and how she had dated her team's starting quarterback. This made her more intimidating, if anything, but I liked it because I didn't really like *being* a news story. Our conversation petered out quickly, and she decided to go right into the interview. The cameraman had set up at the corner of the practice tee, so I made idle chitchat with him while Holly did something with her hair that made me weak in the knees.

"Okay, ready?" she asked me, untangling a large, black "7" microphone. "I'm not going to be in the shot, so just talk into the camera."

"Got it." I waited for a question. She brandished the mike in my face.

"Okay, talk."

"Huh?"

"Talk. Tell me about, you know, your story."

It was not the most elegant interviewing technique, but when Holly asks you to do something, you do it. I stumbled through some short narrative, still keeping my tone excessively casual, trying to maintain that I was as unimpressed with my own story as I was with the length of her skirt, even though I was impressed with both and could hardly keep them separate as I talked.

"Okay," she said after a couple minutes of my drivel. "That should do it!"

Things got more natural from there, well, as "natural" as could be expected during a fake range session with fake conversation for a filler news story. Holly wasn't an Oprah-caliber interviewer, and I for sure wasn't the world's most polished interview subject. But Holly was a 2 handicap—a standout golfer for Michigan State—so what we could both do was hit golf balls. So that's what we did.

I started with an 8-iron. She followed suit—a strong swing with a good turn and a long follow-through clearly sculpted by years on the range. I hit again. She did too. It seemed like one of us should say something.

"You like it here?" I asked abruptly.

"Yeah, it's a great opportunity," she recited with the sort of rehearsed earnestness of a real estate agent. "It's a great community. Everyone's so friendly, and I was lucky to get a chance to come here out of college."

I pured one, a high draw that we both stopped to admire. It loosened me up a little.

"C'mon, Holly," I laughed back. "You're supposed to be the media, not me. You worried I'm going to quote you? No offense, but you do local news in *Arkansas*. You must see some priceless stuff. How much hilarious shit is on your show every day?"

She stopped and looked at me for what felt like the first time as she couldn't help but give a sheepish grin. "Okay, fine, but you said it, not me."

It also occurred to me that maybe she was as nervous as I was, mere weeks into a job and producing a news story about an eighteen-year-old kid who didn't even seem particularly interested in her.

Was that possible? That she was nervous around me? The idea helped steel my remaining nerves. I wasn't anxious, that is, except for the feeling I got when she smiled in my direction. Or the way my stomach felt every time she made solid contact with her 3-wood. Standing behind her as she hit, I tried to suppress every eighteen-year-old instinct I had. *Eyes up, kid. Camera's on you.*

Holly was at home on the driving range—most junior golfers with competitive dreams get pretty familiar with it. I had always hated the range. Every action was of so little consequence. Hit 'em bad and you got frustrated, and so you hit 'em faster, and even worse, and got even more frustrated. But hitting it good on the range was almost worse. You were wasting bullets. You could hit a hundred balls on a tight little three-yard draw with a trajectory that would carve through the wind but still land soft—and you'd have nothing to show for it. It was shooting blanks.

So this must have been my favorite range session of all time. I could make Holly laugh with a fifty-yard slice, and impress her with a low rope hook that whizzed past the range picker. I even goaded her into firing a couple 6-irons in the direction of her cameraman, who had ventured out in search of a new angle. It didn't matter that she had dated the starting quarterback at Michigan State—really—and that I hadn't been to college yet. It felt like we were just a couple of kids trying to one-up each other, and all of a sudden we were having real fun—and not just the type that would look like it on the six o'clock news. Either that or Holly was a lot better at her job than I first guessed.

I tried to imagine what it would be like to hang out with a girl like Holly in real life. What would she say if I asked her on a date? I tried to push the thought out of my mind. I was in town for a day, two max—not setting down roots.

Eventually we ran low on balls, and the cameraman, done with the artsy shots from his perilous vantage point, returned to the tee. Holly and I said good-bye with just a tinge of awkwardness, probably entirely from my end. She asked for my e-mail address—*just in case, for story clarification,* she told me. I took it as a hopeful sign. If it had been *just for the story,* she wouldn't have needed to say so.

It turns out that we were both going to Oklahoma for the weekend—her to cover women's basketball, me to find golf—although watching women's basketball was starting to sound pretty good too. Was it destiny? "You guys should meet up," Jay supplied, and we agreed, each knowing that it wouldn't happen.

Jay, Kim, and I went for pizza that night. Nothing about buffet-style pizza sounded very traditionally Southern, but this place was—both in the unrefined excess of its bacon-cheeseburger pizza and in the oh-it's-so-great-to-see-you smiles that came so easily to the girls carrying fresh platters around.

One waitress, nametag LEANNE, suddenly stopped at the table, touching Kim lightly on the shoulder.

"Well, I hate to interrupt," she said, "but I thought I recognized y'all! It's Kim and Jay, right?"

I wasn't paying attention to the words they exchanged so much as I was to their tones, their expressions. Kim's face had lit up at the introduction. Before long they had established a web of mutual connections. Their voices shifted into a slightly higher register, as though each was upping the ante, ramping up her enthusiasm. I could see Jay watching Kim, and I could see that he was happy, too, to see her happy. It was a moment that the New Englander in me recognized as superficial small talk, but then, here in the South it didn't seem superficial at all. I must have been staring. Leanne turned her smile toward me.

"And is this your son?"

We laughed and glanced at each other, wondering who was going to correct her for more than a moment.

"Just for a few days," I told her.

I said it as kind of a joke, but I realized that in a way, that's exactly what I was—a son for a few days. Kim was beaming; I think she liked that I hadn't dismissed the idea altogether.

By the time we got back to the house, my eyelids were getting heavy. I opened my laptop to scan my new e-mails, and one at the top caught my eye: It was from Holly. The message didn't say much, just thanks for a fun day and that she had a question about whether I was setting any kind of world record.

I sent back a quick response before closing my computer for the night. Kim and Jay were in their room, but Jay came out just as I was raiding the kitchen for a late-night bowl of cereal. Something was on his mind.

"You know, at the restaurant, when Leanne asked if you were our son, well, we liked the idea of that pretty well. Kim and I didn't meet until we were well into our thirties, and by then . . ." His voice caught a little. "Well, if it was a different time in our lives . . ." Now I could feel something rising in my throat, too. "We've just been really happy to have you around."

Every day, people were affecting me—teaching me new ways to think, see, and feel the world. But it had rarely occurred to me that I might be doing the same for others. That my presence would make others examine their own lives in a deeper light— that was a crazy idea. Or maybe not. I was beginning to realize the power of talking about my trip. The road trip. It made everyone wonder if they should be on a similar quest. It was the same feeling that ignited my own urge to journey. But it wasn't just the travel. It was me, and what I represented to people.

A few days living with someone was just enough time for the what-ifs to creep in. I was immersing myself in people's worlds, and they in mine, which gave us both a chance to feel firsthand what it would be like to live a different life. The idea must have made me a particularly intrusive houseguest. But it also gave me an extra sense of responsibility, knowing that I wasn't just a passive learner anymore—I was leaving my mark, too.

• • •

Muskogee Country Club was a half hour south of Tulsa, three hours west of Little Rock, and tucked into one of the nicest neighborhoods in the city of Muskogee. The oldest golf course in Oklahoma had started as a dairy farm, the pro told me, and was first converted to fairways and sand greens in 1907. A couple decades later, renowned golf course architect Perry Maxwell came in to perform a major redesign. Plenty of golf courses make similar claims—that their course has been around for the better part of American history—when all that really means is that there were three gopher holes and six empty milk cans sprinkled around the property when the golf course "opened" a century ago. But rejecting history in favor of tradition is endemic to the golf world. We all like to do that, I guess. Tradition is comforting.

I hit some range balls while Sam, the head pro, scared up a game with some of the locals. We ended up a fivesome. The other guys, in their forties and fifties, were dressed in worn collared shirts and sun-faded jeans that had seen better days. I was glad I had stuck to shorts rather than khakis.

Bets started forming on the first tee, some I understood and some I didn't. Partly I was confused because I hadn't really learned anyone's name, and whatever game we were playing involved swapping partners throughout the round. I didn't know whether I was rooting for a putt to go in or lip out, which really stilted conversation. The guys barely went by their given names. They were mostly "hoss" or "partner" when they were talking to each other, "jackass" or "dickwad" when they were talking to themselves. Only I was called just Dylan, but even that started changing after a few holes, and soon I was "young gun," "junior," or "Sergio."

They could have told me I owed just about anything and I would have believed them as Ross, my partner, added up the scores after we finished the eighteenth. I had played pretty well but had long since lost track of the presses and the front/back side matches and who was getting strokes on which holes. So when they handed me twelve dollars, good enough for dinner and more, I was relieved. I still hadn't learned to avoid the cardinal sin of gambling without a dollar in my pocket.

I splurged on a meatball sub and parked outside a shuttered café with wireless. I wanted to check my e-mail and post a blog entry I had written the night before. It always felt like a weight off my shoulders to post on the blog—I was always behind, but I had a surprisingly loyal bunch of followers.

I had a few new messages, from Colorado and Missouri and Tennessee asking me when I would be there. I usually replied, *Well, I'm not sure, but eventually,* but other people seemed to like things to be more definite than that for some reason. No message from Holly.

In reality, I hadn't expected it. We had exchanged a few more e-mails. I asked if she wanted to play golf or go watch basketball, because I knew she liked doing both and I was planning on it anyway. What did I have to lose? (Note: Really, it was *her* loss. I had tickets for the second round of the men's NCAA tournament, a game pitting number-one Kansas against little-known Northern Iowa. When UNI won, ESPN called it the best game of the year, any sport.)

No, she had said. *I won't have enough time.* It was a nice, concise excuse. No worries. But then: *Let me know if you'd like to meet up Saturday night if you're in town.* And then a little winky face. What the hell did that mean? I wrote back to see when she'd be free, probably too eagerly, even though I wasn't sure what we would do in Oklahoma City on a Saturday night, the eighteen-year-old vagrant and the twenty-two-year-old bombshell. But she had made it easy on my wallet and my schedule by not responding. I hadn't expected her to, really. It didn't make sense. But it still stung a little bit.

I hadn't seen *anyone* twice since September, in the sense of having hung out with a person, left to go somewhere else, and then seeing that same person again. All "See ya," no "See ya later."

For the most part, it had been great. I had been trying on people's lives like sneakers, seeing how they fit. But maybe this wasn't a natural state, being so transient. Humans weren't built to live this way forever. I had loved it in Little Rock. I wanted to stay in Arkansas for a week, a month. But I had to complete my inner loop of the central states I'd missed on my northern sweep. My plan was to head as far west as Colorado and Nebraska before turning back to pick up Missouri, Kentucky, Tennessee, and then the Eastern Seaboard.

But Jay and Kim had been special. They'd given me a feeling of belonging, this sense that I fit right in when I could just as easily have not. It was the perfect, if temporary, antidote for my loneliness. On the other hand, whatever force made me dwell on Holly was something different. I'd largely had to suppress any desire for romance, for some emotional or physical intimacy. But Holly had brought those yearnings to the forefront. Did that make her special? Or was she just a stark reminder that choosing to take this journey had largely separated me from my peers— and the kinds of relationships they were surely developing at college? I felt hollow.

I closed my computer and started to drive away. I would look for a state park to spend the night in, somewhere farther from the city. I liked this part of the night, the tired part, when I could just park, and sleep, and eventually wake up. It wasn't so bad, being alone.

Maybe she would write tomorrow.

CHAPTER 12

Keeping Score

By the time I'd hit Missouri, I'd decided that keeping score was the best—but also the worst—thing about golf. It's probably true that keeping score in any game distracts from the game itself, its essence, the physical actions and settings that make it fun to play. I've always been sure that golf is a beautiful game. But the way we try to reduce the success of a four-hour athletic endeavor shared by friends down to miniature pencil numbers squeezed onto a four-by-six-inch piece of paper is absurd.

We ruin lots of beautiful experiences by quantifying them. Movies get evaluated by colored-in stars in the newspaper. Intelligence, through SAT scores. Jump shots by how often they go through the hoop. Human life couldn't exist without valuations—they're our way of making sense of the world. We categorize and reduce and simplify, and numbers make it easy for us. But sometimes doing so sucks the life out of things.

An empty scorecard is a coloring book. It has the outlines for you—the tee markers and the handicaps and what's par. It tells you how far you have to go and which holes are supposed to be the hardest. And it begs to be colored in, filled up by a smartly sharpened pencil, blissfully unaware that in about twelve holes it could be crumpled in a back pocket, its results either hotly contested over beers and dollar bills or else conveniently forgotten on the seventeenth tee box.

Golf courses, though, aren't made to be painted by number.

They're made of opportunity and failure and creativity, because in reality, the golf course—not the scorecard—is the canvas. For me, watching Adam Scott paint irons on flawless little two-yard draws from fairway to green was art. Writing down 3? That stole some of the magic away. Nobody goes to the Met with a bingo card or a grading rubric. Why bother at Augusta?

Golf isn't about the number at the end; it's about the possibility at the beginning. Not knowing *how* you're going to get there—that's the most important part.

There wasn't much not-knowing in Steve Maritz's life—or at least that's the impression he liked to give off.

And he loved keeping score. Maybe it was because he was so used to winning.

Strong and taller and bulkier than me, Steve had a round face and a quick, jovial smile. If somebody told me his house used to be the governor's mansion, I would have believed him. An old wood-and-brick beauty just off the main drive of the St. Louis Country Club, the house was tucked in among the cherry trees, or the redbuds, or the dogwoods, or whatever floral combinations of white and pink it was that made spring at the hundred-year-old St. Louis Country Club look like spring was supposed to look everywhere.

I had nearly completed my inner loop. I survived a rogue snowstorm in Oklahoma. I skied and golfed back-to-back afternoons in Colorado. In Nebraska, I played in wind so strong it made me cry, although that could have also been from the scent on the wind, because Nebraska smelled the worst. I spent a couple days throwing up in Kansas City (Kansas side)—which I attributed to my inconsistent diet, which I guessed was steadily weakening my immune system. But I managed eighteen there, too. Now, on a Friday in early April, I'd made it to Steve Maritz and his house in Missouri. People call St. Louis "the Gateway to the West." To me it was the gateway east—and it marked the beginning of a trip back home.

The St. Louis Country Club is famous in Missouri and served as Steve's home course, except when he played at Boone Valley, which was the highest-ranked course in Missouri.

And except when he played the Floridian Golf and Yacht Club in Palm City, then owned by his friend Wayne Huizenga, who seemed to own a lot of things, like Waste Management and the Miami Dolphins. Each year, yacht club members awaited notification of their continued belonging—membership was free of charge—or else they would hear nothing, which meant nobody would open the gate the next time they showed up. If he was welcome there, it sounded like Steve Maritz was welcome pretty much anywhere.

But Wayne was selling the club, even though it had been successful and despite having reportedly poured most of $100 million into it. Maybe he just liked building things up and then selling them, as he had with the Florida Marlins and Blockbuster Video. Steve was invited to a party to celebrate its sale, the kind of event that "guys could go to and get to be guys and do things they wouldn't tell their wives about," he said, winking at his wife, Jeanne, who rolled her eyes. This was the sort of decision that Steve Maritz had to make: fly to Florida to attend a party, or keep the speaking engagement that he had already committed to? And to his credit, Steve was the kind of guy who kept the speaking engagement.

It was Masters Sunday, and Steve Maritz was the kind of guy, too, who could have gotten us to Augusta that morning if he'd wanted to. Just because he had chosen Augusta, Missouri, today, and not Augusta, Georgia, didn't mean we couldn't have been in the latter's grandstand on eighteen by noon if he had wanted us to be.

Needless to say, I had entered a new social circle. And I was having fun absorbing the possibilities.

Today Steve wanted to play Boone Valley. I glanced around the locker room in the clubhouse, noting the engraved name plates: Ozzie Smith, Joe Buck, Dan Dierdorf, Hale Irwin, Marc

Bulger. A who's who of St. Louis. It occurred to me that I should punch someone on the shoulder and say, "Hot damn! You see the Wizard of Oz has a locker here?" until it occurred to me that I was with Steve Maritz, and that was his nameplate on the locker right around the corner.

Our drive that morning had taken us from the city into a leafier, hillier Missouri that looked closer to the Ozarks I grew up imagining, where a kid like me could go hunting with his dad and his dogs and never want for a thing in the world. Steve had called the area "wine country." We weren't quite on the same page.

"So what is it, exactly, that your company does?" I asked. He glanced away from the road and over at me, an inscrutable expression on his face. I immediately regretted my question. Was he surprised at my ignorance of what he did? Did he dislike his job? Or was it just that he had hoped to escape that morning, away from his e-mail and onto the golf course with a kid who wouldn't be asking stupid questions about what sort of company he ran? I knew part of the answer to my question. His wife, Jeanne, had e-mailed me after reading the *USA Today* story to say that I was welcome to stay with them. I had done a quick Google search and found his company's site—rife with words like *success, trustworthiness,* and *reliability*. His corporation ran rewards programs, working with other companies to "incentivize loyalty" (a contradiction?).

It was quiet at Boone Valley on this Masters Sunday. Steve and I had the practice range to ourselves as I worked out the stiffness from my night in a real bed. I started with several 8-irons and had worked my way down to the 4-iron when a man and a teenage boy came up behind us.

"Great day for it," the man said.

"Little better'n a kick in the ass, eh?" I'd learned that one in Kansas.

He watched me hit. "Wow. That's a long iron. Say, is that your father down there?" He pointed to Steve. I explained.

"I'm actually not from around here," I added. "This is my first time out, so I'm excited. It's gorgeous, the woods and the water and all this silence."

He agreed. "Where are you from?"

I told him.

"Wait a minute," he said. "I thought I recognized you. You were in the newspaper a few weeks ago, no? You're the kid . . ."

Whoa. This was the first time this had happened to me, a complete stranger knowing who I was. It was weird. And kind of cool. We got to talking—the man was Dan, and he was with his son, Corbin, and they were out-of-state members who drove all the way from Louisville, Kentucky. Corbin, who was sixteen, looked even younger—he was slight with glasses and impeccable manners, and I imagined he might say things like "Golly gee!" or "Jiminy cricket!" when he was upset.

Steve came over to join in on the conversation, extending his hand to Dan.

"Hey. Steve Maritz."

"What is it?"

"Steve. Steve Maritz."

"Oh, Maritz like the . . . ? Oh, wow. My wife used to work for you, when we lived in the area."

"Yeah, we take a lot of pride in being one of St. Louis's largest employers," Steve said. He didn't mean it that way, but I looked at Dan and wondered if he had heard it as I had: *Your wife and I live on different planets.*

It's hard to be the worst player in the group, no matter what. It's hard to be worse at something than your son. It's hard to be vulnerable, period, in front of your kid. It's hard, I was learning, to play golf with a kid that you've read about in the newspaper. And it's hard to play with a guy whose company is big enough that he would have no possible way of knowing that he had employed your wife.

I don't think any of these thoughts entered Steve's mind as he insisted we play from the back tees. Judging from the swing he made on the first tee, Dan, on the other hand, was tangibly aware of all of the above. He waved one into the grass short and right of the fairway, then hurriedly picked up his tee. I couldn't tell if he was feigning indifference or just rushing out of the spotlight.

"Breakfast ball?" Steve called up to him.

"Nah, I'll just drop one up there. Don't wanna hold you guys up."

Corbin, unburdened by the same weights as his father, spent the first few holes absolutely puring the ball. He didn't hit it terribly far for a sixteen-year-old with a 3 handicap, but for the first few holes every shot was dead on line. I couldn't tell if that made things better or worse for his father. Worse, I guessed. Dan lost another ball on the second and another on the fifth, and then did that thing people do when they're self-conscious, insisting we not look for it even though it had barely gone into the woods. This was golf: half the sport is chasing down the stray ball you just hit.

I'd been worried about the dynamic from the first tee shot, but Steve, who was sharing a cart with me, seemed unperturbed. He finally turned to me on the sixth fairway. "He looks a little tight still, huh?"

It's hard to say when things turned around. It might've been on the eighth tee, where I decided my pitching wedge was the correct club and fired three balls in a row into the water to try and prove my point. Maybe it was when we stopped for lunch after nine and got into a discussion about how at night Boone Valley got so still that you could sit on the porch and listen to the fish jump.

Or maybe it was on the back nine, when we decided to play some sort of a four-ball, our cart versus theirs, and Dan and Steve each had six-footers left for par. Dan stepped up first.

"Hey, Dan," Steve murmured. "No need to change that putting stroke now."

Yikes. I thought that one might hit a little too close to home. But Dan looked like he actually enjoyed the ribbing and responded by hitting a firm putt that made a convincing *thud* off the back of the hole and then dropped in. He was elated, gave Corbin a great high five, and turned to watch Steve try to match it.

"Steve," he said eagerly. "Cozy this one up there. Get it real close."

Steve mock-glared at him before he, too, drained his putt. For a moment everyone was happy. Sometimes a foursome is a lot like a relay race—you've got to get everyone to the finish line, and the only way to do that is by making everyone believe that they belong out there. It doesn't always work, especially because any initial failure just makes people less likely to feel comfortable, and bad rounds can turn even worse. But Steve had a way of talking to other people as if they knew as much as he did and were as important as he was, things that were probably not and definitely not true. I don't even know if it was intentional, but Steve really turned on that quality on the back nine. And it saved our foursome. We'd been complete strangers on the range—by the end of the round I'd been invited to come stay at Dan and Corbin's Louisville house.

It may sound as though this would just reinforce their respective positions in the hierarchy of power, Steve in control and Dan learning. But that wasn't really relevant here. Besides, in golf the students almost always make more than the teachers— the pros, the guys who give the lessons—anyway. The power structure of the game is already messed up. So instead of solidifying their positions, with Steve at the top and Dan at the bottom, what happened on the back nine meant something else. Steve was spending his energy trying to make Dan comfortable; the rich guy was worrying whether or not the other guy was having a good time.

Golf is famous for exacerbating class differences. I'd grown up painfully aware of it. But it also has unifying elements: the familiarity of the game, the strokes, and the equipment. Once you leave the trappings of the game behind, it's just you, your foursome, and four hours to explore the strengths and weaknesses of each. All the "other stuff" that people spend their lives worrying about fades to the background. Golf has its own language. At Boone Valley, once we began to focus on the fairways and greens rather than membership and money, the conversation just seemed *normal*. The game kept proving itself to be more democratic than I'd once thought.

CHAPTER 13

The Foursome

There was a hole in my golf bag. It was the same red Sunday carry bag I'd started out with, filled with the same eleven clubs—though fewer golf balls and more Snickers wrappers. A rip had begun to form at the bottom. The tear shouldn't have been surprising, really. I'm prone to walking with my hand on my driver head cover, pressing it into the floor of the bag for hours at a time. My bag had endured hundreds of hours of such abuse, maybe thousands. Still, I was sad to see it this way; my bag was one of the clearest connections I felt to the Dylan who had left Williamstown eight months ago, and as I noticed my 7-iron slip halfway out the bottom, it hit me: I had been away from home a long time.

After you turn right at the Shell station, you'll be driving along a divider. When that ends, you'll see a broken white mailbox on the left side of the road. Turn in there until you come to the chain-link fence. You'll see an intercom. Talk into it.

"Would you freakin' listen to this?" exclaimed Rob as he read aloud the directions he had written down. You'd think we'd found a treasure map. "We could be going to FBI headquarters, y'know? I love it. Oh man, that is so sweet."

We were headed to The Honors Course in Ooltewah, Ten-

191

nessee, and there was something cool about the necessity of *turning right at the Shell station* to do so. It was how we gave directions in small-town New England, on the way to soccer tournaments or ski races or middle-of-the-woods bonfires. Today, though, we were en route to one of the nicest golf tracks in the world.

I had never met Rob before and only vaguely understood the web of connections that had led me to him. Taylor's father's college roommate's brother?

Rob and I had met up at a nearby driving range that afternoon. What little I knew about him I'd learned through his e-mails. He had sent me links to courses and told me that I needed to buy an out-of-print book, Tom Doak's *The Confidential Guide to Golf Courses,* that he figured was around $500 but totally worth it. It didn't seem like a wise purchase, but it tipped me off—he was a golf course nut. He mentioned that he had been a part of Gary Player's course design firm.

With this background, I expected him to dress and look like a slick golf professional. He didn't. Rob was taller than I expected, maybe six four—mostly neck and knees—and just a bit gawky. An old Atlanta Braves hat held a mane of curly brown hair in place, and even though he seemed to have shaved for the occasion, Rob's baggy eyes betrayed the sleepless nights of a new father. His shoes looked too big, had once been white, and now contrasted nicely with his actually white socks. His blue golf shirt had a zipper where buttons should be and kept untucking itself from his khaki shorts.

I was a few minutes late to the range, and I think Rob already had blisters by then; he was so eager to have his game in shape to attack the course. It was probably good I arrived, actually, so I could divert his attention. As I got deeper into my journey, I had begun feeling more confident about my course-design knowledge. I had learned terms like "cape hole" (where the fairway wraps around a body of water, creating a risky diagonal tee shot), and "redan green" (where a deep front bunker guards a right-to-left, downward-sloping green that runs away from the tee box).

But in the face of Rob's barrage of questions about the courses I'd played on—the renovations at Pebble Beach or the landing areas at Sawgrass or the architect at Marquette Golf Club—I felt completely inept. I mentioned a course I had played in Chicago, and he shook his head. "Wow," he murmured. "Legendary cross-bunkering at that joint." Was this guy for real?

Rob maintained this combination: the earnestness of someone who's genuinely interested in the cleverness of a bunker wall, but someone who could speak about it with the twang of a Southern boy and the informality of a college kid. We clicked right away.

Enthusiasm and skill had gotten Rob a job in golf course design, but now he was stuck in limbo. He was looking to get another job in an industry that, like many, was shrinking.

Golf courses don't come and go like houses, don't often get torn down or replaced in favor of new ones. They're big, they're expensive, and they require a certain number of people to play them. In 2008 *nobody* wanted a new golf course.

For me, Rob was the perfect Tennessee contact, a guy who knew the golf and the area alike. For him, I was the perfect guest—and his ticket to the big time. After he'd received my e-mail, he'd gone into overdrive, a blitzkrieg of calls and e-mails, urging anyone and everyone who would listen that I needed to experience The Honors Course (and that he, as my host, needed to as well). Unburdened by teenage uncertainty, he'd sold my story with more earnestness and enthusiasm than I'd been able to muster. And that's how we ended up at The Honors Course. This was Rob's dream—he was from Tennessee, after all, and even in his days designing courses had never set foot on this one.

His point of entry was David Stone, the course superintendent and the third player in our group, whose directions we were now following. We had turned right at the Shell station and driven along the divider until, lo and behold, we spotted the decrepit white mailbox. We turned left into the crumbling driveway and approached the chain-link fence, and the guy on the other end of the intercom did something that made the fence slide away.

Rob and I drove through, the fence closing behind us, and within a minute *everything* changed. At this point in the trip, I didn't get wowed by a golf course very easily—but the transformation in scenery was extraordinary. We'd made it just a few hundred yards from Walmart and Walgreens and strip-mall suburban Chattanooga, but we'd entered a golfing haven that felt a world away. We drove in silence up the driveway, which swerved beneath a canopy of hickories. Huge deciduous trees stood in the fields to the right of the drive, and in the distance they grew denser and the terrain began to rise as the view opened into a set of leafy peaks. I glanced back at the driver's seat and noticed Rob grinning like an eight-year-old about to blow out birthday candles.

The course opened up to our left, but this wasn't just fairways and flagsticks. Meadows buzzed with unseen life, with grasses so thick that it would be hard to find someone who decided to lie flat on the ground, never mind a golf ball. We parked and walked across the practice green as we continued to gaze at the meadows, which meandered down to the edge of a large silver lake. The clubhouse, with simple tin siding and steep beige roofs, had open patio seating and great stone chimneys and was surrounded by trees that seemed to grow from its very foundation. It was a Tennessee farmhouse imagined by Tolkien.

Courtesy of David, this was our playground for the afternoon. I had thought for years that course "superintendent" meant the same thing as it did in middle school—someone who wore a suit and didn't come around too often. Luckily, I had met enough of them by now to know that David's job was nothing if not hands-on. But he seemed in a class of his own, the creator of a masterpiece of golf and nature.

Measured by pure golfing ability, David wouldn't have registered too highly, but as a playing partner he was world-class. A tiny man with a great limp, he wasn't very mobile or long off the tee. But he played fast and he played straight, and he had a neat short game. As for his mobility, well, he found ways around it. David had taken the part of him that needed to run around and explore and he'd given it away, to watch it flourish in another.

Our fourth was a dog—David's dog, Missy.

Seeing Missy, I realized that I'd found someone who could match Rob's pure enthusiasm. Missy had been cooped up in the cart barn all day before she rode with David up to the clubhouse. She sat in the cart, watching our first tee shots. And then she took off into dog heaven, traipsing the meadowlike grasses looking for rats or snapping at clusters of birds on low-lying branches. And then there was Rob, giddy as a puppy, the golf course lover for whom truly great courses were elusive but who now roamed freely at one of the world's very best.

It was a testament to the unique nature of The Honors. David had created a sanctuary, and even if we were just off the city strip, I got the feeling that we were tucked a world away, where the sound track was birdsong and where life seemed to slow down. It definitely passed the dog test, and the Rob test, too.

Rob asked David questions about the underlying "personality" of the course. I was used to people talking about golf courses in hushed tones, like religious sites. But I was taken aback by their vocabulary—the "irritability" of one side of a fairway or the "bipolarity" of a bunker based on a given pin position. It was architecture but also psychology—no, philosophy. *What does it mean to be a golf hole?* Lots of things, apparently. It meant risk and reward, challenging sight lines, and acknowledging traditional course architecture even while interpreting hole designs in a new way. I'd certainly thought about golf holes before. But I'd never thought about paying homage to Bobby Jones's designs or the way a certain type of cape hole was supposed to make a player feel. Rob wondered all these things and guessed at answers as we strode The Honors. And now and then he said nothing at all, knowing that his silence would mean that much more.

The two of them created an infectious atmosphere: *What* they were talking about wasn't particularly important. A lot of the time

I couldn't even understand it. But the *way* that they were talking about it was striking. From bunker placement to green upkeep to general design theory, Rob had all the questions and David had nearly every answer. What was more, I could see pleasure in David's face every time Rob observed a subtle nuance of the course.

We got to the sixth tee and Rob let out a long, low sigh. He didn't need to say anything because I knew what it meant: that this hole was exactly where Rob Collins wanted to be. He was as content as I could imagine a person, gazing out along that remarkable dogleg, temporarily suppressing the instincts of the puppy who wanted to see everything up close.

It was breath-stopping, that sixth hole. The large lake at the core of the course ran all the way down the left side, around to the green. The fairway wrapped alongside the lake, but then, as my eye moved farther right, the ground did something different: It dropped. The lake was the top of the hole and the grass ran away from it, a role reversal, as if nature was momentarily confused and we were the beneficiaries.

"Shit, would you look at that," Rob said, pausing on the tee, almost seeming reluctant to taint the idyllic view with something as coarse as a golf ball.

Golfers always talk about their "dream foursomes," the group they'd pick if they could choose a round with anyone. You weren't really supposed to settle on one group—it was more of an exercise, the arguing about criteria, the combinations of personalities, the matches you could have. I figured Tiger, Phil, and Obama would round out a foursome pretty well. Two righties, two lefties. I would never have guessed that this foursome—an unemployed golf course architect, a short-hitting superintendent, and his wild dog—would be a damn near perfect combination. Golf never failed to surprise me.

Two days later, I was sitting impatiently in a cart, staring expectantly out at the parking lot, waiting for a very different foursome to arrive.

The starter noticed me checking my phone and walked over. "You waiting for someone?" he asked.

"Yeah, three other guys, actually. And we're supposed to tee off in"—I checked my phone again—"one minute. I'm hoping that won't be a problem?"

"Son, there's one thing that's nice about being at this end of this driveway instead of that one," he said, pointing in the direction of the rest of the world. "We don't really *have* problems up here."

I smiled when he said it. It sounded true.

FarmLinks would have passed the dog test, too. I'd made it to rural Alabama, quiet, slow, open Alabama. We were an hour southeast of Birmingham, in the land of the firefly and the cicada, governed by God. Psalm 111 adorned a large rock on the edge of the driveway (Great are the works of the Lord/He has made wonders to be remembered), suggesting to visitors that this would be an otherworldly experience. It wasn't far off—this was just about the finest golf that rural Alabama would have to offer. A pair of rocking chairs sat on the front porch of what was essentially a farmhouse. I could imagine a pair of old-timers in straw hats and overalls seated in them, watching in contented silence as the world meandered by.

The guys I was waiting for were a group perfectly suited to disrupt the serenity of the place. Andy had written to me after reading the *USA Today* piece, offering up an Alabama round with his buddies Scott and Sean.

"You wanna know why we wanted to play with you?" Sean asked on the fourth hole, once we'd settled into the round. "Because you're not doing this for charity."

Scott started laughing. "That's a good sound bite there, man."

"I'm kidding. Actually, no, I'm really not. Most stories like yours, people trying to travel and do something cool, they've got some agenda, some BS to take other people's money and pat themselves on the back. Y'know? And here you are, just a kid out on his own, doing this for you. Awesome."

I'd never been complimented for not giving to charity before. But this was a very different round than what I'd gotten used to. Andy, Scott, and Sean were best buddies in their thirties, normal fun-loving guys who worked in sales and real estate, guys who had enough free time at their jobs to unleash a full afternoon's worth of hilarious trash talk over e-mail the day before. They respected my trip by ridiculing every part of it. Playing with these guys was like playing with older versions of my own friends. They became so instantly familiar and ridiculous. They wanted to hear everything about the journey while making fun of it every step of the way. It was refreshing.

"Where'd you stay last night?" Andy asked.

"Uhh, a parking lot, I guess. In the back of my car."

"Oh, nice. Hear that, Hays? Kid slept in a parking lot last night."

Scott shrugged. "Oops. Sorry man. They asked if you wanted to stay in one of the cottages here but I told 'em you'd probably rather be on your own."

I grinned. I liked Scott's attitude—and he may have been right. Rolling over to go to sleep in Subi had grown pretty comforting. Humans are so adaptable. "No worries. I had Wi-Fi, anyway. I was fine."

"Wi-Fi? What parking lot is this?"

"I was at the Holiday Inn in Sylacauga."

Sean chimed in. "No fucking *way*! I used to date a girl from Sylacauga. Think I mighta lost my virginity right where you spent the night."

Everyone was cracking up now. "In the hotel? Or in the parking lot?"

"What was I, a damn Alabaman teenage entrepreneur made of money? The parking lot. Dark and convenient. Same reason you chose it, I'm sure."

It was a hot bluebird day, and we played slowly, examining each shot, particularly those shots key to our match, Sean and me versus the other two. Nobody was quicker with a one-liner than

Sean, particularly at the expense of his own game. His swing started and finished powerfully, but somewhere in the transition his hands got so far out in front of the club that he spent most of the day hitting pop-slice tee shots down the left side.

"Oh, the things I would do for that ball flight," he said after I hit a nice sweeping draw. "Dirty things. Unspeakable things."

The vodka came out on about the fourth hole, or about eleven A.M., just as the sun was beginning to get hot. This didn't change things immediately—but as the day wore on and the vodka-and-Gatorades started flowing, things grew more absurd. The stories started to flow along with the booze.

They particularly liked the fact that I slept with an ax.

"Now when you say *ax*, are we talking, like, a full-on maul?" Scott asked as we began the back nine.

"Can't be that," Sean countered. "No good in close quarters. You need something lighter, with some versatility."

"Don't worry, it's pretty small for an ax," I reassured him. "Good swing weight."

Scott started laughing again. "I still don't know what I would do if I was walking through a parking lot at night and saw some kid sitting up in the trunk of his car holding a freakin' ax."

"Good point," Sean returned. "Hey, Dylan, remind me to not give you my business card or home address."

"Speaking of swinging axes," Scott continued, pointing at the woods. "Andy, what're you doing in there? We're watching you! You drop a ball without telling us, you're sleeping in the Subaru tonight."

Andy spent a lot of time in the woods as the afternoon wore on—peeing, searching for his ball, punching out to safety. The sun and the alcohol and the high-octane conversation began to take a toll on his attention span and his energy as the day wore on. Needless to say, they were losing the match. Andy got to the fourteenth green and sat down in a small patch of shade as we putted out.

"Do you have any idea how long I could sleep here right

now?" he asked. "Y'all could play another round and wake me up when you got back to this green."

We each put tee shots into the water on the next hole—effectively ending the competition. It didn't really matter.

"I don't need any details," Scott began as we got to the final hole. "But tell me that you've met some Midwest girls, girls from the farm, y'know, wearing plaid and overalls or something, cute as could be. Tell me you've gotten to know some of those."

"Not enough who fit that description," I laughed back. "But yeah, I've got you covered. Just know that they're out there."

I loved the round: It was fulfilling, memorable, hilarious. These were the kinds of friends I hoped I'd have, the sorts of rounds I hoped to play for years to come.

"Thanks for getting us out," Scott told me. "We've been meaning to try this track for years—now we finally get to, and for free? We owe you big-time."

The gratitude reminded me exactly of what Rob had said as we drove from The Honors. Both rounds had been a blast, but so different—this round had been rollicking, Rob's reverential. The Alabama boys weren't so concerned with the *philosophy* of the golf course. They were concerned with playing golf, with ribbing their friends, and keeping a good match going.

But then, of course that was a philosophy of golf, too. It was just a different version. And as I considered it, I wasn't sure which I'd liked better, the foursome on the elite private course with the golf course experts in Tennessee or the trash talk and laughter of the Birmingham boys at FarmLinks. There's more than one way to make par, and there's more than one way to look at the game. I was damn glad that I'd experienced both of these ways.

"Oh, man." Andy was smiling. "That was the most fun I've had since the last time I played golf. C'mon, let's go get a picture with the hatchet."

CHAPTER 14

Walking with Phil

I t was just the two of us sitting on the tee box, and Phil Mickelson looked like he was about to lose his lunch.

This isn't the first time someone has said this about Lefty. He is the second-best player of his generation, but the way he plays serves as a constant reminder not of how good a second he is, but of just how far he is behind number one. He's had an affinity for near misses, for failing to win the big one, for putting three-footers as if he were using one of those trick balls that's half sand and rolls crooked. And he also has the look.

I thought I recognized the look from the eighteenth hole at the 2006 U.S. Open at Winged Foot. He needed par to win, bogey to force a playoff, and I remember watching TV in my basement as he sliced driver left of everything—over the crowd, through the trees, and finally down next to a hospitality tent. He bounced his next one off a tree and plugged his third in a bunker, and then came the look. It was the look of a man who was feeling something come out the wrong way.

His post-double-bogey meltdown interview was even more difficult to watch than the collapse itself. *"I—I still am . . . in shock that I did that. I just—I just can't believe that I did that. I am, ah, such an idiot."* I was a merciless fourteen-year-old Tiger fan who had been rooting for that exact sequence of events, yet even I found myself squirming at just how profoundly Phil seemed to have lost his way. At its most cruel, professional golf leaves you wholly and completely exposed. There are no teammates to hide behind, no bad referees to blame. Here was a player who, instead of making a case for himself as the best player in the whole freakin' world, was reduced to blurting out word vomit.

Now, four years later, here I was, sitting next to Phil at the Quail Hollow Championship. But this time the vomit was no metaphor. The group in front of us had slowed to a near halt, and the rest of our group was still by the previous green, talking to fans and officials. So we waited: me, standing, and Phil, slumped down on a drink cooler, head in his hands.

The PGA Tour's pro-ams are charity exhibitions, glorified practice rounds, and they're also part of what separates golf from the rest of the sports world for fans. Typically held on the Wednesdays before a tournament begins, the events pair one pro with several amateurs, and fifty-some groups compete in a form of best ball. Big Lakers fans don't get to go shoot around with Kobe Bryant, and deep-pocketed Red Sox fans don't get a spot in the rotation during batting practice. But for a few thousand dollars, golf fanatics can enter a pro-am and get the chance to pick the brains of the guys at the top, guys who *have* to be there whether they like it or not, just to be eligible to play in the weekend's event.

We were on the fifth tee of the Quail Hollow Championship's pro-am in Charlotte, North Carolina. It was a Carolina-blue spring day and I was caddying for Tim Belk, who was the CEO of the largest privately owned department store chain in the country and, more important, a 22-handicap with a bit of a slicing problem. His daughter Katherine had become friends with my brother Evan, so when word of my trip traveled from Ev to her to her father, he sent me an e-mail with the generous offer to carry his bag in the event. Tim was one of Charlotte's premier business figures and Belk was a big sponsor, but the "draft" at the preparty the night before played no favorites. There was no guarantee where our pick would fall. There was also nothing fake about his excitement when he called me on the way back.

I was just hoping that we got someone I had heard of—a tour regular, a journeyman, the kind of guy whose name fell midway on the leaderboard. Still, part of me held out for someone special—Tim had said that Fred Couples was taken (nabbed by Michael Jordan), but nearly everyone else was available. "Guess who we got?" Tim asked me from the other end of the line, the excitement thinly masked in his voice. I had a suspicion from the way he said it, but I didn't want to guess too optimistically. "I'll give you a hint," he told me. "His initials are P.M."

Hot damn. This raised the stakes immediately, and I was stoked. Phil was endlessly intriguing, a guy I'd watched for hundreds of hours, whom I'd rooted for and against, whose game I'd analyzed thoroughly. The rumors about him were wild, too—how he'd reportedly racked up millions of dollars of gambling debt and had to switch to Callaway just so that the company would pay them off. Gambling Phil was a hard image to reconcile with the guy with the J. Crew–catalog family that swarmed the eighteenth whenever he won a tournament. Who was the real Phil Mickelson? Was I about to find out?

In this tournament format, two amateurs were paired with one pro in a best-ball game, the amateurs getting strokes based on their handicaps. (Tim's 22 meant he got one stroke off on fourteen holes and two strokes off on the four hardest ones.) This worked out well for the pros, who seemed to tolerate these events in a good-natured way (and preferred the Quail Hollow threesomes to the foursomes they usually had to deal with). I thought they seemed fun to play from either end: The pros got a chance to host some of the folks responsible for keeping them on top—they surely garner any number of small favors from playing with the rich and successful—and to raise money for charity without it coming out of their pockets. Tim's friend and business associate Bruce Rockowitz, who was in from Hong Kong for the day, rounded out our group.

I had gone to the practice round the day before, parking miles away and riding the shuttle to the course with a horde of other fans. I had never been to a practice round before. Several thousand fans were there with me but milled around the gift shop, driving range, and the few holes close to the clubhouse. Since I was scouting out the course (and the competition) for the next day, I walked the entirety of the layout, and on the far reaches of the course, few spectators competed for space. The contrast in practice-round styles was fascinating. Several players, Vijay Singh among them, went out with just their caddies, discussing shot shapes and landing areas meticulously hole to hole, shot to shot, before taking any physical action. Others played in foursomes, exchanging genial trash talk. All players—no matter whether alone or in groups—would each drop several balls in different places around the green and would chip and putt, rapid-fire style, to get a feel for how the surfaces would react. I watched as Alex Cejka hit several quick sand shots on the ninth before hopping out to look over a flop shot much more carefully from the rough. He studied it from both sides, walked down to the green's edge to check out the slope and the break, and moved back up the hill, where he started taking practice swings.

"What's that all about?" an official asked him, looking on.

"I've got a match going," Cejka replied, grinning. "Two bucks down the drain if I don't hole out here." This from a guy with $10 million in career prize money. He lipped out the chip.

It was a cool look into the world of being a tour pro, the practice and focus it takes but also, well, how much damn fun it would be. They were casual and yet attentive, nonchalant but focused. What would this life be like day in, day out?

Maybe I already knew. After all, I spent my days traveling across the country playing golf—how many people could say that besides these guys? They walked many of the same courses, they knew the same cities, they knew about traveling to play where the warm weather would allow. I had the same calluses they did, the same aches and pains, the same scared feeling that my game would leave one day and never come back.

I had Subi; they had the Ritz-Carlton.

It was strange watching them. Why were they here anyway? Was it because they loved golf? Or was it because we were here watching them—paying to see them play, studying their every move, cheering because they could do things we spectators never could—and making them rich by doing so? Even if they had started off with a pure love of golf, surely the idea of netting a million dollars for a week's work would go to their heads. I thought of the guys I'd been playing with all year, and I thought about these guys I was watching now. We may have had some surface-level similarities, me and Vijay and Cejka and Charles Howell III. But I guessed that for many of these pros, the reason for playing the game was far different from mine. I was here for adventure. For many of these guys, it was just money—either to make millions or even tens of millions, or, for the ones without a boldfaced name, to eke out a comfortable living.

The pro-am was thus a fascinating cross section of players. There were the guys who loved the game so much that they'd pay thousands to play, paired with the guys who got paid so much to play that they may have forgotten what it meant to love the game. So it was strange that Wednesday as Tim (we'd long since dispensed with "Mr. Belk") and I drove in through two security checkpoints and one special gate. My instinct was to fear these types of gates, to turn back when I saw them. I didn't associate with the kind of people who would be waved through. But now we *were* the event, and a few minutes later we were pulling up to the clubhouse itself, where a valet service was waiting to take the car. Tim went into the locker room while I took his clubs around to a waiting area for caddies and players, and it hit me just how surreal all of this was.

I passed Australian star Adam Scott on the stairs and made eye contact; he seemed to recognize my facial expression—shy recognition?—and smirked. "What's up, man?" he offered as he passed. I glanced around, recognizing more players. Charles Howell III standing in the corner chatting with a security guard. Camilo Villegas walking from the locker room with his caddie. Chad Campbell munching on an apple from the hospitality table. It was bizarre.

This same strange feeling persisted as we moved to the driving range, which was overrun with people battling for spots on the tee. Pros were lined up on the left side, amateurs on the right. We ended up in the middle, next to pro Charley Hoffman and his caddie. Even Hoffman, a veteran who has never been one of the best in the world, was wild to watch on the range. He hit the ball impossibly high and far, with a swing of impeccable rhythm and surprising strength—especially for a guy with a blond ponytail. Every swing was made with intent, sculpting out a shot shape before he stepped up and then an evaluation as he admired or belittled the result afterward. In contrast, the amateurs were of all shapes and sizes and hit the ball in every direction. Some barely made contact at all.

Each time a notable figure emerged onto the tee, the murmur of the crowd swelled. The chatter grew loudest when Fred Couples arrived with his playing partner for the day. Freddy, a fan favorite, would always get a good reaction, but in this case he was accompanied by Michael Jordan—a superhuman presence.

As chaotic as the range was, when we switched to the chipping area things got infinitely worse. Balls whizzed from the sand and the rough in the vague direction of the greens, and I kept expecting someone to get clocked as I absentmindedly brushed down Tim's clubs. Tim hit a couple short chips to the adjacent green before requesting the sand wedge. I saw him turn and take aim at the next green over, some thirty-five yards away, with a pin tucked tight beyond a bunker. Several layers of people stood between us and the hole. It would've been an ambitious shot for a pro to hit; people were moving around so much, and any of them would've given Tim twenty-five shots a round. I cringed but didn't say anything. I couldn't. I was the caddie, the guest. His first attempt was pretty good, actually—the ball hit just over the bunker and ran out to somewhere near the hole. But he skulled the next one, which dove on a line past the left knee of Charles Howell III before skittering into the sand.

"Hey, boss," a voice said from behind us. "Not sure that one looks like a good idea. Gonna hurt someone, yeah?" I turned. It was Alex Cejka. I couldn't tell if Tim heard him, but he switched back to the closer green, playing a series of safer pitch-and-runs. Cejka's next swing, meanwhile, sent a high flop to the far green. "Oh, shit," he exclaimed. "Fore!" But it was too crowded for any warning to be effective, and the ball collided squarely with the back of a caddie who had just wandered onto the green to collect balls. The caddie scuttled off the green, looking more embarrassed than hurt. "Guess I should mind my own business, eh?" Cejka said to his own caddie.

After lunch in the clubhouse, we moved onto the putting green for the last few minutes of practice before our tee time. As Tim practiced a short left-to-righter, I noticed that a large group of people had moved into the area from the eighteenth green, enveloping the gated putting area six, seven, eight people deep. The cause of all the commotion soon became clear. A wave of excitement ran through the crowd. Heads turned toward the walkway by the eighteenth hole and a figure in fluorescent green. Tiger Woods walked into the clubhouse from the back steps, having just finished his round. It was so surreal, his being *right there,* the man responsible for so much in my golf life—for my even having a golf life. The real reason I was standing here now.

There are two Tiger Woods posters hanging in my room at home. In one, he has just hit an iron and is holding his follow-through, posing as he glowers at the ball, willing it toward the flag. In the other he is in the midst of a signature fist pump—a violent uppercut that's nearly too much for golf's collective high blood pressure to handle—following a particularly meaningful hole-out.

These two images, one of determination, the other of elation, represent all I really ever wanted from Tiger. But it took me a long time to realize that. It had taken me the past few months, at least. Something in me would never recover from the fall that Tiger had taken from the top of the world to the very bottom, revered and idolized to derided and loathed. I just wanted it all to go away.

Tiger had always held an appearance of complete control off the course and took great pains to build up a careful image. He had his gorgeous wife, Elin, who played the role of enthusiastic mother to their pair of genetically flawless children and who, like her husband, never said anything controversial—or really anything at all. He had the house in the gated community and the big boat called *Privacy* and the reputation of just wanting to live his own life. He had his Tiger Foundation and learning center, which he claimed meant more to him than anything else in the world. And he had a work ethic and training regimen that bordered on ludicrous, the lifestyle that proved to everyone just how badly this guy wanted to win.

Any holes in that image I was more than happy to fill in on Tiger's behalf. *He doesn't act overly friendly to a lot of fans because he's such a private person. He really values his privacy.* Or, *He shows his temper more than anyone else on the course because he cares the most. That's part of what makes him such a great player.* These excuses had elements of truth, but so did the dimmer view that Tiger was a bitter kid with little respect for the game and no appreciation for his fans. But I never would have admitted anything of the sort.

When messy details had started coming out about Tiger just after Thanksgiving (I was in California), starting with his fishy car accident and continuing with tabloid allegations of infidelity, I naturally reverted to stick-up-for-Tiger mode. *Of course they would say that, it's the* National Enquirer. And, *This girl's just trying to get her fifteen minutes; it'll all blow over in a couple days.* And although both those thoughts were true, it didn't blow over in a couple days. It got worse and worse until everything came to a head, an insurmountable wave of proof.

Tiger had made golf cool. He made it high stakes. Hit a good shot, fist pump. A bad shot? A quick, sharp cussword and a slam of the club—at least. It made for compelling television and even more compelling attempts at emulation. Like countless other kids, I was awed by just how dynamic he had made this slow-paced game.

It broke my heart, thinking about Tiger. He had been larger than life, with unparalleled success on the course and a fault-free existence off of it. Not only had this been a lie, but the entire basis for my interest in the game felt like a lie too. What was I supposed to stand on? "Should he apologize to the public?" radio hosts pondered. "Does he really owe them an apology?" *Maybe he doesn't* owe *anyone anything,* I thought. *But jeez, I* want *an apology.*

I snapped out of my mind and back to my spot at the edge of the putting green. The crowd had swollen to its largest size yet, with folks ringed around the practice area and adjoining first tee, waiting for the 1:07 tee time. Our tee time. Tiger's crowd was still there, too, and they'd become Phil's crowd. This was a significant transition for them, though. Rooting for Tiger had always been like rooting for a chainsaw—ruthless, efficient, and likely to win. But if Tiger was revered, Phil was beloved, because being a Phil fan was more like rooting for a cheerleading squad— there could be high-flying success or there could be spectacular failure, and either way there was a good chance people would be crying at the end.

Phil walked down the stairs from the players' locker room and onto the edge of the putting green. Everyone was ready. He led the way, daughters and dads alike shouting and reaching from the edge of the ropes. Tim picked up his Nike ball from the bottom of the cup and followed him through the throng and onto the first tee.

That's when it really hit me, the feeling of being inside the ropes. The entire first hole was lined with fans several rows deep—twenty or thirty deep by the tee box—and on the tee were Phil and his caddie, Bones; Bruce and his caddie, Buzz; and Tim and me. That was it. We were so exposed. I felt a tightness rising in my chest, and I hoped my nerves wouldn't get the better of me.

But then I realized. *Wait, Dyl, you're not doing anything hard.* I was carrying a bag and saying helpful things like "straight's good here," or "this putt should be pretty fast." There was zero pressure. I strode over to the refreshments tent to the right of the tee and emerged, taking a big, confident bite out of a fresh apple. This was so cool.

Phil striped one about 330 yards down the center, a powerful cut with a slight left-to-right draw, and smiled to the crowd, which was frothing at its collective mouth. But then it was Tim's turn. "Nice and easy," I told him as I uncovered his driver, fearing the worst. He had a decent swing, actually. But a decent swing isn't damn near good enough when all the feeling in your body is gone.

Only part of the crowd was paying attention by this point; the rest were busy clamoring annoyingly, as they would all day, for Phil's autograph, or wondering where they could buy a four-dollar water. *Good, talk amongst yourselves,* I thought, glad that Tim wouldn't be subject to the same wait-wait-wait-scream scrutiny as his playing partner. But then I picked up on a thread of conversation from the semidistracted throngs.

"You hear about Boo Weekley's partner this morning?" a kid my age asked his friends. "This guy steps up over the ball on the first and whiffs. Totally missed it. The ball didn't get off the tee. Looked like such a *loser*. It was hilarious."

Yikes. Now I was a little more nervous. Who knew that the fans of my-upset-face-is-still-a-smile Phil would be such sharks? I hoped Tim didn't hear. I don't think he did, because he was already standing over the ball. *Make contact. Make contact.*

Tim did, and even got the ball off the ground, but only in a line-drive-to-the-shortstop kind of way that bounded into the gallery on the left. Oh well. Bruce, president of the mysteriously named Li & Fung Limited, had mentioned at lunch how golf was the only thing that could still make him nervous. But he managed a low cut that found fairway, generating polite applause (and some teenage disappointment). And we were off.

The format we were playing was a forgiving "par is your partner" style, where there was essentially an invisible fourth player in each group who made par every hole. This meant that the pros didn't need to worry about tapping in for par and the amateurs could pick up (and were encouraged to) if a particular hole was carrying on a little long. We took advantage of this on the first two holes. On the first hole Tim went from the left crowd to the right woods to his pocket. On the par-3 second hole, both he and Bruce threatened the lives of several patrons off the right side and struggled to what could've been a pair of big numbers.

As he got to the second tee, Phil was swarmed by a group of kids from The First Tee, a program that focuses on teaching good morals and character lessons through the game of golf. Some shied away, but a bold group of four youngsters attached themselves to him on his way down the hole, badgering him with questions. One girl took his bag from Bones and dragged it down the hole. Luckily it was a par-3, as the bag was just as tall and nearly as heavy as the poor girl. He sidled up next to her. "I've been thinking about getting rid of Bones anyway," he whispered, with a hint of mischief. "You good at reading putts?"

We had spent so much time in the woods on the first two holes that it wasn't until the third tee that I officially met the man. He had hit his tee shot and continued up to the amateur tee box, where we waited for a crowd to clear before Bruce could hit. "Hey, Phil," I said, extending my hand. "I'm Dylan, I'm caddying for Mr. Belk." He tugged off his glove and returned the handshake and said it was a pleasure to meet me. "Are you Mr. Belk's son?" he asked. No, I told him, and explained briefly what I was doing. "Oh, that's cool," he said with the enthusiasm he might've evinced if his straw changed from purple to green at Friendly's. This didn't really surprise me; I figured everyone who meets Phil wants to tell him something about themselves and, after a while, it would be hard to really *listen* to each thing. (Not *that* hard, but whatever.)

Everyone had kept their drives in the fairway, so for once the group walked together down the center. Tim asked Phil if I had told him what I was doing.

"Yeah, a little," Phil replied. "So what're the states that are hard to play in? Can you play golf in, like, South Dakota?"

It struck me as a particularly stupid question for a professional golfer to ask, someone who traveled the country playing as his *job*. C'mon. There was golf everywhere. He knew that. I told him briefly about playing the Dakotas, the West, the appeal of the evening round in the middle of nowhere. We had slowed, Phil and I, walking behind the others now. I had caught his attention.

"Wait a minute," he said, really looking at me for the first time. "Who are you doing this with?"

"Just me," I said. "Big solo road trip."

"Just you? Wow." He grinned, then shook his head slightly. "That's really impressive. I'm not sure I could do that."

Tim's mediocre start may have taken the pressure off by the time we got to this third hole, where he bounded a low iron shot from the left side of the fairway up onto the green that settled about ten feet above the hole. He smiled at me and gave a relieved little wave to the crowd.

I realized as I approached the green that this was my first big moment. I crouched over the birdie putt and I felt Phil, who had a longer putt from the back of the green, approach behind me. "What do you think?" I asked over my shoulder.

He walked away, toward his ball, leaving me with a subtle smile, letting me know that this wasn't up to him. "What do *you* think?"

I saw it a cup outside left, and fast. Tim agreed, and proceeded to pull it at least twice that far outside. It tracked right into the center of the hole: a birdie and a net eagle.

"Great putt!" Phil called out, coming over for a high five. A little forced, but nice. "Good read, caddie."

Walking with Phil was like following the Wave around Fenway. Noise and attention and people all swelled as he passed, drawn to him like some sort of audiovisual magnet. They lined the roped-off walkways to try and get an autograph, a fist bump, anything. Hell, kids were asking for *my* autograph. "If you want," I told one kid, grinning as I scribbled something onto his hat. "But I don't think you do . . ."

Cheers of "Go get 'em, Lefty!" and "Nice win at the Masters, Phil!" and "You da man!" trailed us. Walking from the fourth green to the fifth tee, kids continued to plead with Phil for his autograph, and again and again he patiently replied, "Sorry guys, I can't sign now, I'll sign after the round, after the eighteenth." Again and again and again. He tried to respond to every compliment, too, turning to say, "Thanks, man," to well-wishers. Several teenage guys stuck their fists out to get one of his signature fist bumps. One connected and immediately turned back to his buddies in amazement, as if to say, "You see that? You see what happened there?" And on it went relentlessly. Say what you want about the guy: He was patient.

"Jeez," I said to him as we made it onto the fourth tee, a moment of respite. "It's tough being Phil Mickelson." He thought about that for a second. "Yeah," he agreed. "But it's a pretty good thing." Hard to argue with.

I had noticed him grimacing a couple times, like there was a rock stuck in one of his alligator-skin shoes. And then I noticed he was getting quieter, more withdrawn. He was having several low, serious conversations with Bones. And he walked briskly from the fourth green to the fifth tee, ahead of everyone, and for some reason only I had followed.

So that's how, after eight months and about thirty-one thousand miles, I came to be sitting on a tee box with Phil Mickelson, watching him put his head in his hands.

"I feel like I'm going to explode from one end or the other," he said aloud.

Phil birdied the fifth and headed quickly to the hospitality tent nearby. We waited, unsure. Would someone replace him? Bones mentioned that he'd be interested. For a moment I thought maybe I'd get to play the back tees. I was bummed, but it was weirdly cool knowing that I could see the tent where Phil was ralphing.

As we stood on the sixth tee, Rory McIlroy's group caught up. Rory, a rosy-cheeked twenty-year-old Northern Irishman and golf's biggest rising star, was signing a few autographs. Arriving late to the tee box, he was surprised to find us still there. His group was in conversation with Tim and Bruce, so he turned to me. "What's up? You guys are still waiting?" I explained the situation and turned to the rest of the group to consult. "What's the deal? Are we letting them through?"

Nobody knew—not the players or the marshals or the officials on the tee. Rory took charge. "Okay. We'll just come on through then." It wasn't much, but it was a moment that stuck out to me. *This kid has it all in control, the whole situation.* And so that part of the day was over as quickly as it had begun. Once Rory passed through, our following thinned. Jonathan Byrd, a cheerful pro from South Carolina, replaced Phil—but our time in the spotlight was through.

Rory's wasn't. He just made the cut on Friday, shot six under Saturday, and put up a ludicrous final round of ten-under 62 to win the tournament by five shots. Second place? Phil Mickelson.

I sat outside the Belks' house that evening, staring into the sprawling garden. I had promised Mrs. Belk that I would help Louisa, their eleven-year-old daughter, with her geography quiz, but it hadn't taken Weezy long to convince me to play Mario Kart instead. Eventually she went to bed and I went to the back patio to think.

Whether its players played for love or for money, the PGA Tour was so cool. The pros got to travel everywhere and play with their friends in front of enthusiastic galleries. I loved the idea of playing for your salary—what other job rewarded success and punished failure so fairly? There were real pressures: make putts to make cuts, to stay in the top 125, to make it back onto the Tour the next year.

The relationships seemed real, too. Play with your friends on Tuesday, make some new ones on Wednesday, and go to work on Thursday—playing golf. It was every man's dream. Plus, they had figured out how to play the game and make *other* people happy. And they got to do it every week.

But something Phil had said on the walk to the fourth hole still stuck with me. "Gosh," he'd said. "Y'know, I wish I could do something like what you're doing."

I could've dismissed it as a throwaway line. But he had said it unprompted, in a second of silence as we walked together. What's more, everyone had been saying that. I wondered what it was. He had found success in just about every measurable way. He had lots of money, a beautiful wife and smiley kids, and his work was playing a game—which only a handful of men had ever played more successfully than he did. He *was* happy. He should've been. Nearly everyone would take his life.

What was it about youth that made people so green with envy? Everyone pursues the kind of success Phil has. But he seemed to wish for a little of what I had, too. Freedom. Possibility. He could buy anything. Go anywhere. But his pursuits involved winning golf tournaments. That was exciting and fun, but it was also a reminder that as we grow, our pursuits shrink. Not literally— Phil's pursuits involved millions of dollars and millions of fans, and he certainly wielded more influence than most. More than me, that was for sure. But he knew just about how his days would end, whether he won or finished last. That was what I figured he meant when he said he was jealous of me. He was already Phil Mickelson. Dylan Dethier could still be whomever he wanted.

My day hadn't been quite finished when we walked off eighteen. I had been in touch with someone from the PGA Tour who had said I should come up after the round to the media tent. It was now pretty late, and the big names—Tiger, Phil, Anthony Kim, and pretty much everyone else—were off the course, and the media was mostly gone. The remainder seemed to be focused on NASCAR driver Jimmie Johnson, paired with Davis Love III in the group behind us—but I figured I would go check out the setup anyway. I dropped off Tim's clubs in the holding area as he went into the locker room and went in search of the tent, tucked back in a corner of the property.

The path to the media center cut through the players' parking lot, and I entered from one corner, peering at the crisp white spaces, half of which were empty in the early evening. I was the only person in the lot, I thought as I walked in the direction of a jet-black Mercedes. As I neared, though, I noticed that I wasn't alone. A man was bent over his car, putting something in the backseat. He straightened up for a second. Oh. A large man, with an unmistakable shiny bald head. His Airness, Michael Jordan.

I had to say something. My buddy Than would've killed me if I didn't. *I* would've killed me. But what were you supposed to say to the guy?

"Hey, Michael," I called over, my voice only half cracking as I paused even with his car. "How'd it go today?" He raised his large, polished head to catch my eye for just a moment before reaching back into his car. "Oh, you know," he said. "Pretty much the same way it always goes, I guess."

Yeah, I thought to myself. *For you, maybe.*

CHAPTER 15

Spoiled

"**S**ome days it just seems so easy and then some days you can just barely hit the ball, y'know what I mean?"

I didn't know what he meant. I had always been able to hit the ball. Hitting the ball was easy. Sticking it close? Going low? That was hard. Vincent, it seemed, just sucked at golf.

Where was this snark coming from?

Get it together, Dylan, I told myself. *You're a guest here.*

I gave a knowing shake of my head. "Totally. Crazy game."

I couldn't completely shake my irritation. For most of the morning I had watched Vincent, a sixty-five-year-old semi-retiree who'd spent his career in the finance sector in D.C., bumble around in the right rough. I hadn't known Vincent beforehand, but I'd been put in contact with the head pro at this starchy northern Maryland country club, and Vincent had agreed to serve as my host.

And we were playing completely different games. It was eighty-five degrees and my entire body felt loose, and I had been bombing the ball over trees and past corners and hitting it once for every three shots of his. His driver maxed out at about 150 yards and never got more than about fifteen feet off the ground in a predictable boomerang slice.

In the cart between shots, the disparity in our game had created an inevitable awkwardness. Was I allowed to vent my frustration when a bad drive had gone more than a hundred yards farther than his? Was he allowed to be happy that he got the ball airborne? It requires a certain lack of self-awareness to play seriously with someone so much better or worse than you are, and if he was unaware, then I was hyperaware, because his every move hurt to watch. Just the way he drew the club away from the ball looked painful, like he was dragging a net through a frog pond. And by the time he got to impact, it felt like a miracle that he was still vertical.

Why did I feel I was entitled to something better? What was wrong with me? I was playing a nice, old, well-maintained course with a successful, well-traveled guy who had taken an interest in showing me around. Every golfer is used to playing with people much worse than him—you root for them, and you encourage them, and you deal with it. What was wrong with me?

I had zigzagged my way up the East Coast for the past month, playing the best country clubs in each state—Tennessee and Georgia and up, through the Carolinas and the Virginias and into the mid-Atlantic region. I hit major championship courses, regular tour stops, East Lake and Valhalla and the Greenbriar and the Country Club of Virginia and TPC this and that, with plenty of other invitations that I no longer had time to accept. Being featured in *USA Today* had helped plant a seed, and now word had spread—from newspaper readers, from the guys at the Tour headquarters, from the Williams alumni network, and from each set of hosts to their friends. I'd gone from guiltily shelling out twelve dollars for cheap municipals to being treated to the crème de la crème as a special guest. As a result I'd gotten to know a lot of older guys, mostly good ones, who were successful in life and strove to be successful on the course. They were friendly, helpful, and welcoming. And they owned houses with guest rooms. Subi had started spending nights alone.

I had grown comfortable at places like this—suburban country clubs where your shorts had to extend to the top of the knee but couldn't extend any further, where you'd *better* not enter the dining room after six without a jacket on, where any sign of denim would get you expelled from the premises.

That day with Vincent, I didn't feel especially lucky or privileged—more like I was being deprived of something that was rightfully mine. How dare this man ruin the round of golf he had set up and paid for? That's what I couldn't help but think again as we stepped to the fifteenth tee and gazed out at a 530-yard par-5 with sand down the left that guarded a slight dogleg.

I looked down by the green, where a careless collection of bunkers served as protection before a narrow opening to the putting surface. It was a great hole, rewarding aggression off the tee while punishing poor execution, the way any good risk-reward par-5 should. Driver and then a cut 3-wood, I thought, or a 4-iron if I really crushed it. I looked at Vincent. Getting to the green in three was a pipe dream, even from the up tees.

He had offered a meal and a bed, but somewhere early on the back nine I had decided I wasn't going to stay with Vincent. I told him I had to get to New Jersey by the next morning, where I had an early tee time.

I didn't have an early tee time and I wasn't going to New Jersey. But I was tired, and I was lonely. I think I just wanted to go home—but since I couldn't go there, sitting in the sun for a while before retreating to Subi sounded better than putting on my houseguest face for another one-night stay. I felt bad saying no—but then I could picture how the night would go. At dinner we'd review the afternoon's events with Vincent and his wife, where he would be complimentary and self-deprecating and I would get to pretend that I wasn't that good and he didn't suck that bad. Then his wife would agree with me that he must have done *great* because golf wives married *successful* men and could never believe that their husbands could spend so much time doing something and just be bad at it. I knew I was being an ungrateful teenager—I wasn't proud of that.

• • •

I assumed that the Arnold Palmer I had originally ordered must have been free, or close enough, because I sat outside the clubhouse all afternoon sucking down lemonade and iced tea in equal proportion, doodling a schedule on my napkin but expending most of my energy on keeping my feet up on the chair in front of me as the sun started to creep beneath the shade of the umbrella above.

The napkin schedule would have impressed any course guru. I had five top-hundred courses lined up for the next ten days, including meccas Merion and Oak Hill just two days apart. And those five didn't even include Wilmington Country Club, the pride of Delaware, or the implied possibility in an e-mail I had just received from a recent host with the subject line "Pine Valley??"—a course that, if you had told me about the offer eight months earlier (after explaining first what Pine Valley was), I would've said I had less a chance of playing than getting a private tour of the White House.

Pine Valley was *the* country club. To get there, I had heard, you drove for a while through an old water park, a good nighttime site for a horror movie. Then, once you got past the edge of the park, you turned right on a small dirt road, which you took to the dead end, but then you continued through a turnaround area and past a railroad crossing sign, and then you turned again—and *then* you saw the gate. Beyond the gate lay the best golf course in the entire world, as it has been dubbed multiple times by *Golf Digest*. I had heard that when you ate there, they didn't give you a menu, you just ordered whatever you wanted and they'd make it. I heard that women were welcomed with open arms, so long as they were members' wives and it was a Sunday afternoon, and if it wasn't, then, well—sorry.

In reality, I had no idea what Pine Valley was like, and yet for some reason I knew that driving in would still excite me. It took a lot to really get me going at this point, but driving through the gate in the enormous wall that guarded the place—even if it wasn't literally a wall, and even if it didn't have a moat, and even if there weren't ninjas standing guard—would literally mean driving into the course I'd dreamed of now for months. For an eighteen-year-old with no long-standing connection to the game of golf or to the game of being really rich, getting invited to play there would be a miracle. Penetrating golf's most inner sanctum: That would still be an accomplishment.

As I reviewed the napkin's contents, I started making mental notes of which commitments I could blow off if the invitation from Camden County presented itself.

"Mind if I join you?" a voice suddenly asked as I was lost deep in my thoughts. "The in-laws just got here and I'm about four drinks away from happy to see them."

I looked up to find a man in his midforties with graying hair and a face that looked kind but tired. I tugged the chair next to me slightly, giving permission. "For sure."

He introduced himself—James—and then he sat and sighed a little thoughtful sigh that I guessed was somewhere between "content" and "my wife's going to be pissed later."

We were silent for a while. I was focused intently on matching up my breathing to the faint ticking of the grandfather clock just inside the door. Maybe I was tired of these places, in a way, but I had taken to their easy way of life, too. It was a contradiction—the fact that I was jaded and skeptical and yet still here. What *was* I doing here?

"When you were eighteen," I started eventually, "did you know you were going to belong to a place like *this*?"

I had gotten good at asking questions that provoked but fell just short of being offensive.

"Eighteen? God, no," he responded. "I think what I knew at eighteen was that I wanted to grow my hair out and that our band was going to make it big. There were three of us on the same hall at Princeton—drummer, bassist, lead guitar, and vocals. We were gonna go on tour."

"Well, damn, you guys must have hit it big to belong to a place like this." I grinned—I was being playful, if a bit sarcastic too. "Which of your songs do I know?"

"Actually, my parents told me they'd stop paying if I didn't get my grades up, which I was fine with at first. But I started trying to sleep with a girl in my biology class, and all of a sudden being a doctor seemed like it would be pretty cool."

"And?"

"And that's why I'm here, I guess. My hospital's ten minutes that way." He pointed in the direction of the sun.

I mulled this over for a while.

"So you're happy?"

I could feel him looking at me but I kept my gaze forward, exuding nonchalance as best I could. "What do you mean?" he asked after a moment.

I started my answer slowly, carefully, but as I started to speak I realized—I was afraid that James was exactly who I would become. "Are you happy that you stayed in school? That you made your parents happy and got rich and started paying twenty grand a year to belong to WASP nation and finish third in the mixed-doubles club championship every year? That you never found out if your little band was actually the coolest thing ever?" I felt bad. I was being rude for no reason. But I had gotten the wheels churning behind James's eyes.

"Well," he started, "I guess it's not bad, here."

The waitress came outside right as he finished this first sentence, interrupting. "Can I get you anything to drink?" she asked him.

"Gin and tonic," he said, looking at me. "Actually, better make it a double. And I'll pick up whatever he's getting."

"I'll have the same," I told her, feeling rebellious, leaning back to make eye contact for just a second before refocusing on the fading sun. "Thanks."

I could see her start to walk away, then stop for a moment, then keep going. I felt no small amount of satisfaction in pulling off the under-age order, although I hoped that James hadn't just picked up the tab for six nonalcoholic Arnold Palmers as well. But I was invested in the rest of his answer.

He didn't seem interested in giving it, and instead turned the scope on me.

"Are you in school somewhere?" he asked.

"I'm kind of . . . self-enrolled," I responded, hoping that would somehow stop him from asking any follow-ups. I was tired of thinking hard about the answer to *So, what's your favorite state?*, especially when the asker didn't really care.

But James did seem to care, and he picked my brain for a while as we worked our way through courses and cities and what was still to come, and through another round of gin and tonics, which, by the way, I hated.

During a lull in the conversation a slim, leggy girl I guessed to be about my age wearing a swimsuit, a towel, and a pair of over-size sunglasses approached from the pool area. She waved to us. James returned the gesture.

"Hey, Mare," he called out.

"Hey, Dad," she replied, climbing the back steps to come talk. "Monsters-in-law here yet?"

"Yeah, they're with your mother inside. You should go say hi."

She lifted up her shades and pushed them back into her wavy brown hair, which looked as though it had been dried as an after-thought on her way out of the water. She was very cute, and care-lessly so, which suggested she knew exactly how cute she was.

She rolled her eyes. "I was thinking I might just go lie in the road instead."

"Oh, come on," he said, glancing at me, still conscious of my presence. "They're not that bad."

"Dad, the last time I talked to Grandma we showed her pic-tures from Winter Formal. She said my date had a big Jew nose and that I looked like a little slut. Besides, *you're* the one hiding on the back porch drinking." She climbed the steps and came up behind her dad, putting her left hand on the top of his head as her right grabbed his drink. She took a long gulp before she set the glass back on the table. "Holy shit," she winced, tossing a glance at me. "You trying to pass out before dinner? And who's your friend?"

"Oh, yeah," he said. "Dylan, this is my daughter Meredith. Meredith, Dylan."

"Don't listen to him, everyone calls me Mare," she told me. "Nobody can call me Meredith until I hit seventy-five years old or two hundred pounds."

I grinned. "Nice to meet you." I was impressed by this performance. She was funny, this girl, and full of life. Plus, anytime I got to meet a girl my age was a welcome relief from the parade of middle-aged white dudes.

"Yeah, I gotta go shower and put a dress on," she continued. "Maybe something with sleeves. I don't need to get called a whore in front of the whole party. See you there?"

It was hard to tell who she was looking at—she had lowered her sunglasses again. And I had no idea what party she was talking about. But I was getting the feeling that I wouldn't mind being at the same party as this girl.

"Uh, yeah," I responded. "Definitely."

The party was some kind of beginning-of-summer social. Cocktails and dinner and, apparently, more cocktails. I was several drinks deep by this point, and I drank so rarely that several drinks had expelled my inhibitions. *Let's do this.* I went to my car and extracted my least-wrinkled pair of khakis and a too-small blazer that I'd gotten for my cousin's wedding in ninth grade. The blazer, along with two dress shirts—one blue, one yellow—had been hanging in Subi's backseat all year long, blocking any view I might have wanted out the driver's-side window. I wondered if one dinner party could make up for a year's worth of well-here-goes-nothing charges into the left lane. Probably not. I chose the blue shirt.

Walking uninvited into a country club dinner party would

have both disgusted and terrified me several months earlier. Maybe it was the gin, but now I happily headed back into the maze of a locker room, where I showered, shaved, and changed before reemerging into the dining area, where a buffet had been set up. I loved buffets.

For the next hour or so I wasn't exactly the life of the party, but I kept my head above water. I didn't really want to be Dylan, in case word got back to Vincent that I had crashed his members' dinner, but I was rarely even asked my name, because everyone either figured that they must kind of know me if I was there or assumed I was some kid named Jared, who apparently went to Villanova.

Eventually I told one guy what I'd been doing, and he told his friend, and they started asking me about what kind of golf I'd seen, and I started telling them about Hawktree Golf Club in North Dakota, where the bunkers were a deep black, filled with coal slag instead of sand. Even though it was an exciting golf course, it wasn't a particularly exciting story, and yet after just a few sentences three more guys had joined in. Now I had an audience—and a good one. They laughed at my jokes and didn't butt in and shook their heads at the sheer *possibility* of the whole thing. Mare walked by and I noticed her grinning and shaking her head, too, except her grin recognized the absurdity of the situation, while the grins in my audience looked like men lost in daydream.

I held court for a while by the grand piano, shaking lots of hands and pocketing business cards by the handful and telling strangers who didn't look like they slept in cars about my experiences sleeping in cars. It was rewarding—but eventually exhausting. I excused myself, making my way over to the TVs, where *Baseball Tonight* was on. I sank into a leather armchair, feeling the ache of relief as I did so. I laid low for a while, chatting about baseball with the guy in the other armchair who looked at least as relieved as I did to not be in the heart of the party.

A few minutes later I spotted Mare across the room again, wearing a forced smile and backed into a corner by a short older woman who I guessed was Grandma. I tried to make eye contact but decided that might make me look creepy, so I gave up and turned back to the TV.

I hadn't moved from the corner when, twenty minutes later, I noticed her approaching with a grin on her face. She was wearing a three-quarter-sleeve dress that was green with yellow shapes and clung to her in a way that no doubt displeased her grand-mother. Her hair had a slight wave to it, and even with too much eye shadow she was striking. "You look like you're having fun," she said, handing me a drink. "Thought you might need this."

"I was doing pretty well," I responded sheepishly. "But I guess being at a party where you don't know anyone gets tough after a while."

"Hey, I saw you taking over the party by the piano. But now you just look like either a total loser or someone who wasn't actually invited." She slowed her delivery on the last three words, a mock accusation.

I chose to ignore her and took a sip of my drink, which looked like Coke but tasted different. Rum, I guessed. I noticed she was holding a glass of wine. "Wait, how'd you get these?"

"Relax, it's not like the real world here," she told me. "And I'm tight with the bartender. He's hooked me up for like the last three years. Grandma says I'm an alcoholic and I'm going to turn out just like Dad. I had to fake a coughing attack just to get out of there." She glanced over her shoulder.

"She's still there—uh-oh, she's looking over here," I said, watching Mare's grandmother as she eyed the two of us. I nod-ded toward the door. "You, uh, wanna take a walk?"

I caught the glances of a couple members as we walked onto the deck out back. If they'd been inspired before when I'd just been talking about golf, well, now they were downright jealous.

Our conversation flowed easily, aided by the drinks and our respective versions of country club cockiness—mine recently acquired, hers encouraged and cultivated from an early age. We strolled down the stairs and along a cart path behind the eighteenth green.

"Here, leave your shoes," she said, kicking off her own. "I hate golf, but these green things feel so cool under your feet."

The ground was wet; it was thick in the rough. On the green, though, she was right. Greens were really cool. The grass was mowed to ice-rink height, and the ground was firm yet soft, spongy beneath my toes. I walked around slowly, watching as my feet left marks on the putting surface, little indentations that disappeared as quickly as they formed. I showed Mare.

This was *fun*. I'd been missing this part of being a kid for too long—for that matter, I'd been missing this alternative use of a golf course, too. It felt just scandalous enough, just teenage enough.

We walked down off the front of the green and along the fairway, one foot in front of the other so as to create a single line in the dew. We turned at the dogleg and continued down the center, then made it all the way to the seventeenth green. I wished I had brought out a putter—the moon was so bright that I could've seen the ball's entire ride to the hole. Instead I sat down. A breeze was beginning to pick up through the course. Mare, who had joined me on the ground, shivered.

"I'm cold."

"Well, we can go back if you want to," I replied.

"Not yet." She drew a little closer. "It's kinda nice out here."

I leaned all the way back until I felt the moisture of the green coming through my shirt. She followed suit, and I let her fall onto my arm. We lay there in silence for a while, looking up at the clear sky. I traced a line with my finger down her shoulder and along her arm.

She turned slightly to face me and gave a slow sigh before she began to talk. "Well, I think that this is where I have to tell you that I have a boyfriend."

Ah. Bad news. "If you have to," I said back, grinning.

"I'm sorry." She patted me on the chest to echo the point. "Don't be. This is nice." We didn't move. Whoever her boyfriend was, I couldn't imagine he would enjoy stumbling onto this scene. Maybe she was thinking the same thing. A few minutes later, she gave me a quick kiss on the cheek and bounded to her feet, skipping around the green with nervous energy before returning to where I was sitting.

"I think we need to go back."

I had realized that it would be idiotic to drive anywhere—besides, there was nowhere that I could go—so I pulled to the corner of the parking lot, away from the party's stragglers.

As I lay in Subi that night, I was soaked in thoughts.

I felt happy, mostly. I wasn't worried about Meredith or her boyfriend, not for more than a minute or two, at least.

But what stuck out most in my mind was her father, and what he had said about golf at the club. "I guess it's not bad."

It was a weird way to say anything. Out of context he would've sounded smug, but that wasn't the impression I got. I felt like he was being honest. And I agreed with him. It didn't suck, but it was far from perfect. Was it the homogeneity? The exclusivity? It would eat at me. Maybe it already was eating at me. I'd had a great night, talking and walking and lying around. But if I worked my ass off for a few decades and reached the top, is this where I'd end up? I pictured myself as one of the guys who'd still been inside when I left, who'd watched me go. Was that the dream?

It was weird when I really thought about it: *Golf* was the cornerstone for this type of community. Wasn't golf just a game?

It had been easy being me the last few weeks—before I started thinking about things like this. Because they hadn't just let me in, these pillars of society: They'd been actively seeking my approval. They'd showed me their stuff, seeking validation that what they were doing with their spare time was cool. Sure, they lived pleasant lives, and they seemed happy, and not just in a look-at-all-my-things way. But still they queued up at this party, asking if I'd played here or there, at the places where they'd played. I wondered if that's why they played golf, to be able to ask questions like these. If they did, well, I'd gotten better at the answering too.

I woke up early enough the next morning that the sun was still rising, early enough that most of the maintenance crew hadn't even arrived yet. My head ached from the final rum and Coke and so I sat up, rubbing my temple. It was getting bright and it was already humid, but the air was thick, misty, so much so that I could barely see the edge of the clubhouse, which loomed in the distance like some sort of anchored yacht. More sleep seemed out of the question, so I popped a couple Aleves and wrestled on a blue T-shirt before rolling out the passenger door. I made my way, almost by default, to the practice green, where I whacked thirty-footers for a while, my head as hazy as the air around it. There was a light dew on the green and my putts left a faint trail along it, like those dumb new putt trackers they show on golf telecasts.

Before long I heard the unmistakable sound of iron on golf ball, and reading putts was starting to make me nauseous, so I went to investigate the range. I made myself invisible as I approached silently, hoping only to watch and not disturb. My jaw dropped.

It was Vincent.

Here he was, the 25 handicapper, standing alone on the range at 5:30 A.M., firing balls into the mist. My first reaction was to laugh. The display I had seen the day before hadn't just been the careless effort of a now-and-then social member—it was the honed craft of an early-morning ball beater. But I stopped, and watched, and started to feel my incredulity disappear.

There *was* a reason that Vincent belonged to this club that had nothing to do with status or dinner-party conversation. I doubted he even wanted people to know that he was out here.

Even here, I realized, the pursuit of the game could still be the foundation. Maybe not for everyone, and maybe not all the time. But the idea that Vincent was making an honest effort to improve made all the difference.

It was peaceful watching Vincent, and I stayed for a few minutes, for some reason unafraid that he would see me seeing him. His swing and his mind had looked as though they couldn't escape the rough the day before, but they had settled down here, too. He brought the club back in an easy arc that still came back too close to his body and came through too far away, but the ball popped off the club like it was supposed to and faded gently to the right as it neared the ground.

Eventually I stole away back to Subi, but the image of Vincent remained in my head; it comforted me. I wondered if he was trying to find something in the mist. I felt like I already had.

CHAPTER 16

Crossroads

I was running out of time.

I checked my watch: 7:04. Maybe an hour and a half left before complete dark. Most pro shops closed by seven. It didn't matter, really, whether I got a full nine in. I had played eighteen every day for most of the last month at places that weren't state parks in the beyond-Amish-remote region that was the Pennsylvania–New York border. But I always liked to get a full front nine in before it got dark—I hated leaving things mostly completed.

I was closing in. It was May now, which meant the beginning of final exams in places with final exams—and it meant that the end of my school year was approaching, too. My lone remaining test was the New England loop. I'd knocked out forty-two states—I just needed the northeasternmost six. This was my first solo round in several weeks. I hadn't even been planning on playing that day. But it had reached about 5:30 and I had no concrete plans, so I headed to the golf course.

Sure enough, as I got out of my car a young man was just walking to the parking lot, name tag still on, and the pro shop had gone dark. I took it as a sign that I was welcome to play for free. I ambled down to the first tee and bent over to stretch my back a little as I tried to check my e-mail on my phone. I was hoping for a response about Pine Valley—it wasn't on the way home in any sense, but for Pine Valley you rerouted everything.

Loading. That's what my phone spent most of its time doing. That and losing battery life. This phone had e-mail the way McDonald's had salad—it was there, but didn't quite *work*.

"You going out?" Another guy had joined me on the tee. Still loading.

"Yeah, about to. Wanna join?" I didn't look up, still midstretch and midphone.

I heard a couple practice swings and glanced over as he roped a driver down the middle. Smooth customer. I stood up straight and arched my back, feeling a satisfying crack between my shoulder blades.

He stuck out his hand. "Hank." He was a wiry guy in his thirties wearing a gray T-shirt and khaki shorts, and a swath of brown hair fell easily across his face. His handshake was firm.

"Dylan."

I hit a swinging hook that started well right but came back to bounce in the middle of the fairway. It rolled out to the edge of the left rough.

"Haven't seen you out here before."

"No, my first time, actually." I gave him the rundown.

"Oh, wow. That's something." He thought about it some more. "No, man, seriously. That's something else." He seemed really moved by the idea.

"Thanks."

He pushed for more details, asked me what I'd learned.

"Well," I told him. "The whole thing has really taken on a life of its own. I've gotten to play some unreal courses. Pebble Beach, Bandon, Valhalla, Sawgrass, Merion, even Oak Hill in a couple days. I've been some places I never imagined I would get to."

Recently, that story had earned me instant validation. With Hank, not so much.

"Pebble Beach; I heard that's a special one."

"Yeah, it's not bad."

• • •

Still loading. *C'mon.*

"Mind if I ask what's so important that's on your phone?" he asked.

I tried to explain Pine Valley, how it was a one-of-a-kind thing, how if I could get on there, well, wow. The trip would have reached a whole new height.

"Oh. So it's more that you're collecting golf courses?"

"No. Not at all. I mean, I've been playing some pretty unbelievable ones recently, but, I mean, I'm here, aren't I?"

"I don't know," he retorted, taking a pointed glance at my phone. "Are you? It's just, when you first said it, it sounded different. Not something some kid from Greenwich could do by flipping through his daddy's address book, you know, and smiling at people."

Ouch. I didn't have a quick reply to this—I knew that he was wrong, or at least that he wasn't completely right. I'd given him a lazy description of my last few weeks. It was my own fault.

Hank had stopped talking, but his face looked troubled as we walked up the fairway. He had forty yards into the green and hit a low pitch shot that bounded up to just short of the hole, some six or eight feet from the flag.

"Wow, great shot!" I told him, trying to cover the awkwardness with enthusiasm.

"Thanks," he responded without affect.

I felt distinctly like I had done something to offend him. Hank walked ahead of me like a kicked dog, ears tucked behind his head, bent over in thought. We putted out and walked to the next tee in silence.

"Sorry for not saying much," he said. "It's just that this is eating at me. You've got a million different things you could do, places you could go. What're you doing wasting that, impressing old dudes by telling 'em that you can go places that they've already been anyway?"

This was a far cry from the coddling I had grown used to. Could he be right? I was worried that I couldn't come up with neatly packaged answers about what, exactly, I'd learned—and now I'd met someone who was suggesting I hadn't learned anything at all.

Maybe he just didn't get it. Maybe he was just an overworked family man trying to sneak in a quick nine. I *hoped* he was wrong. And I kept my phone in my bag the rest of the round.

Two days passed. I drove to just outside Rochester to play Oak Hill—Ryder Cup, U.S. Open, PGA Championship Oak Hill— which was a tremendous, historic golf course. I had fun, played a good match, and met some generous members. But Hank's words still gnawed at me. Why was I here? Was I "collecting" Oak Hill?

I left Oak Hill and drove for a couple hours in a fog, first following all the signs that said north, then the ones that said west, and then the ones that said south. I still had a few days to kill before I was scheduled to hit Connecticut—and I knew this was really my last chance to wander through unknown America. I wasn't sure where I'd ended up, but I jumped at the sight of a hotel for $39.99 that didn't look particularly dangerous—I had enough money left to justify a night of comfort and hygiene.

I took a short shower, partly because it was getting late for dinner and partly because the weak, lukewarm stream that trickled from the showerhead gave the distinct impression that I was being urinated on.

There was only one other person in the diner as I entered, a middle-aged guy with a goatee at the counter. I chose a booth at the other end of the room.

I was thinking hard about Hank, and about Oak Hill, as I pretended to read the menu and wondered if I could get through my order while only saying one word—"cheeseburger"—and not come off as rude.

Thinking too hard always made me go quiet and stare, expressionless, into space. Girls complained that they never knew what

I was feeling, although I figured the ones that liked me did so for that reason also—I was nice . . . and a little confusing. But right now the thinking just made me feel empty, and maybe reckless, or something.

The waitress came over. She was a little older than me, I guessed, and cute—a slight brunette with freckles and a bouncy ponytail.

"Can I get you anything to drink?" she asked, smiling faintly. I cocked my head as if I were thinking, and tried to look friendly. "Or just water?" she continued. I smiled, and nodded. Water.

"And do you know what you'd like to eat?"

"Cheeseburger?" I tried to make it sound like a sentence, to add depth to an uninteresting word, but it came out an abrupt question instead. I got the one-word part, but that was definitely rude. Oh well.

"Okay, I'll be back with your water." She picked up my menu.

What was it about this past month that had changed things? That my tabs got picked up wherever I went? That I was invited in the front door instead of sneaking around the back? That I'd gotten used to one-time-only social interactions? Had I played *too much* golf? Or maybe I was just scared that a one-of-a-kind year was almost over.

A few minutes later, she returned with my water.

"Thanks." I gestured to the booth across from me. "Here, sit." I wasn't sure what made me say it, and I could see her pause, uncertain. "I mean, unless you have to attend to all your customers."

I was lonely, possibly emotional, and had turned quietly sarcastic; I hoped her company might distract me from my own thoughts. I was in a weird mood. But this somehow came across as confidence, because she smiled again, and sat.

I hadn't thought of what I would say if she actually sat down. I looked at her, and then at the table, and I picked up a bottle of ketchup.

"I was at this place for lunch the other day," I started, "and they had burgers, and sandwiches, all this stuff. And they were serving ketchup with a spoon. You ever serve yourself ketchup with a spoon?"

She shrugged. "Not that I can remember."

I shook my head. "Something wasn't right about it. It was unnatural. If someone comes over to my house in twenty years for burgers and I'm spooning 'em ketchup from a special ketchup dish, I hope someone shoots me."

"Well, what'd you do the other day?"

"What do you mean?"

"When they were spooning ketchup. What'd you do?"

"Oh. Well, I already had my burger . . ."

"You took it?"

"I guess so."

"So you'd rather die than have a ketchup dish, but you'd rather have spooned ketchup than no ketchup? You should stop eating hamburgers. It could get dangerous."

I laughed. "What, you think it's a good idea?"

"Ketchup in a dish? Nah. Sounds like something for douche bags." She stood up. "I've gotta go check with the kitchen."

She brought back my burger a few minutes later. She mopped the other end of the restaurant for a few minutes, then came back over. This time she sat down on her own and stayed for a while, watching me eat while we talked about nothing in particular.

"You're not from around here," she told me after a pause in the conversation.

"No," I agreed.

"So, where's home?"

"A small town. Western Massachusetts. That's where I grew up, at least—I haven't been home in a while. What's it like, living here?"

"What, this place? I don't know. It's pretty good, I guess. Quiet. Small. Everyone's really nice." She paused. She wasn't smiling anymore.

"You hate it, huh?"

"Kind of."

"Well, how come you're still here?"

"I left, you know, for college. But then I graduated, and I didn't have a job, and . . . I dunno. Where would I go?"

"Sorry," I said sheepishly. "I shouldn't have brought it up. I liked it better when you were smiling."

The goateed guy was calling her over. Maybe he was jealous. As she got up, her hand lingered a moment, grazing my shoulder as she passed.

I dropped twelve dollars on the table and penned out a quick note on the napkin in front of me.

> Room 107, Days Inn.
> —Dylan

I probably should have stayed there, asked if she wanted to hang out. But then I would've risked rejection face-to-face—and besides, I had the sense that I'd managed as well as I could in conversation. She was intrigued and entertained, and anything more I said would probably work against me. I didn't have an end goal in mind—it just seemed like a fun thing to do. So I left it.

And I got up and walked out, all while she was settling up with her other customer. I was excited as I made my way out the side entrance. I could tell: She'd come. I turned on the radio and turned up the volume, started playing the drums on the dashboard. Here, on the back roads of Pennsylvania, I was the coolest guy around.

The feeling didn't last long. I pulled into the motel parking lot and was instantly reminded of the chipping paint and the piss shower and the fact that my door didn't lock, key or not. It wasn't threatening so much as it was just kind of gross. A girl would be insane to come to a place like this, never mind to follow through based on a napkin note from a guy several years her junior after twenty minutes of conversation, no matter how dark or intriguing or existential, about ketchup.

It was a quick psychological reversal, and soon I was convincing myself that I didn't care that she wasn't coming. I didn't make my bed, didn't move my dirty clothes from the spot where I had discarded them on the floor. Why bother? I flicked on the television and quickly found *The Bourne Identity,* one of my all-time favorites.

By the time Jason Bourne had taken out an entire U.S. embassy, I was resigned to the situation. It wasn't bad, really. I had a bed. I had Internet. I had a shower, more or less, and a mirror—two mirrors, if you counted the crack down the middle as a divider.

A half hour later, I heard a car pull up into the gravel outside. I muted the TV. Nothing. I waited for a while, convinced myself it was nothing, and turned the volume back on. Jason was taking down a sniper in a cornfield. Badass. It must have been a full ten minutes before I heard the slam of a car door, and then a knock on the door so timid that I wondered if the knocker actually wanted to be heard.

I hopped off my bed, kicked a pair of boxers and a dirty polo under the table. I flipped the comforter back over most of the bed. And I went to the door.

She had ditched the apron, but she was still in the stained diner T-shirt and tight blue shorts she'd been wearing earlier. What was I supposed to do with this woman who had shown up at my hotel room at 11:15 at night? This was weird. Reckless was gone, and, I realized, so was Mr. Badass.

"Hey," I said.

"Hi."

"Do you wanna come in?"

"Um, yeah. Sure."

I closed the door behind her. "I think it's four stars, maybe four-and-a-half." She didn't laugh. But then I turned around, and she was looking at me, and then she kissed me, except I wasn't quite ready for it, so it was kind of a glancing blow. But if it was awkward it didn't matter, because she kissed me again, and then we were on the bed and she was kicking off her shoes, and it was seeming less and less likely that we were going to watch much of the rest of the movie.

She was smiling again, except now it wasn't a shy smile it all. It shouldn't have been; even though my nerves had settled down, it was still pretty obvious who was in control. She pushed me away for a second, looking at me, and gave a little laugh.

"I just realized, you're like, a lot younger than me, aren't you?"

I had been painfully aware of this the entire time and was just glad someone had addressed it. "Maybe. I don't know how old you are."

"I didn't know when I was talking to you before. Or maybe I did. I still don't know. And actually, let's keep it that way."

We kept making out, although her hands were starting to do some exploring. I had pictured a little more of this going on throughout the trip, really. Well, better late than never. She stopped again.

"Okay, how old?"

"You first."

"Twenty . . . two."

I wondered if I was supposed to lie. "Eighteen. Not that bad."

"Holy *shit*. Eighteen? I was lying. I'm twenty-six." She paused but then shrugged, as if to say, *Oh well, too late.*

And then *it* happened.

I guess I was okay with the idea. But I'd never had sex before. Most all of my high school friends had, and by the end of high school, I'd started to feel self-conscious about being a virgin. I wasn't holding out for marriage or anything. Things just hadn't worked out that way. I'd never had a girlfriend, and the girls who had been around who weren't girlfriends didn't stay around long enough for things to get to that point.

I tried to play it cool as articles of clothing hit the floor, one by one. I kept picturing myself like I was in a high school comedy—

the overmatched boyfriend in the after-prom scene. I couldn't help but smile.

"Why are you laughing?" I stopped smiling. This poor girl.

"I'm not laughing . . ." except now I was smiling again, which made it a tougher point to prove.

"Maybe . . . we shouldn't talk so much," she said. Yikes.

Now I was nervous, and overly conscious of the way our bodies were moving. Was I messing up? I could feel a cold drop of sweat rolling down my cheek. I was so afraid of the encounter lasting briefly that I couldn't relax at all.

She seemed to be enjoying herself, at least—was I? Too scared to tell. Jason Bourne was shouting faintly in the background. Everything was getting faster, louder, her breathing, my heart rate, and now the bed was complaining, until finally it was over, and we pulled apart.

I felt empty as I lay there afterward. She was in the bathroom. I felt relieved as she said a quick good-bye, sweet and awkward, and left. No phone number—no last name, even. And then I felt emptier still.

It was kind of a crazy story, I knew that. Taylor would be pumped for me—all my buddies would if I told them. They would think that it was funny. *Badass*. But I was lonely, and now, after we'd had sex, I felt even lonelier. Real connection, I guess, isn't just physical—which was a sacrilegious thing for an eighteen-year-old boy to think, but maybe it doesn't happen between two strangers in a motel room, at least not at this price.

I didn't ask her why she came. Was she as lonely as I was? I couldn't imagine that I had helped at all. I chose to go on this trip—to wander into her life. She ended up in this town because she'd run out of options. Maybe she'd hoped that through me, some part of her would escape out into the greater world. Maybe she was using me to feel like she could get out of this town just as much as I was using her to come into it. I wondered if I'd let her down just as I'd let down Hank—I wondered if my trip wasn't good enough. Would he say I was collecting experiences, just like I was collecting courses? I wondered how much this journey belonged to just me anymore.

I turned the TV back on. *The Bourne Identity* was starting again. I watched it all the way through.

CHAPTER 17

The Back Nine

I had stopped looking at anything but road signs for directions. My broken GPS lay on the floor of the passenger seat, and I still had a day to kill before I was supposed to be in Connecticut. It was mid-May now. Here, in central New York, I was navigating by feel: back roads, vague directions, low speeds, and no precise destination. It was an inefficient but soothing way to travel, the same way I'd begun the trip, and the way I still liked best.

My meandering turns had led me past a local park. I felt the urge to get some exercise, and there were several guys playing basketball. It was too hot for shirts, so I shot around barechested with two other guys doing the same. Several of their friends lounged under a nearby enclosure, blasting music and drinking beer. It was a redneck scene, happy and loud; the otherwise empty park didn't seem to mind.

My compatriots, each about five years older than me, were a complementary pair. One was extremely short, no more than five foot four, but thick and heavily tattooed. His friend must have been a foot taller, but he was pure pale skin and bones, a body that called to mind a sheet of printer paper. On the court the short one was quicker and could often sneak by his friend for a layup. Other times he would try to put up an off-balance shot and his friend would swat it away like a tetherball, then crow in delight.

We played one-on-one-on-one for a while before the short

243

one gasped for a break. I grabbed the ball, waiting for the game to continue, and swished a few. I still couldn't really dribble and didn't understand the pick-and-roll—my basketball career had ended in fourth grade—but I had gotten pretty good at shooting jumpers in an outdoor park. Golf wasn't the only sport that could get you to talking.

"You guys from around here?"

They were. Was I?

I told them my shtick—that I was from western Massachusetts, an hour east of Albany, that I had been traveling around the country for about the last year, that this was the closest I'd been to home in nine months.

"No shit, all over?" the short one asked. "Just shooting hoops?" It may have been the most flattering thing I'd heard all trip. I tried to clear the matter up, told them that I'd been playing golf some of the time, and not been playing golf most of the time.

"Damn, that's cool." The short guy had stopped dribbling, tucking the ball under his arm. It was the first moment I had seen him motionless. "I'm glad people still do stuff like that. Y'know? I dunno if I could do it, but I'm glad people do."

"I'm gonna do something like that," the taller one announced suddenly. "Just waiting to get some money together."

"Yeah, okay, maybe once you can leave the state," his friend pointed out, rolling his eyes. "Mr. DUI over here . . ."

The group by the picnic tables had stood up to leave, drawing the attention of my two playing partners. "Hey, Kev!" the short one yelled. "Where you headed?"

"We're going swimming," his buddy called back, turning as he jogged toward the sputtering red pickup. "At Kelly's house, up Boonville way." He hoisted himself into the bed of the truck and waved to my new friends. "Just meet us up there."

He turned back to me. "I think we're done for the day."

"Did he say Boonville?"

"Yeah, we got a friend whose house is up there, like ten minutes away, lives on a lake. We're gonna go get drunk. Wanna join?"

The Back Nine

• • •

Boonville. I had known I must be close, but still—it hadn't really occurred to me that I would be right around the corner from the first golf course of the entire trip. I declined the invite—hopping in a truck with Mr. DUI seemed like it could end badly—but followed their truck out of the park and up the road until we hit Route 12. I *remembered* Route 12. I turned left.

It was nearing five o'clock as I turned into the driveway for the Alder Creek Golf Course and Country Inn. I felt like I was seeing a place from my childhood, deeply familiar and yet as though it belonged to some part of my life far gone. It was a place I had explored often since I'd first been there, in my memory, thinking back about my first day on my own. People often asked about the first course, thinking it must have been a special one. It had been special, but not because I had planned it out or chosen it with any particular criteria. I'd wanted to play golf and I'd driven by it, the unassuming country inn with the nine-hole golf course. And it had only gotten more significant since then, because with every new place I visited, the place where I began it all meant a little extra.

The Alder Creek of my memory was both better and worse than the one I now found in real life. The driveway wasn't impassable. The practice area wasn't a disaster zone. The clubhouse—well, actually, the clubhouse still did look like it could use some serious work.

No doubt I'd embellished it a little bit in my imagination since I'd last been. It was a cheap public course with a ramshackle clubhouse down a crumbling driveway in a place so clearly in the boonies that that's what they had literally named the town after. It had been the perfect course to start with, the poster child for obscure golf.

But if the bad wasn't as bad as I remembered, the good wasn't as good, either. The whole property seemed smaller, less significant than it had become in my mind. Some of the country elegance I remembered was gone; September's late summer beauty

245

had been replaced by May's tire tracks, lingering in spring's left-over mud.

Alder Creek was an average public golf course. I'd seen better, for sure, and I'd seen worse, too. Had I remembered it wrong the whole time? I circled the clubhouse. The bad wasn't so bad. The trampoline was still standing. There was a pool I had forgotten about, and it looked almost clean.

Nobody was really around, so I teed off alone, and this time I hit a driver even though it wasn't really a hole for a driver. My ball sailed happily through the fairway and ended up by the seventh tee box. It wasn't down the middle, but it was a definite improvement on my sixty-yard effort from September. I banged a long iron up by the green and even got up and down for birdie.

We see things differently over time. Is it faulty memory? Shifting perspective? Golf courses didn't really change. Some got makeovers and became longer or more extensively bunkered versions of themselves, while some merely aged—although if you were around long enough to notice *that,* it was probably you that was aging. I'd played a lot of golf courses in the last year. But I knew Alder Creek was about the same as when I'd seen it last. The golf course hadn't changed—I had.

I tried to remember what I'd been looking for as I walked these same fairways my first day on the road. I'd gone looking for America, and for golf in America, and for a way to justify my love of the game. I was on a trip hoping to glorify the lowest ranks of American golf and satirize the elitism at the top. It was a journey with simple aspirations, really. I didn't think I was escaping anything, and I didn't think I was on a trip to find anything within myself. I had gone on a journey to learn about my country, to find its best and worst, and to figure out where—and *why*—golf fit in.

But I'd stumbled onto answers I hadn't expected—answers about the game, about myself. I'd gone searching for answers in golf courses. But it wasn't the golf courses that held the secrets.

Those had been in the golfers themselves, and they'd been there the whole time. Why did people play? That was the mystery: their motivation, their path, their hopes at the beginning of a new round. Everyone who tees it up is in search of something—hoping that by the time they putt out on eighteen, they'll be a little different.

The saddest parts of the America I saw were the cities and towns where people had lost hope. Sometimes it had disappeared with unemployment; other times it had been replaced by loneliness or old age. You might think the institution of golf reinforces some of this hopelessness, separating the haves from the have-nots, splitting people not by score but by wallet size.

But golf is a game built on what's possible. Everything is going to get better the next shot, the next hole, the next round (unless, of course, it gets worse). Golf just keeps people coming back, and it's not because they're sure to do better—but shoot, they might. For the American who will be just as unemployed, just as old, and just as lonely tomorrow as he is today, having that *might* is everything. And for the CEO who controls everything in his life except the hook on that damn 3-wood, the not-knowing is just as important. I learned that golf can pick you up or knock you down, and it won't play favorites. Life, even in America, is famously unfair. But golf? Golf is fair.

Golf, I'd found, has little to do with where your course is and everything to do with where *you* are when you play it. I met guys who were looking to play their way back into youth. I'd met sad people who were looking to play their way to happiness. I'd met young guys for whom golf meant camaraderie, the antidote to their problems beyond the course gates. And I'd realized something else, what every kid eventually stumbles upon, one way or another: that I could go it on my own. I'd never wanted to grow up. That was a big reason I was taking "a year off" at age eighteen. But whether I had intended to or not, I was playing my way straight into being a man. Playing eighteen in America meant that I was on a farewell tour of my childhood. When I putted out on the last green, I realized, a big part of my life would be over.

Scorecards have little boxes where you total up at the end—
there's your front nine, your back nine, and your total. "Out" is
for your front, "In" for your back, and "Total" for the two added
together. I'd played my first nine at Alder Creek nine months
earlier, just as I was heading out. Now I was playing my back
nine, thirty thousand miles later, walking into the summer sunset.

What was my total?

There were a lot of things I didn't know when I left Williamstown—about myself, about my country, about how they fit
together. The fact that I'd grown comfortable with so many different types of courses and so many types of Americans meant at
least one thing: I was comfortable in my own skin. I knew my own
game, and I knew where I fit into this big nation.

And Pine Valley? Whatever lay behind its gates could stay
there. I didn't need it—not yet, at least. In a game that's all about
pursuit, it's good to have some unopened doors.

But here in Boonville, walking down the short downhill par-4
ninth hole, I was content with the round I was completing. I was
ready to total up. And that meant that I was just about ready to
be home.

CHAPTER 18

My America

The last few weeks of the trip challenged me. Some days were fine—actually, some days were great. I could start to see that a happy future awaited me at home. Life would go on. In Connecticut, I played with a future Williams teammate, Cody, who was relieved that I was "pretty normal," socially and financially, and not a trust-fund dweeb like those he'd pictured comprising most college golf teams. Life would go on for others, too, including Brad, a high school junior I met in Rhode Island who was so affected by my trip that he told me after graduation he was going to do "pretty much exactly what you're doing."

I was playing well, too—better than I'd ever played in my life. I shot even par at TPC River Highlands, a regular Tour stop near Hartford. I played Rhode Island Country Club with Matt Broome, the defending New England Amateur champ, and even got up and down from the sand on eighteen to—however improbably—win our match.

I played a final few elite eighteens, and I tried to remind myself that I wouldn't always have such privileged access to the best of the golf world. I teed off at my final top-hundred course, Myopia Hunt in Hamilton, Massachusetts, at 5:30 A.M., and played a quick eighteen before my host, Mark, had to go to work. I played at President Bush's favorite course, Cape Arundel, an absolute gem in southern Maine, and broke 70 for the first time since Truth or Consequences, New Mexico.

People were starting to find out about me. Word had followed me back to New England, and I agreed to some interview requests: ESPN.com, *Golf Digest,* and—gulp—the *New York Times.*

But the last few weeks had been as purely lonely as any stretch of the trip. Being so close to Williamstown, a mere morning's drive away, had been more isolating than comforting as I circled my way around New England. I would get into a guest-room bed some nights and look at the ceiling and feel myself getting choked up, and I wasn't sure why. All I knew was that I was ready for home.

On May 31, Evan came to play with me in Vermont.

It was the last state of the trip, and we were playing Ekwanok, a private club in Manchester, with his friend Will.

Seeing Evan and knowing that we were back together was an incredible relief. How does anyone ever get separated from his brother? I didn't have to be cautious around him, navigate any social land mines, see whether I could be myself or not. I'd finally found the person who knew me best—and I was purely happy. It was he who got me started in the game back in Maisie and Gramps's driveway what seemed like a lifetime ago. And here he was by my side for the conclusion to a major stage of my golf career—and of my life. There's nobody I would've rather had there.

The three of us, Will and Ev and I, met in the parking lot just before four P.M.

"The real question," Evan told me, grinning, "is how you're going to feel when I beat the pants off you this round."

I was glad that he felt sentimental, too. We snuck on—there was a party going on at the clubhouse, and nobody seemed to notice—and about three hours later, we walked off.

I'd made it. But it was a moment of anticlimax. This didn't quite *feel* like the end. How do you end a trip like this?

• • •

We stopped at an outdoor burger place on the way home. Evan had to pay—I had only four dollars left.

It was at once surreal and normal to arrive home that night. I'd spent my whole life coming down the gravel driveway to this house.

Mom came out onto our front porch in the dark. "Hey, guys!" she called out, her voice cracking slightly. She ran over to us, giving big hugs, laughing in happiness and in genuine relief. Dad wasn't far behind, striding down the front steps, a tight squeeze for an embrace.

We sat in the living room for a while as I snacked on chocolate-chip cookies and told them about how good it was to be home.

"What do you want to do now?" Mom asked, hoping she could help give me something.

"Sleep," I told her. "And not go anywhere. For like, a week."

First, though, we went to unload the car. I opened the trunk and Mom gasped. I couldn't tell if it was from the smell or the clutter. "You slept *here*?"

It *was* hard to imagine. There was no open space. My supplies had been replaced by souvenirs. Scorecards littered the back seat. Golf balls rolled everywhere. Tees and ball markers, pamphlets and maps, parking tickets and business cards, all the books that people had just kept giving me—these formed the trunk's base layer, like a nest I'd been building to sleep in.

Dad grabbed a pair of golf shoes in one hand and my laundry sack in the other, extending his arms as far from his nostrils as possible. He chuckled. "You think a certain amount of this would do pretty well in a fire?"

I grinned back, but it quickly turned to a yawn. "Let's just do this tomorrow." I knew it was a disaster back there—but it didn't matter anymore.

I was exhausted as I brushed my teeth and got into bed. But I couldn't manage to fall asleep. Maybe I was too used to being scrunched up in the trunk. I wondered—how long would it take before I got used to a bed again? How long before I got used to staying in one place, to being at home, where I could fall asleep just because I was tired?

About an hour.

My family had organized a cookout for the following afternoon. Dozens of people showed up—my friends, my parents' friends, people I barely knew—and for a few hours, all was well at the Dethier house. My buddies were back from college with stories of their own, big life changes that would demand more than a cookout conversation. We had a whole year to celebrate. And to most, what had happened in between then and now didn't matter so much as the fact that here we were, back together. I felt no need for grand speeches about life lessons. I told everyone I was happy to be back—which was true—and then I played Wiffle ball and ate ice cream cake and reveled in the contentedness of small-town New England.

Real closure had to wait one more day.

"Well, you're back."

Cathy Pohle, pro shop manager of Taconic Golf Club, stood in front of me, her lips pursed together in a subtle smile. The world, to Cathy, was matter-of-fact—she was friendly, polite, and never surprised.

I felt an easy grin come over my face. Everything seemed *easy* those first couple days back in Williamstown. "I am back," I said. "It's good to be back."

"Well, you must have seen some very interesting things," she said, and without bothering to wait for a response, continued, "So it'll be you, Taylor, Evan, and Sammy?"

I shook my head as I left the shop. Maybe nothing had changed.

It was a familiar foursome—Evan, Taylor, and Sam, who'd been my closest friend and playing partner on our high school team. Taylor was early as always, Sam was on time for once, and Evan and I got there two minutes before the tee time, which was pretty good for us. It certainly didn't faze Cathy.

We decided not to set up any sort of match; we would just play. My game felt polished—I'd become a slightly refined version of the free swinger who had walked these fairways the previous summer. I hit more 3-woods than drivers and more fairways than trees. The round didn't feel like the end of anything—it felt like the next chapter. The continuation.

Our conversation flowed easily, musing on Evan's new girlfriend and Sam's freshman year and Taylor's impending graduation. It was a round we'd played a thousand times before. A local reporter joined us for a few holes, but even that was familiar—this guy, Patrick, had been around our high school sporting events for years.

On the sixteenth tee it began to rain. *Damn.* How would I ever get dry now? It was a brief moment of exasperation—except then I realized that after the round I wasn't returning to Subi. I was returning home.

I thought of all the rain I'd seen in the last year. I thought of Marquette Golf Club, in the sideways freezing drizzle. I thought of huddling up in Subi as winds battered the car and raindrops crashed against the windows, trying to get in. I thought about snow in Minnesota, and slush in North Dakota, and sleet in Wyoming, and how it poured outside as I was stuck inside the Morongo Casino, nearly drowning.

And then I thought of West Texas, and the round I'd played there in a midwinter downpour—a round I'd barely thought of since then.

I'm not sure the place even had a name—the sign just said GOLF COURSE. The clubhouse—had it been open—was essentially a Porta-Potty connected to an old lemonade stand. There was a cash box next to the first tee where golfers placed greens fees on the honor system. I'm not sure who looked after any of it except the cows—they mowed the fairways, unperturbed by my presence.

When the clouds grew dark and the drops had started falling on the third hole, I stared back in the direction of Subi. But then I stopped. I turned back and continued playing—all eleven holes. I had nowhere to be, nothing to do except learn and play and wonder. What was golf doing here, in the furthest reaches of America? What did it mean to people? I kept playing even as the cows retreated to the edge of the trees, where they cozied up together, watching the drenched eighteen-year-old sloshing his way through a round he would never get to play again.

And with that memory rushed a flood of more: I saw Lamar and Randy and the glory gone by of Flint; I was beside Larry and Rick on the Bully Pulpit tee, atop North Dakota; I traipsed behind Ford Shaper as we scrambled through the woods of East Texas, enemies lurking behind every tree. I awoke to a police officer rapping on my window, and tiptoed along a cliff in the Big Horns, and watched a five-hundred-dollar putt lip out in Las Vegas. I saw golf holes: number seven at Pebble, seventeen at Sawgrass, sixteen at Merion—and I saw number four at Brechtel Park in New Orleans, number eight at Rolling Hills in Iowa, number nine at Alder Creek Golf Course and Country Inn. And I saw people—hosts opening their doors, playing partners showing me their courses, distant cousins and complete strangers, cowboys and Indians, skeptical cops and would-be robbers—except I could hardly distinguish one face from the next, and they blurred together into a single picture: my America.

And now here at Taconic, I looked out from the eighteenth tee. The rain had slowed. The final hole was a gorgeous par-5 with a tee shot that carried over a pond and right at the mountains, the familiar leafy Berkshire Hills. I was wet but content—nothing a hot shower and a fresh set of clothes couldn't fix.

I teed off first before retreating to the corner of the tee, and then I felt it: A large lump was rising in the back of my throat. This was the end. There were no more rural Texas downpours to play through. No more continental breakfasts to raid. No more days that began with the question "What if?" and proceeded however I saw fit. It was great to be home, but it was just occurring to me that Subi and I were going to be parked in a familiar driveway that night, and the next night, and the night after that, too. I was scared that I was losing the possibility of the open road.

Maybe one day I could find it again.

The sky was clearing as we made our way off the tee, leaving us with soaked shirts and matted hair as we walked down the fairway. The clouds were parting—the sun would be out soon. I noticed Mom standing behind the green, watching us approach. There was Dad, too, walking up beside her.

We putted out, Evan first, then Taylor, and then Sam. As I rolled in my two-footer, I heard my parents applauding.

And I could feel myself smiling.

Acknowledgments

I have a wish for people with big ideas: I wish that those who tell you what you *can't* do will always be outnumbered by those who tell you to follow your dreams.

No journey—nor any book—is completed without the help and encouragement of just about everyone in your life.

I was lucky to have enough people believe in me that I could start to believe in myself. These pages are a testament to all those people, only some of whose contributions can be recognized below.

My deepest thanks:

To everyone who taught me to love golf, from my earliest partners—Than and Alvand, Nico and Sam, Pat and Ian—to my current ones, Cody and Jake, Matt and Ross, Taylor and Evan.

To Mark Mills, for opening up a foreign game to a pair of brothers who just wanted to play.

To Rick Pohle and Erik Tiele, for trying to teach me that it's okay to punch out to safety, and that golf takes place on a six-inch course—that space between my ears.

To Blair Dils, who helped me understand games and lives, and who made it clear that when it comes to comma placement, there are no mulligans.

To Brian Gill, Nick Fogel, and Matt Voisin, who taught me to do everything with passion and to never sacrifice what I wanted most for what I wanted at the moment.

To Rob White, for being the first and most consistent voice of optimism when I made the bold suggestion that I was a teenager who wanted to write a book.

To Paul Lieberman and Gage McWeeny, who prodded me in all the right ways to keep my wheels moving forward.

To the team at Scribner, who threw their support behind a writing rookie.

To Paul Whitlatch, the best editor I've ever had, who took a chance on a kid with a big idea and took the disconnected ramblings of a college kid and turned them into a story.

To Rob Weisbach, agent extraordinaire, who gleefully gave me the keys to a car I didn't know how to drive, who sees potential in every conversation, who has the uncanny ability to understand me better than I understand myself.

To all my hosts from coast to coast, who cemented my faith in the goodness of people, the power of America, and the ability of sport to unite us all. To the Balderstons and Belks, Costleys and Cranshaws, Dethiers and Elliots, Finans and Foehls, Fogels and Foxes, Kourajians and Lunds, Maritzes and McNaughts, Nylens and Rasers, Shapers and Thompsons, Voisins and Williamses— and so many more.

Finally, to my brother Evan, for taking up golf so that there was finally something that I was better at than you, and for always being there to play whatever game lay before us.

And to Mom and Dad, for teaching me everything, and for letting me go—and knowing that I'll always come back.